Money, Autonomy and Citizenship

Alessandro Pinzani • Walquiria Leão Rego

Money, Autonomy and Citizenship

The Experience of the Brazilian Bolsa Família

Springer

editora unesp

Alessandro Pinzani
Centro de Filosofia e Ciências Humanas
Universidade Federal de Santa Catarina
Florianopolis, Santa Catarina, Brazil

Walquiria Leão Rego
Instituto de Filosofia e Ciências Humanas
Universidade Estadual de Campinas
Campinas, São Paulo, Brazil

Translated by Katie Gray Craven

ISBN 978-3-030-01360-8   ISBN 978-3-030-01361-5 (eBook)
https://doi.org/10.1007/978-3-030-01361-5

Library of Congress Control Number: 2018957079

Translated from the Portuguese language edition: *Vozes do Bolsa Família – Autonomia, dinheiro e cidadania*, 2nd edition, by Walquiria Leão Rego and Alessando Pinzani.

This Springer imprint is published by the registered company Springer Nature Switzerland AG
The registered company address is: Gewerbestrasse 11, 6330 Cham, Switzerland

Like a dog
is thicker than an apple.
Like the blood of the dog
is thicker
than the dog itself.
Like a man is thicker
than the blood
of a dog.
Like the blood of a man
is far thicker
than the dream of a man.
Thick
like an apple is thick.
Like an apple
is much thicker
if a man eats it
than if a man sees it.
Like it is even thicker
if hunger eats it.
Like it is even thicker
if the hunger that sees it
cannot eat it.

João Cabral de Melo Neto

To Luciana, Waldeni, and the others

Preface to the English Edition

This work presents the results of 5 years of field research on the effects of the Bolsa Família program (henceforth, PBF) on the subjectivity of its participants: on how they perceived themselves after having enrolled and receiving regular money income for some period (often for the first time in their lives). Since its first publication in Portuguese (2013), many things have changed in Brazilian politics, but we believe that our findings are still valid, since they do not depend on a specific social policy, but are more widely applicable.

In order to familiarize non-Brazilian readers with the PBF, we will provide some background data and describe some aspects of the present situation in Brazil.

When Luiz Inácio Lula da Silva assumed the presidency of Brazil in 2002, one of the explicit priorities of his government was to combat poverty, a problem that still affects a significant percentage of the Brazilian population. Several programs were launched or extended (Lula's predecessor, Fernando Henrique Cardoso, had already taken steps in this direction), but none were as successful and as widely debated (and criticized) as the PBF. At its height, it was the widest ranging social program in Brazil (serving approximately 55 million out of a general population of 200 million people). Contrary to other programs that directly distribute food to poor families (e.g., the *Banco de Alimentos*), the PBF is a CCT (conditional cash transfer) program that distributes money instead of goods.

The *Bolsa Família* is neither a credit scheme nor a loan: its participants do not receive money in order to start an economic activity or their own business (even if they might use it for this purpose), and they have no obligation to repay anything. Its aim is neither to increase economic inclusion nor economic development, even though it has had both of these impacts. According to the Institute for Applied Economic Research (IPEA), every *real* paid by the government via PBF and spent by families in consumption contributes 1.78 R$ to the Brazilian GDP (on the whole, the sum spent by the government with the PBF amounts to just at 0.48% of the Brazilian GDP).[1] It is a program of civic inclusion: it aims to help

[1] www.ipea.gov.br/portal/index.php?option=com_content&view=article&id=20244&Itemid=75 (accessed on 05/15/14)

citizens meet their most basic necessities and sometimes just to survive. Its goal is to create *citizenship*, not to merely train the entrepreneurial spirit.

At the time of our research (2006–2011), the allowance was granted to individuals or families (defined widely as a unit formed by one or two parents and their children, by one or two grandparents and their grandchildren, by an aunt or an uncle and her or his nieces or nephews, etc.) whose per capita monthly income was equal to or less than R$ 70 (US$ 35, 2011, or US$ 21, December 2017).[2] For comparison's sake, 2011 Brazilian average income/month was R$ 783 (US$ 390, 2011), while the minimum wage was R$ 678 (US$ 335, 2011). By 2017, the minimum wage had increased to R$ 937 (US$ 282, 2017).

At present (December 2017), the threshold for entering the program is a per capita income equal to or less than R$ 85 (US$ 25.6, 2017) or between 85 and 170 R$ (US$ 51.2), if there are children between 0 and 17 years of age. The basic allowance amounts to R$ 85 (US$ 25.6, 2017). For school age children under 15, there is a per capita variable allowance of R$ 39 (US$ 11.7) for a maximum of 5 children. For teenagers under 19, there is a per capita variable allowance of R$ 46 (US$ 13.8) for a maximum of two young people. In any case, a family will not receive more than five variable allowances. Therefore, the maximum allowance for a family with three children under 15 years and two teenagers under 19 years is R$ 294 (US$ 88.5) There are also special allowances for pregnant women and for babies under 6 months (R$ 39, or US$ 11.7), but they have strict time limitations, due to their very nature. At the time of the interviews, the allowance was significantly lower, and the maximum number of children was just three.

After the parliamentary coup that ousted President Dilma Rousseff at the end of August 2016, the new government under Michel Temer has drastically reduced anti-poverty social programs while, however, keeping the PBF. However, it has offered incentives for local governments to reduce the number of participants. As a result, millions of people have lost the benefit. According to the Ministry for Social Development data, almost 14 million out of over 26 million poor families are currently participating in the program. Interestingly, the Ministry does not publish the current number of individual recipients. The 12 million families in the lowest income cohort (earning between 0 and 85 R$ per capita per month) comprise 38 million people. If this proportion is respected, the 14 million PBF families should encompass 44 million individuals, which represent a decrease of around 11 million relative to the administrations of Presidents Lula and Dilma. During recent field work in the Brazilian Northeast (states of Ceará and of Pernambuco), our local contacts told us that the Federal Government was not financing over 50 social programs introduced by President Lula and his successor President Dilma. As a result, poor families in the *sertão*, but also in the peripheries of big cities such as Recife, were once again suffering hunger and even thirst (as in the case of the millions of families dependent on federal programs for building family water reservoirs). As a consequence, after many years of absence, Brazil may once more be listed in the FAO Hunger Map.[3]

---

[2] The exchange rates of the *real* to the dollar and the euro at two points in time, 2011 (at the end of the research) and, at present, December 2017: 1 US$ = 2 R$ and 1 US$ = 3.32 R$; 1€ = 2.40 € and 1€ = 2.40 R$.

[3] https://www.youtube.com/watch?v=QguB2PUJzw8

Preface to the Second Edition

This book was published on June 11, 2013 (the first day of the demonstrations that began in São Paulo and spread over many cities throughout the country, primarily protesting against increases in bus fares; these were the largest national demonstrations since 1992). The first edition of our book sold out exactly 3 months later. We never could have imagined that this would happen nor that the book (it is worth keeping in mind that this is an academic work) would prompt so much debate, even on the social networks. Of course, the rumors about the end of the program that led to a run on the bank by Bolsa Família beneficiaries in May 2013 and helped bring the program to the attention of a much broader range of people than just those academics who had been the original target audience. However, we are of the opinion that interest in our work was not just a fluke since the work did indeed fill a lacuna among the many studies of the topic. While most investigations have either focused on the economic impact of the program or have presented quantitative analyses, our book provides a qualitative analysis of the impact that the program has had on the lives of its participants. Furthermore, it allows readers to hear these people's voices directly. The way in which the book allows its subjects to tell their stories may have been what provoked the greatest interest on the part of readers – including professionals directly involved in implementing this social program. Subsequently, we have received not only innumerable invitations to round tables, interviews, and to write articles, but we also have received emails many from readers who wanted to share their own experiences with the Bolsa Família (managers and social workers as well as students from families covered by the program). The book went so far as to inspire filmmakers like Sérgio Machado and Eliza Capai, whose beautiful short-film *Severinas* portrays in a striking and immediate way the world of the women we interviewed.

During debates that followed the publication of the book and the discussions that we participated in throughout Brazil (from Santana do Livramento in the far south of the country to Natal in the extreme northeast), some questions have arisen that we would like to address briefly in this preface to the second edition. In the first place, our intention in writing this book was not to defend the program from a partisan point of view, even though both of us consider ourselves to be leftist intellectuals.[1] We were motivated by mere intellectual curiosity, and, if the book at a certain point openly defends the program against its critics, it is because we realized from early on that most of the criticism arose from unfounded and morally questionable biases. In some cases, these biases suggest a true class hatred (or simply hatred, since we are often describing the *survival* of people who are lacking the most basic human needs). So, even though we state at the end of Chap. 1 that we have no intention of taking on the attitude of Brazilians toward their impoverished fellow citizens, that attitude is frequently analyzed and criticized. Perhaps we are dealing with a "performative contradiction," as one says in philosophical jargon, but we find it necessary to reject the criticism that the program and its beneficiaries face, which is ideological and, at times, hatefully cynical. Therefore, we took on this self-contradiction (as Walt Whitman said, "Do I contradict myself? Very well then I contradict myself"[2]).

In the second place, we have no intention of affirming any automatic association between receiving a regular monetary income and the creation of autonomous individuals (including in the sense of the emancipation of women from their husbands or families).[3] We merely state that regular monetary income represents a necessary, if insufficient, condition for prompting the process of building a sense of autonomy on the part of the people who receive it. Our intention is to describe that which, together with Theodor Adorno, we have identified as a trend in society that has nothing to do with predictions or hopes. According to the German scholar, it is a tendency that is recognized when, in the context of carrying out a theoretical analysis of a certain state of affairs, something comes up that is qualitatively distinct from the previous status quo and that points in the direction in which things are evolving (Adorno 2008, p. 43). We are not speaking of a secondary concept, since it is impossible to imagine a society without making use of it (ibidem, p. 38): a society is not static, but it is constantly in evolution. A true social theory, therefore, cannot limit itself to describing the current state of affairs (as many contemporary social scientists appear to believe). Such a social theory must point to exactly that novelty that is more than a mere casual deviation from the regular patterns that describe the state

[1] In fact, it should be unnecessary to make this point clear, but the political polarization surrounding the *Bolsa Família* has made it necessary. By way of example, one of us recently received the following message from a student who received a bad grade on an exam in a subject totally unrelated to the *Bolsa Família* or to Brazilian politics. The course, in fact, dealt with seventeenth-century political philosophy. The student wrote: "Isn't this typical of people on the left who, when their ideas are contested, take desperate measures, as human history shows. Next time, don't ask my opinion. Just ask me to write an article about the stupid things that you believe to be true. Without further ado, good night. Happy dreams of the Workers' Party (PT)." We have also received many offensive messages on social networks or the comments from readers following interviews or academic articles.

[2] Whitman, Walt. "Song of Myself". In: *Poetry and Prose*. New York: The Library of America, 1996, p. 246

[3] There have been articles in the media that present our work as arguing that there has been "a feminist revolution in the *sertão*" (sic). We cannot tell whether this misguided interpretation arises from an overly quick or superficial reading of the book or bad faith on the part of the writers of such articles.

of things. This deviation, in fact, might represent the beginning of a process that may lead to the formation of a new pattern, of a new social "law" (ibidem, p. 48). Our book intends to take note of, precisely, one of the differentiating moments that might indicate a new trend in the heart of Brazilian society, namely, a trend toward greater inclusion into the citizenry of a great number of Brazilian hitherto excluded. This exclusion was not voluntary but was due to the situation of almost total privation of the minimal material conditions for a person to be an autonomous individual and to act as an active citizen, as has been described in this book. This does not, however, mean that such a trend will automatically and inevitably lead to real inclusion, since this process depends on a series of circumstances including the continuation of government policies like the Bolsa Família or the institutionalization of similar mechanisms for implementing constitutional rights.[4]

In the third place, we would like to answer a few criticisms about our concept of autonomy and the risk that the Bolsa Família would contribute to maintaining women in their state of submission relative to men as a result of their roles as women and mothers of families. Our concept of autonomy (p. 57 s.) should not be understood as merely atomistic or individualistic; in fact, we would like to emphasize its intersubjective nature, particularly, as it relates to what we consider to be one of its main aspect, namely, mutual recognition as moral and legal subjects. The women that we interviewed tended to see themselves as part of a broader network of moral relationships, particularly responsibilities that accrued to them due to their roles as wives, daughters, mothers, etc. Although accepting these roles might be seen as a consequence of an oppressive education, these people consider their abilities to fulfill these obligations as a central aspect of their individual liberty. As social researchers, we cannot ignore this aspect just because we have different ideals of autonomy (particularly regarding women's emancipation). Criticizing these women because they want to be good mothers or good wives instead of hoping to be emancipated women would be to judge them based on values that they could not have developed autonomously and it would, therefore, represent an act of cultural domination. However, this situation is changing, to the extent that some of these women (and particularly their daughters) are beginning to question their traditional roles, as we describe in the book.

Finally, we would like to put forward some concrete proposals relative to the Bolsa Família. One question that deserves to be investigated is the possible humiliation of the "beneficiaries" of the PBF due to the very fact of receiving it. We are not so much interested in the humiliation that arises from stigmas or hostile attitudes on

[4] We would like to remind readers that the positive impact of the program has been proven in many different pieces of research, including some conducted by physicians. The decrease in the infant mortality rate between 0 and 5 years of age was more than 95%, as was the reduction in the hospitalization of children in the same age range. In general, the improvement of the state of health of children and other grantees is well documented. Illness from malnutrition (in other words, illness caused by conditions of extreme poverty) has fallen almost 100%. As far as material life conditions are concerned, there has been a significant improvement, thus forming a trend full of political and democratic meaning and potential.

the part of neighbors or fellow citizens,[5] because this refers to a process of social evolution that is difficult to change by social policies and that requires civic or humane education in the long term. No, we are referring to the possibility that beneficiaries of social programs like the PBF might feel humiliated by the very fact of having been officially declared to be needy, in other words, to have been branded as people unable to guarantee the survival of their families. This might cause the impression that they are receiving some sort of handout or free aid from public institutions (this might partly explain the tendency that we took note of in many interviews where many of the women considered the program to be a favor from the government). We would like to make the following proposals in this respect:

1. The term "beneficiary" should be replaced with that of "grantee." Anyone who receives a grant (for study, research, or training) can be referred to as a grantee and not a beneficiary. The idea is that a grant remunerates one for a certain activity (studies, research, training) and is not merely a gift. The same takes place with the Bolsa Família: the activity which is remunerated is that of supporting a family under difficult conditions, taking special care of the education and well-being of the children and future Brazilian citizens (these are, in fact, set up as the only two conditions imposed upon the grantees). We believe that if the competent governmental organizations were to adopt the term "grantee," this would constitute a first, symbolic change that would, however, be particularly useful. Recently, some official documents have begun using the term "program participants" which we find to be a good alternative – much preferable to "beneficiaries." In this work, we opt for the term grantee.
2. It would be advisable that the mayors and program managers receive training in treating grantees in a more respectful and humane fashion. Several cases came to our attention where this did not take place and in which the authorities responsible for implementing the program did so in a humiliating fashion. One of the most blatant examples of such a disrespectful attitude that is indifferent to the human importance of the relationship between institutions and citizens might be, for example, using deliberately abstruse and highly bureaucratic language in letters directed to illiterate participants. Both the Ministry of Social Development (MDS) and the Ministry of Education (MEC) are putting together specialization courses to train and qualify the managers and other people involved in the on-site implementation of the program (e.g., school principals). It would be important that such training courses include not only technical information but also the question of respect and institutional humiliation.
3. From our point of view, it is imperative to help grantees organize themselves so that they may share their experiences with one another (as well as sharing them with the institutions) and so formulate their demands and communicate them to the local and federal authorities so that they might finally escape the vicious

[5] For more information about this point, see the doctoral thesis *A construção de fronteiras simbólicas entre os "pobres": o caso do programa Bolsa Família*, by Mani Tebet de Azevedo Marins at UFRJ, Brazil in 2013.

circle of dumbness on the part of the poor and deafness on the part of institutions so that grantees might cease to be mere political objects and become political subjects, as we hope for in our book.

4. Finally, the economic support provided by the Bolsa Família should be transformed into a positive constitutional right, especially to avoid that, as a governmental program, it is seen by grantees themselves as a favor instead of an expression of their right as citizens.

Taking full advantage of this opportunity to achieve greater social political and civic inclusion on the part of more than 50 million grantees constitutes a huge challenge to the democratic imagination of a policy intended to promote the growth of autonomy of Brazilian citizens.

Florianopolis, Santa Catarina, Brazil — Alessandro Pinzani
Campinas, São Paulo, Brazil — Walquíria Leão Rego

Contents

Introduction

Poverty is a complex problem and, like all complex problems, it has no simple answers. Therefore, it cannot be simply resolved by a program of direct monetary payments like the *Bolsa Família* (henceforth referred to also as BF).[1] However, such a program faces important concerns related to poverty and offers at least a partial solution; even better, it deals with some of the facets of the issue. It would be a mistake to limit itself to ensuring the material survival of extremely poor and destitute families (although this would obviously be one of its principle merits).

It is important to remember that poverty has long been a topic of discussion in Latin America – starting with the fertile essays of the 1920s–1930s and extending to the academic research undertaken by many differing teams of researchers. Several traditions of research on poverty have cross-fertilized each other, starting with ethnographic studies carried out, in great part, by anthropologists. Such research has become rooted in the cultures of their respective countries, particularly those with significant indigenous populations. The economic exclusion of the native peoples and their location amid the lowest social levels of these Latin American societies made them the central figures of the most shocking poverty. Due to the large numbers of these populations, they were more visible. This visibility, in turn, makes them the most undesirable people of the large cities. The systematic attacks against these populations, marked by extreme violence by those in power, were designed to destroy them completely. They were targeted in many manners, including actual assassinations, but mostly by trying to deny their identity and cultures.

[1] For more about the history of the program, see Silva et al. (2008). The basic grant of R$70 (US$ 38.72) is paid to extremely poor families with an income/person of R$ 70 (US$ 38.72) even if they do not have children, teenagers, or young people. The variable grant is paid to poor families with an income/person of up to R$32 (US$ 17.70) as long as they have children or teenagers up to 15 years of age. Each family can receive up to three times the variable grant, in other words, up to R$96 (US$ 51.10). The variable grant for teens/BVJ is paid to all families in the program who have teens of 16 or 17 that are attending school. Each family can receive up to two times a BVJ or R$76 (US$43.04). The extraordinary variable grant (BVCE) is paid to families when the migration of previous programs such as gas aid, school grant, or the food grant and the food card to the family grant (BF) would lead to economic losses. The amount of the grant varies, therefore, from case to case. [Translator's note: November 30, 2011, the values listed in US$ (1.8079 $/R) equivalents.]

In Brazil, poverty generally has color: it is black or mulatto. This serves as a reminder of slavery, the main institution for the accumulation of wealth in Brazil for 300 years. Slavery, founded on the ultimate expropriation of the very person of the slave, formed structures of sentiment and patterns of public morality that are incompatible with the normative demands of a decent society.[2] Their history among us has always been accompanied by the "procession of harsh and calamitous customs," in the words of the nineteenth-century Brazilian liberal Tavares Bastos (1837–1875).

In Brazil, as in the rest of Latin America, the abovementioned tradition of sociological research on poverty emphasized, for the most part, social class, especially in the case of Marxist-inspired investigations. Naturally, this inspiration led researchers to focus on the life and work conditions of the rural and urban working classes. The investigation revealed the conflicts that existed between the differing social classes, since they were carried out in a period during which grave repression was violently carried out against any social movements: these were the days of the Cold War when military governments ruled almost all of Latin America.

For this reason, these studies focused on the arduous struggle for unionization and the long, punishing working days, in other words, the pain and suffering of the working class. They described the pitiful housing conditions and low wages and revealed the magnitude of the exploitation of the work force. They brought to light the abiding vestiges of an authoritarian, slaveholder mentality averse to human rights of any kind. The mechanisms of marginalization, as were commented on during the period, produced excellent works of historical reconstruction as well as theoretical analyses about the production and reproduction of poverty. The goal was to study the idiosyncrasies of the development of capitalism within this adversity and, in our case, the peculiarities of Brazilian capitalism, which was never predated by a democratic revolution that might have opened up even a few cracks in the foundation through which the practice and culture of rights might have come to place (see Chap. 4, p. 85). The most marked characteristics of sociological studies of the topic visible throughout that period emphasized the study of the rural to urban migrations, the poverty of the areas surrounding the city centers, as well as the *favelas*, or shanty towns. They looked into the living conditions of these regions and the lack of urban facilities even within the cities themselves. However, these analyses usually portrayed this marginalization as a "natural" consequence of the functioning of capitalism, historically speaking. The "reserve army of labor" and "structural unemployment" were the concepts most commonly used within the narratives of the period. Few, if any, of the pieces of research dealt with the day-to-day life of the unemployed, their specific adversities, or their worldview. After all, who were these people who made up this reserve army of labor? Who were the people who were structurally unemployed? It was known that their existence was an inevitable facet of the reproduction of capital. However, almost nothing was known about their ways of life, their dreams, or their expectations. They were only dealt with by Latin American art. Literature and the cinema constantly portrayed these marginalized peoples, and, so doing, they revealed among many other things, the darker than

[2] For the concept of decent society, see Margalit (1996) (see Sect. 2.1 of the present work as well).

dark destinies of those who, under the auspices of capitalism, lacked not only any job at all but any expression of their voices.[3] They were always there in line, waiting for the next expansionary cycle of the system where they might, who knows, finally find a place. Normally, those marginalized people were wandering individuals, without schooling. They were always the everlasting reserve awaiting the most degrading jobs. They moved frequently, and, thus, they reaffirmed their complete incapacity for work seen as a professional or qualified job.[4] Their stereotyped image as bums or vagabonds figured as one of the most brutal phenomena of Brazilian society. It was as heinous and cruel as the reputation which arose during slavery, according to which the black slave was stigmatized and portrayed as being lazy, indolent, and lascivious and who would only work under the most absolute coercion, in other words, under the most brutal physical violence, after being whipped to shreds by the foreman.[5]

These brief thoughts indicate that, in our intellectual tradition, it was not very common to focus on people who are disorganized, those who lack a voice, and those who at dawn fall into line in hopes of getting the worst jobs, if any. As for the women, their fate had been sealed long ago: they would become domestic slaves, almost completely robbed of their voices by the ambiguous links established within private work environments. According to a century-old stereotype, they are those whom you should not trust because if you do, they will turn up their noses, since they don't know anything. If you treat them well, "Watch out! You'll lose all your authority." Completely divorced from a world that is organized around the concept of rights but practically grants them none, their pain and suffering never surfaces. It has been dampened by the ambiguity of the very work relationship they are subject to.

Today we study poverty, those destitute of voice, the "invisible" ones. We have realized thanks to many recent studies that millions of Brazilians were, and in many cases still are, totally without access to the most basic benefits of civilization.

Our intention with this research was to investigate the political and moral effects of the *Bolsa Família*, which are far from secondary, in the light of a concept of individual autonomy based on the capability approach devised by Amartya Sen and Martha Nussbaum. We also relied on the theoretical link between monetary income

[3] Luis Bûnuel made a touching film in Mexico about these forgotten ones in 1950, *Los Olvidados*, de 1950. Marx in *Critique of the Gotha Program* to a certain extent alerted us to the danger regarding the treatment of workers, when the only factor considered is their inequality when faced with the same situation of exploitation. He was calling attention to disequality in life conditions and criticized the theoretical perspective that lost sight of situational disequality and, thereby, people's characteristics as individuals. "Unequal individuals (and they would not be different individuals if they were not unequal) are only measurable by an equal standard in so far as they are brought under an equal point of view, are taken from one *definite* side only, e.g. in the present case, are regarded only as workers, and nothing more seen in them, everything else being ignored" (Marx 2008, p. 26).

[4] See Sect. 2.4 for more about the concept of *capability*.

[5] The relationship between slavery and Brazilian poverty is portrayed in a caustic fashion in the film *What Is It Worth* by Sérgio Bianchi.

and individual autonomy outlined especially by Georg Simmel.[6] A particular inspiration for this work is the Frankfurt School of Critical Theory, a fact which will be made clear in the first chapter.

In order to carry out this research, we spent 5 years traveling, during which time we interviewed BF grantees in the most underserved regions of Brazil, namely, the northeastern *sertão*[7] (Alagoas state), the outskirts of the city of Recife (Pernambuco), the coastal region of Alagoas, the Jequitinhonha Valley (Minas Gerais), the interior regions of the states of Piauí and Maranhão, and the outskirts of the city of São Luis (Maranhão). Using Rawlesian terminology, we went to hear the most disadvantaged people, i.e., the worst off.

We did not undertake a statistical or quantitative project but one that is fundamentally qualitative. We used an open interview rather than a questionnaire as our data collection instrument because we felt that it was the only tool possible, exactly because we wanted to gain access to various levels of the interviewees' subjective experience.[8] Our basic method, as is well known, consists of a long interview supported merely by a series of questions and of listening as intently as possible to

---

[6]We have based ourselves fundamentally on *Philosophy of Money* by Simmel and very little on Marx's reflections on the same question because we do not discuss money as capital and its respective fetish (amply discussed by Marx). Simmel did not treat money in the same fashion, and we therefore were able to use his ideas widely to the extent that our goal was precisely to study the effects of a cash income on people's subjectivity (a central theme of Simmel's work).

[7]Translator's note: The *sertão* refers to a huge region in the inland areas of the states of Alagoas, Bahia, Pernambuco, Paraíba, Rio Grande do Norte, Ceará, Maranhão, Piauí, and northern Minas Gerais. It is an impoverished region marked by very little economic diversity, in which the great majority of the population depends on subsistence agriculture in a semiarid climate marked by frequent draughts.

[8]We chose to undertake qualitative research, using open-ended interviews instead of the questionnaires that are usually used by economists and by researchers interested in the quantifiable, material effects of the BPF (e.g., by the researchers of Brazilian governmental institutions such as the IPEIA and the Ministry for Social Development). Two reasons justified our choice. Firstly, we realized almost immediately that the women interviewed found it difficult to answer direct questions about such objective questions as the amount of money they spent weekly or monthly for food, clothes, etc. (most individuals would probably have these difficulties, if they had to answer to such questions without going through their bills and bank statements – but these women do not receive bills and have no bank account). Questionnaires also tend to neglect or to overlook the peculiar language of the interviewed persons, but this is a necessary evil, if they want to obtain data that can be summed up, compared, and treated statistically. On the other hand, by ignoring the linguistic problems faced by the interview participants as well as their particular view of things (which might not be translatable into numbers or into preformulated multiple options), questionnaires are prone to present contradictory results or distorted data. By way of example, in our very first interview, we asked a woman how much she typically spent on food in a month and the answer was simply unrealistic (hundreds of *reais*, she claimed). We then reformulated the question and asked her how often she bought food at the market or at the grocery and then what she would buy and in what quantity. Finally, by asking her and our local informants, we would ascertain the price of the items she purchased. This allowed us to come up with a sum that was much more realistic and probably closer to reality. We repeated the experiment several times, and we always registered this discrepancy between the first answer to the more abstract questions and the following answers to the more detailed questions.

the freest possible speech of the participants. In order to collect changes in grantees' moral and political views over time, repeated interviews were needed. That necessitated returning to the field at least a second time. It also required the building of a closer relationship so that, as Pierre Bourdieu would say, a "contract based on trust" could be built up with the people (Bourdieu 1999, 1). The interview was intended to understand as well as possible the deepest changes taking place within the people interviewed.

For this reason, the investigation required long periods of time, both in the data collection and in the analysis of the data.[9] The interviews varied in length, as people are different, especially when they are talking about themselves, opening themselves up to dialog, telling their stories, and describing the changes that have come about in their lives with this new situation. The experience of *Bolsa Família*, which has brought a regular income to these women, is very new to most of them. It has had an impact on their lives. Nevertheless, they continue to be poor and lack numerous rights. It takes a while for them to reveal the most complex changes, especially those related to moral decisions, such as marital breakups or the desire for such. One of the topics that they were able to speak about most freely relates to experiencing, sometimes for the first time, a greater level of personal freedom. They also spoke about gaining a precious feeling: having gained more respectability in their local community. We felt great obstacles in our ability to understand the issues in the type of research that we undertook. We sought to get around them as much as possible.

We recorded the interviews, then, we had them professionally transcribed so that the oral statements were turned into written text. As Bourdieu has warned, this is a crucial step. Speech has its own rhythm which is often lost in written text. As he said:

> Transcription already transforms the oral discussion decisively. To point the reader toward factors easily overlooked in a distracted, cursory reading, we have add titles, headings (always taken from the interview), and, especially, prefatory remarks. These benchmarks and observations recall the social conditions and conditionings of the men and women talking, along with their careers, education, and work experiences – everything that is at once hidden and disclosed, not only in the transcribed discussion but also in the pronunciation and intonation, everything transcription eradicates, from body language, gestures, demeanor, mimicry and looks, to silences, innuendos, and slips of the tongue. (Bourdieu 1999, 1f)

[9] We approached 181 women; only 12 refused to be interviewed. We decided not to include another 15 interviews by women who did not respond freely. Some were evidently trying to give us the answers they thought we wished to hear, while others were influenced by their husbands who refused to leave, or they seemed scared despite the fact that we always were accompanied by local contacts in order to gain their trust, as described above. We selected the women according to family size and age, but we also carried out blind interviews (one or two for every place we visited, for a total of 21) in order to make sure that our contacts, who helped us select the persons to be interviewed, had not chosen people whom *they* judged to be likely to give us certain answers and not others.

In summary, such an investigative technique requires that the voices of these women be listened to repeatedly and carefully, so that we might capture a dimension that might remain inaccessible to other methods researching the same issue.

Throughout the work, we made use of local contacts. On some occasions, we found people directly responsible for the implementation of the program such as social workers, managers, mayors, etc. At other times, we were lucky to receive help from people involved in local social and intellectual movements: all of them provided us with precious information about the situation in loco but most of the time we sought out the grantees directly, in order to avoid any type of bias.

We chose to interview grantees who lived in the countryside or in small, towns far from the coast, as we thought that their situation would be quite different from that of the urban poor, who have already been the subject of much research. The rural poor face very different problems, beginning with geographical isolation that results, almost always, in a lack of access to basic public services. In some cases, we were unable to obtain access to grantees in isolated regions without roads (in the Jequitinhonha Valley) since we would have had to ride in on horseback. This isolation means that their privations are deeper and harder to remedy. To this extent, they are more destitute than the urban poor; they are truly the worst off of Brazilian society.

This work blends empirical data collected from grantee interviews with theoretical reflections and incorporates a view of citizenship from different perspectives. This choice arose from our intention to not lose sight of the individual characteristics of the people who were the focus of this investigation, namely, women who live in a state of extreme material poverty, social marginalization, and almost always, submission to their families. For this reason, our narratives have taken advantage of many reflections by feminist thinkers who agree with the central concerns of many sociological theories of citizenship as well as normative theories about the subject. The issue of women's liberation, the possibility of their progressive increase in autonomy in the face of the many types of domination that they face, allows for this pluridimensional appropriation.

During the research, many questions were raised about the potential liberation of the women. One of the basic hypotheses is linked to the fact that they received monetary income. For this reason, this text discusses, if not exhaustively, the liberating role of such income. To this end, we turned to classic texts about the topic, as well as more recent sociological studies that have investigated and debated the many social functions assigned to money, in other words, topics which are common in the sociology of money.

Our work intends to explore several possibilities that were empirically observed throughout the research. The changes that were wrought in the subjectivity of the women interviewed, even if they were visible to the perception of the observer and the research methods used, are slow and, obviously, ambivalent. This research aimed exactly to collect the dimensions of ambiguity and, at times, even the paradoxes included in the experiences of those who had begun to receive a certain monetary income. For this reason, they began to become subject to a certain empowerment that took place due to the direct transfer of income. We also sought to understand, by way of the speech of the grantees, the potential cultural changes (not only the subjective ones) inherent to the *Bolsa Família* program, as incipient as they might be, but which had not yet become an object of specific cultural policies aiming at these women. The program lacks the political and institutional conditions for being implemented with the goal of realizing a more complete policy aiming at creating citizenship.

In this book, we will firstly present the necessity of listening directly to the *Bolsa Família* grantees and the difficulties associated with this task (Chap. 1). Then, we will briefly discuss the theoretical bases of our research (Chap. 2) and, particularly, those related to the already mentioned link between monetary income and individual autonomy. We will rely on many authors whose theories offer us precious conceptual and analytical tools that have enabled us to attempt to analyze the empirical data collected. In the following chapter, we present the interviews carried out between 2006 and 2011 in narrative form, with quotes from some of the women (Chap. 3). Next, we will comment upon many characteristics of the women interviewed and the extent as which they are representative of the poor in general; we also discuss problems peculiar to Brazilian poverty (Chap. 4). Finally, we will present our main thesis: that regular monetary income is an important instrument for individual and political autonomy (Chap. 5). Those readers more specifically interested in the analysis and discussion of the effects of the *Bolsa Família* on the grantees can skip ahead to Chaps. 3, 4, and 5, keeping in mind, however, that our evaluation of the interviews is supported by the theoretical foundation discussed in Chaps. 1 and 2.

The authors of this work come from differing intellectual backgrounds, philosophy, and social science, as they also come from different countries, namely, Italy and Brazil. This leads to different ways of seeing and differing theoretical perspectives which might lead, at certain times, to different emphases and tones, despite the fact that the book was written by four hands. One of the reasons behind our taking on this collaboration was our attempt, on the one hand, to bring political philosophy closer to an empirical analysis of social reality. On the other hand, the desire was to strengthen the interdisciplinary dialog that has existed since the birth of sociology. For these reasons, we consider this book to be an interpretive experiment in which a dialog took place between various contemporary normative theories of citizenship and which came face to face with the reality of these extremely poor women who were *Bolsa Família* grantees.

While carrying out a piece of research, one accumulates unrepayable debts. First and foremost is that to the very women interviewed who gave of their time and allowed us to glance at some of their most intimate emotions and their deepest torments arising not only from their situations of material deprivation but also from their emotional backgrounds. The second debt is to those people in the various locations who helped us with information and practical suggestions. In particular, we would like to thank Luiz Sávio de Almeida, Cícero Péricles de Carvalho, Golbery Lessa, and Genivaldo "Geno" Vieira da Silva and his son Claudemir in Alagoas; Ana and Sandra, nuns at the Araçuaí diocese in the Vale do Jequitinhonha, Zeca (student at Unicamp, who was born in Araçuaí), and Zé, a labor unionist who accompanied us on our visit to Itinga in the Vale; the staff at the Secretariat of Social Welfare in Teresina, Jean Teixeira da Costa, João Paulo de Assis Neto, Maria do Socorro Brito Cavalcanti e Menezes, and Roseli Oliveira Ramos, as well as the State Secretariat for Social Welfare in São Luiz no Maranhão; and, finally, João, Juju, and Marcos Costa Lima, in Recife.

We would like to thank Silvana Gentili for the dedication and skill with which she carried out the transcriptions of the tapes, which was crucial for the writing of this book.

We would also like to thank all of the following people who, in different ways, contributed to the elaboration of this manuscript: Fernando Coelho, Gisleine Aver, Gilberto Bercovici, Rubem Murilo Leão Rego, Debora Spini, Alberto Cupani, and Lara Bethânia Zílio; Nadia Urbinati, Pedro Meira Monteiro, and the other participants in the debate about this topic that took place at Princeton University, USA, in September 2007; Rahel Jaeggi, Axel Honneth, Kathya Araujo, Marek Hrubec, and the other participants in the IV International Symposium on Justice that took place in September 2009 in Porto Alegre, Brazil; the participants in the international colloquium "Philosophy and Social Sciences" that was carried out in Prague in May 2010; Barbara Fritz, Sérgio Costa, and the participants of a workshop about the topic of the book organized by the *Freie Universität* of Berlin in June 2010; and André Singer and Cícero Romão de Araujo, who in two different seminars (such as those that took place at CENEFIC in December 2010 and another in October 2011 at CEDEC), helped significantly to form our thinking on certain issues.

References

Adorno, Theodor W. et al. *Philosophische Elemente einer Theorie der Gesellschaft*. Frankfurt a. M.: Suhrkamp, 2008.

Bourdieu, Pierre (ed.). *The Weight of the World*. Stanford: Stanford University Press, 1999.

Margalit, Avishai. *The Decent Society*. Cambridge (MA): Harvard University Press, 1996.

Marx, Karl. *Critique of the Gotha Program*. Rockwille (MD): Wildside. 2008

Silva, Maria Ozanira S.; Yazbek, Maria Carmelita; Di Giovanni, Geraldo. *A política social brasileira no século XXI. A prevalência dos programas de transferência de renda*. 4ª edição. São Paulo: Cortez, 2008.

Chapter 1
Hearing the Voice of the Poor

> A sense of shame bids philosophy not to repress George Simmel's insight that its history shows amazingly few indications of the sufferings of humankind.
> Theodor W. Adorno[1]

During the course of our research, we came across several methodological problems. We are not referring so much to the undeniable hermeneutic challenges of understanding and decodifying the women's language and the way that they perceive and understand their world and their situation. The biggest challenge is, in fact, to find the right stance, not that of a mere impartial and omniscient observer, nor, on the other hand, that of participants who are excessively involved in the phenomena that they are trying to describe. This issue is worthy of considerable discussion before we go on to present our results.

1.1 Critical Theory from an Ethical Perspective

This project works from the perspective of critical theory. It presents the results of our research by way of a narrative that reveals the links between the empirical data and theoretical assumptions. We feel it is important to make it clear what these theoretical assumptions are and what we understand critical theory to be.

Various scholars have pointed out how social criticism is an essential component of any reflection on society (see, e.g., Boltanski 2010). In Durkheim's work, there was already constant attention to the risk of social disintegration arising from the very nature of modern society, which goes to show that, from its very beginnings, sociology has tended to criticize reality and its pathologies. Contrary to traditional political philosophy, however, critical sociology does not make use of ideal and universal models of society like the Platonic Republic cited by Kant in

[1] Adorno (2004, 153)

A. Pinzani, W. L. Rego, *Money, Autonomy and Citizenship*,
https://doi.org/10.1007/978-3-030-01361-5_1

his *Critique of Pure Reason* (B 372 s.). In other words, critical sociology has to find the criteria on which to base its critique of society in actual social reality. It does not offer, in summary, a critique that is external like that based on the above-mentioned ideal models but an internal one that seeks to unveil the tensions and even the contradictions that prevent society from achieving its own view of itself. Accordingly, society might not keep its promises and might not respect the values and ideals that make up its moral and ethical foundation. Therefore, these promises are sometimes seen to serve only as ideological cover for unconfessable interests. Society can, in sum, be accused alternatively of being hypocritical, traitorous to its own ideals, or incapable of reaching them. One can also call into question the ideals themselves and show how they end up contradicting important phenomena within society (as happened with the bourgeoisie critiques of the French *Ancien Regime*). By way of example, our contemporary capitalistic, globalized society can be criticized for not fulfilling its promise to guarantee full individual autonomy (individuals remain prisoners of impersonal mechanisms that make it impossible to decide their own lives in a truly autonomous fashion), or, alternatively, one can call into question the very ideal of personal autonomy (either because it serves as a basis for that individualism that leads to social disintegration and results in the typical forms of alienation that characterize today's society or for being an empty concept that has no resemblance to an economic system which, like capitalism, is governed by supraindividual forces).

Critical theory, as well as critical sociology, is characterized by its intention to renounce ideal models of society. It tries to carry out an internal critique of society, either by pointing out its contradictions (resulting from a failure to keep its promises) or by calling attention to the negative consequences for its members caused by the realization of its ideals and values (e.g., alienation). Thus, it is important to distinguish between several perspectives which serve as a starting point for an internal critique of the society and its systems: economic, political, legal, etc. The first is a merely functional perspective: The target of criticism is the poor functioning of the system. A classic example would be a critique of capitalism that accuses it of not producing the well-being that it has promised (at least according to its greatest supporters such as Friedrich von Hayek or Milton Friedman). This type of critique believes it to be possible to adjust the system by way of a few changes: It takes seriously the promises which have not been kept and does not find it impossible to achieve them due to any inherent logic within the society or the system in question. The second perspective is a moral one that points out the fact that a society, or the system, is contradicting a moral norm or ideal that they have themselves accepted. An example is a critique of capitalism for exploiting workers and for thereby violating the concept of justice that it claims to follow (e.g., through the ideas of fair exchange and of the free contract between employer and employee). In this case as well, the opportunity is left open for change to take place within the system (through its moralization or the elimination of a specific case of unfairness) so that the system lives up to its own values and moral ideals; however, this is not always possible (e.g., from the perspective of the Marxist theory of surplus value, capitalism is intrinsically unjust since it is based on the exploitation of the workforce and cannot renounce such exploitation without ceasing to be capitalism).The third perspective is an ethical one that highlights how life in a certain society is not a good one, according to its own criteria of a good life. One example is when capitalism is criticized for leading to alienation, instead of helping people become autonomous. From this viewpoint, once again, it can be argued that society manages to eliminate the obstacles that prevent people from living a good life, or it can be claimed that alienation appears to be irreparable.[2]

The various scholars who claim to be or who can be thought to be representatives of critical theory normally take the second or third position. While Adorno and Horkheimer obviously describe capitalistic society from an ethical viewpoint that does not allow itself to be fooled about the possibility of capitalism enabling a good life, Honneth and, to a certain extent, Habermas position themselves as looking from the moral point of view, and they still believe in the possibility of moral progress within contemporary, capitalistic society (in the possibility that society can become more fair). A theory informed by critical theory, therefore, should, first of all, take one of these perspectives. In our case, we chose the ethical perspective.

Such a theory must, in the second place, base itself on empirical social scientific data, but without falling into the trap of believing absolutely in said results (in other words, without taking a blindly positivistic view). Instead, it should contextualize said data, either by critiquing the social scientific methodology, such as in the example of the writing about the epistemological states of sociology by Adorno and Habermas in the 1960s (Adorno et al. 1976), or by critiquing the ideological assumptions of said methodologies, namely, the biases and the interests that may lead the social sciences to offer a distorted view of social phenomena. The type of position that we are taking starts from empirical data about the way in which people recount experiences of injustice or describe their situations so that we might compare such stories with the ideals and the dominant values of society in order to display points of tension or even contradictions.

In the third place, a position inspired by critical theory should criticize the dominant images in society relative to certain social phenomena, i.e., poverty. This task is intimately related to the critique of the social sciences mentioned above, since there is a relation of reciprocal influence between these areas of inquiry and the dominant images. In other words, the way in which poverty is habitually defined by social sciences and the image of it held by society exert reciprocal influence on each other. This becomes particularly evident in the case where poverty is defined by a lack of connection with the world of work and economic productivity. This third task goes hand in hand with the second (listening to the voices of the people involved) so as to provide instruments of critical interpretation of the empirical facts, since the stories in question are strongly influenced by the dominant images within society.

---

[2] We have taken up once more, with some modification, this distinction between the three perspectives of the cycle of lectures about critiques of capitalism by Rahel Jaeggi at the Humboldt-Universität, Berlin in 2010.

1.2 The Role of the Social Researcher

In his essay "The Poor" (1903), Georg Simmel spoke about the "exclusion of the poor." In saying this, he did not merely refer to their invisibility but to the fact that they lack any voice with which to influence public political decisions that concern them (Simmel 1965, 123). Apparently, things have not changed much: Most anti-poverty measures are taken on the basis of statistical, quantitative, or macroeconomic data. Poor people, in sum, are seen merely as objects of public policies rather than as subjects of politics, and this represents a form of loss of autonomy. This might lead to the demand that the poor should begin to participate directly in decision-making about their situation, but such a demand faces a theoretical as well as a practical issue. The theoretical issue consists of the very definition of the phenomenon of poverty and the identification of who is poor. The practical question refers to the difficulty of the poor in organizing themselves in order to choose representatives to speak in their name – a difficulty that arises precisely from their poverty (particularly in the case of misery or extreme poverty). When we approach the first issue in Chap. 4, we would like to point out that it is not our intention (nor was it so throughout the research) to speak in the name of the poor or to play the part of their representatives. On the contrary, we started from the position that it is necessary to hear their voices and to let them describe their own circumstances. This need, however, should take into account the problem of the potential distortions that any understanding of their situation might undergo. Does this might mean that we researchers found ourselves in a privileged position from which we were able to observe this situation without distortion?

With respect to this, in a 2009 interview, the French sociologist Luc Boltanski criticized his teacher Pierre Bourdieu for making an excessively marked distinction between the social actor, on the one hand, and the sociologist on the other. While the former is never aware of their motives, even if they are able to make calculations and strategic choiches, the latter has privileged access to the truth, since they are able to reveal the hidden motives of the agent (Boltanski 2009, 82 ss.). The sociologist becomes the only active subject in social criticism, whose goal is to open the eyes of the blind masses who play a passive role. We will not go into whether Boltanski's criticism of Bourdieu is or is not correct. What is of interest is rather the warning that social critics may easily take a paternalistic role and think that they know more about the situation they are describing than those involved in it. They tend to negate the legitimacy or, at least, to negate the value of what the objects of their studies say about themselves, about how they see themselves, etc., since these descriptions are presumably tainted by an ignorance of their "true" situation which only the social critic is able to observe. From this perspective, one can object that the victims of injustice have privileged access to their own knowledge, that they know it better than any observer (cf. Renault 2004, 44). The American philosopher Michael Walzer refers to the same issue when he states that social critics are themselves members of the society they are criticizing (Walzer 1987). Notably Walzer condemns what he calls the "heroic philosopher," i.e., the scholar who judges society based on normative ideal models that are built up in an abstract fashion (Walzer 1981). In other words, the idea of the social critic as an external observer can be criticized either because it takes on a paternalistic attitude (Boltanski's critique) or because it takes a sort of political Platonism according to which one ought to observe society from a spot that does not exist and modify it working from an Archimedean point (Walzer's critique).

On the other hand, and contrary to Walzer, it can be seen, as Boltanski himself has done, that "in order to carry out sociology, one must place oneself outside of society, for those who are inside the social world are merely experts, specialists" (Boltanski 2009, 95). The same can be said of social criticism: It should distance itself from the object of its critique so that it can work on it. This is to say that it should keep itself free of the mechanisms of domination or alienation that it intends to study and censure in order to avoid becoming a prisoner of them, just as specialists might limit themselves to thinking within the molds and according to the logical and intellectual categories of their own society. The difference is radical. One example would be the difference between showing how the logic of the market ends up dominating public health policy and even the criteria that guide its implementation – which is what one expect from a social critic – and, on the other hand, applying precisely such logic to planning public health policy or hospital management and prioritizing profitability over patient health, which is exactly what is expected from specialists. However, it becomes hard to defend the idea that the position of the social critic should be that of someone who is completely external to society. In the first place, this is true because this Archimedean point does not exist, as Walzer has pointed out. Secondly, it is true because it goes against the very goal of critical theory, which is to perform an immanent critique of society so as to avoid falling into the abovementioned Platonism of abstract ideals raised up by heroic philosophers. Contrary to Walzer and Boltanski, it can be noted that, with Adorno and Horkheimer, it is impossible to hope that people living in a society characterized by alienation and ideology are capable of adequately describing their situation and arriving at a point of view from which they are able to criticize it. A concrete example, people who live in a situation of poverty or misery, who are deprived of the basic conditions for satisfying what many scholars believe to be basic necessities, and whose voice is not only inaudible but dampened, these people are often unaware of the fact that they are victims of some form of injustice. They are not always aware of having been treated unfairly.[3] In other words, what may attract the attention of an observer as having resulted from an injustice might be interpreted very differently by the very victims of said injustice. The American philosopher Brooke Ackerly has an excellent statement of this dilemma: "because it is difficult to recognize oppression one has not experienced and because it is sometimes difficult to understand and articulate oppression one has experienced, social critics need a method" (Ackerly 2000, 15) – namely, a

[3] This is precisely the greatest difficulty with a theory of recognition based on the idea that what counts is people's subjective experience and the objective situation in which they find themselves – this appears to us to be the best critique of Axel Honneth by Nancy Fraser (cf. Fraser and Honneth 2003).

method capable of criticizing unfair aspects of social life without being paternalistic or platonic in the ways described above. To put it in another way, in order to carry out our research, we had to adopt a stance that listened to the voice of the victims of the mechanisms of social exclusion while taking into account the possibility that this voice might have been distorted by the very mechanisms in question. However, despite the risk of distortion mentioned, we found it and we still find it essential to hear these voices, not only for a methodological reason but also for a moral one, which we will now elucidate.

1.3 Why Listen to the Voice of the Poor

The Italian philosopher Salvatore Veca alerts us to the importance of language in relation to individual dignity and autonomy. Language is a social institution in which it is possible to articulate the experience of suffering and that evokes the existence of a community of speakers and agents who know each other. Dignity is related to inclusion in said society that is based on communication and recognition. "Exclusion and a lack of recognition give rise to that peculiar form of suffering (which is perhaps the epitome of social, political or civil suffering: in the sense of being typical of those who are actors in a community of actors in space and time) which we define as the experience of humiliation or debasement" (Veca 1997, 107). Such humiliation represents an erosion of individual autonomy, as it represents a disconnection from the community and implies a loss of self-respect. Exclusion from the community, by breaking the connection between the individual and the community (which Veca calls the interpersonal chain), erodes the bases of the subject's formation of the self (intrapersonal chain). Thus, the affirmation of individual autonomy is linked to the capacity that individuals have to use a certain expression to describe themselves without being subject to a vocabulary (or a description) imposed by others (Veca 1997, 111 s.). There is a double humiliation here. On the one hand, individuals are silenced. On the other, they see themselves as subject to a description that does not correspond to their view of themselves, a view that, in fact, disrespects their own self-image. This can be seen daily in Brazil by the way in which the poor are described by the members of the middle classes and even by the media (e.g., when a poor person is described as "a lowlife," as "lazy," and as a "bum" or if they are accused of being responsible for their situation, without ever being asked for their view of their poverty[4].") Once they are labeled as dangerous, useless, and outsiders to the community, the poor are expressly excluded from it. Yet, at the same time, these excluded people are expected to act like they are committed members of that society. The poor in Brazil live continuously under tension. On the one hand, they are excluded and humiliated by a legal and economic system

[4] Translator's note: It may be seen as a confirmation of the writers' point that Brazilian Portuguese is especially rich in pejorative terms for describing people of lower classes who they suspect to be of being morally suspicious.

that mistreats them. On the other hand, they are called to participate in a system and, thereby, to respect the rules and the social and legal norms.

It is in this light that we are reminded of the comments of Charles Taylor (1995, 97 ff.), who we believe has clearly explained the importance of the linguistic aspect in the economics of the feelings of self-respect and self-esteem:

> If language serves to express a new kind of awareness, then it may not only make possible a new awareness of things, an ability to describe them; it may also open new way of responding to things, of feeling. If in expressing our thoughts about things we can come to have new thoughts, then in expressing or feelings we can come to have transformed feelings. [...] If language must be seen primarily as activity, if it is what is constantly created and recreated in speech, then it becomes relevant to note that the primary locus of speech is conversation. We speak together, to each other. Language is fashioned and grows not principally in monologue but in dialogue or, better, in the life of the speech community. [...] The language I speak, the web I can never fully dominate and oversee, can never be just *my* language; it is always *our* language. [...] Speech also serves to express different relations in which we stand to each other: intimate, formal, official, causal, joking, serious. In naming them, we shape our social relations, as husbands and wives, parents and children, as equal citizens in a republic, subjects of the same monarch, or followers of a war leader. From this point of view, we can see that it is not only the speech community that shapes and creates language, but language that constitutes and sustains the speech community.

Following on from Veca and Taylor, we argue that the linguistic dimension is fundamental for the expression of human dignity since it is based not on an innate quality of human beings[5] but on the recognition of the right of people to participate in the justification of the state of things that affect their lives, when similar states depend on human action (as in the case of legal norms or political, institutional, or economic decisions). This right to justification[6] is central to the formation of respect for the self and for others. Therefore, it is essential for the formation of individual autonomy. We are dealing, in other words, with a basic right in the sense of Henri Shue, i.e., a right which is necessary for the enjoyment of other rights (Shue 1996, 19). From this perspective, the social existence of individuals implies processes in which one demands justification by others and the others demand justification by us. It then follows that society can be seen as an ordered entity that is organized around justifications that sustain its legitimacy but that can also be called into question (cf. Forst 2011). For this purpose, however, individuals must have the capacity and the ability to criticize, to demand justifications, and to elucidate their positions regarding the reality that they feel and experience to be unfair or that needs to be altered for some reason. The inability to articulate their demands or even to describe their situation in terms and from a point of view other than that of the dominant classes leads to an inevitable loss of autonomy. Autonomy presupposes that individuals are able to affirm themselves vís-a-vis the other as actors who are capable of verbally justifying their actions, intentions, wishes, and needs.

---

[5] A transcendent basis for human dignity, as based on the Christian doctrine of humankind's likeness to God, appears to us to be neither philosophically demonstrable nor sociologically feasible within a secular society.

[6] This concept receives special attention by Rainer Forst in Forst (2011).

It is fundamental, therefore, to ensure that the individuals in question are able to define for themselves the relevant aspects of their situation. This is the strategy chosen by scholars such as Pierre Bourdieu with his *The Weight of the World* interviews (Bourdieu 1999) or like Emmanuel Renault with his idea of an "injustice clinic" (Renault 2004, 2008). As stated above about the work of Bourdieu, the data gathered in interviews with many types of poor people (long-term unemployed, or other people at the margin of a rich society like that of the French, or people living in a traditionally poor society, like in the case of other research works that will be described below) "makes accessible to social criticism the daily suffering that is normally banalized as the 'generic misery' either by those involved or by public discourse" (Sonderegger 2009, 71). Such interviews allow the individuals in question to express their perceptions of things, offering up a view of themselves and an explanation of their situation that is of their own construction. A good example is offered by the project *Consultations with the Poor* that was carried out by the World Bank in the 1990s (Narayan et al. 2000a, b). The goal of the project was to "to enable a wide range of poor people – women and men, young and old – in diverse countries and conditions to share their views" about poverty (Narayan et al. 2000a, 3). The study showed that on many continents and in many countries, in the most different cultural situations, there is a general consensus about the elements that define not only human well-being but especially its opposite. The coordinator of the project, Deepa Narayan, calls our attention to such elements:

> Experiences of illbeing include material lack and want (of food, housing and shelter, livelihood, assets and money); hunger, pain and discomfort; exhaustion and poverty of time; exclusion, rejection, isolation and loneliness; bad relations with others, including bad relations within the family; insecurity, vulnerability, worry, fear and low self-confidence; and powerlessness, helplessness, frustration and anger. (Narayan et al. 2000a, 21)

Now, as it has already been mentioned, one could counterargue that people who live in poverty are not good judges of their situation, as the situation itself makes them incapable of articulating their needs in a relatively autonomous fashion. The lack of education and the urgency to satisfy basic needs might lead them to a distorted view of their problems and of the potential solutions. Naturally, people will always run into obstacles to understanding and expressing their needs – obstacles linked to their biographical experience, education, religious beliefs, etc. These obstacles challenge all people, independently of their social or economic situation. From this point of view, the poor are as likely to err as the rich or the middle class. Unlike the latter, however, they will always lack the ability to organize themselves to defend their interests and to try to realize them by way of appropriate political action. One of the main reasons behind this consists of the internalization of the negative image of poverty and the poor that is held by the rest of society or at least by the most ideologically powerful segment of the society. The negative image starts by making the poor out to be responsible for their situation (as if they had chosen to be poor, to be born in a poor family, a poor neighborhood, a poor rural region, i.e., in a poor country or one that neglects them) and may arrive to a kind of racism that sees them as being anthropologically or – in more "modern" terms – genetically different from the rest of the population. This attribution of responsibility gives rise to the negative (self-)image of these people. At best, poverty is stigmatized as a humiliating situation that – whatever its origin – imposes silence and shame on those who find themselves in it. This is what makes it practically impossible for the poor to raise their voices, since, for that to occur, they would need a minimum level of self-esteem that is denied them, in several ways, by the negative image mentioned above, which they tend to internalize. The loss of voice is equal to the lack of recognition of the individual as a subject by those who have silenced them or do not want to hear them or even to see them. It is as if, in addition to having been silenced, they have been made invisible as well, as in Ralph Ellison's novel *The Invisible Man* (Ellison 1952).[7]

This invisibility becomes obvious when the poverty of a large number of people is simply forgotten or removed from the moral conscious of their fellow citizens. In the words of Thomas Pogge, it is not merely hypocrisy. We are dealing with an outright lie relative to our moral responsibilities. If we really thought of ourselves as having a morally responsible attitude toward others, we would not be able to tolerate the absolute lack of resources, the deprivation, the humiliation, and the suffering that so many people live in: "We would seek to develop a full understanding of morality's demands on our conduct in these areas, and we would try to live up to these demands. In fact, we do no such thing even while we traffic heavily in moral" (Pogge 2010, 3). Pogge is speaking here of the inhabitants of wealthy countries and their attitudes toward the "poor" countries, but this type of reasoning can also be applied domestically[8]. Our focus in this work, however, is not on the attitudes of Brazilian citizens toward their poor or miserable compatriots but the public policy and the position of state institutions toward the problems of the poverty and misery faced by a large percentage of the population.

[7] For more about the theme of invisibility, see Honneth (2003).

[8] Pogge's work (e.g., Pogge 2002, 2010) is fundamental for understanding the question of poverty from a global perspective and within international relations. However, the scope of our research is limited to the Brazilian context, and we will therefore not make use of Pogge's analyses and arguments.

Chapter 2
Theoretical Background

> Can people be considered as truly free if they are hungry, live in misery, are unemployed, are humiliated by their inability to feed and educate their children? These people are not free.
> Sandro Pertini[1]

This chapter will set out the theoretical bases that guided the formulation and evaluation of the interviews. Special attention is given to the *capability approach*[2]of Sen and Nussbaum and Marx and Simmel's theories of money. Other scholars who were relevant for our research include Emmanuel Renault, Avishai Margalit, Richard Sennett, Pierre Bourdieu and Iris Marion Young. Since this project focuses on women, we have also found inspiration in works of writers such as Susan M. Okin, Viviana A. Zelizer, Giovanna Zincone and Nancy Fraser, but most of all in John Stuart Mill.The theories of Sen and Simmel are especially pertinent, as we want to highlight the relationship between monetary income and autonomy: our basic hypothesis is that, at many levels, the presence of a regular monetary income facilitates the processes by which individuals gain autonomy. We begin with the capability approach in order to define the concept of individual autonomy and go on to look at some theoretical questions linked to understanding the phenomenology of poverty that will be laid out in the fourth chapter. We opted for this theory, because it is not "primarily interested in investigating the question of how much resources are being spent in total but rather whether the resources are directed appropriately, taking the needs of the individual adequately into account" (Goerne 2010, 12).

Alexander Goerne (2010, 10 s.) pointed out that the capability approach is a potentially useful concept for evaluating public policies, such as in our case. However, this must be based on one or more normative points of reference that help identify the valuable functionings[3] that are the subject of the policies in question. Our intention

[1] Pertini was a socialist politician who was President of the Italian Republic between 1978 and 1985.

[2] Capability is a term used by Sen that fuses 'capacity' with 'ability'.

[3] The concepts of capability and functioning will be defined below in Sect. 2.4.

A. Pinzani, W. L. Rego, *Money, Autonomy and Citizenship*,
https://doi.org/10.1007/978-3-030-01361-5_2

was not to apply Sen's categories of capability and functioning so as to provide a detailed evaluation of public anti-poverty policies (Others have done so, such as Deneulin et al. 2006; Comim et al. 2008; Anand et al. 2009; Deneulin et al. 2009). Our goal, rather, was to make use of said categories, firstly, for descriptive ends and, secondly, to support a more generalized evaluation. We had two normative points of reference: (1) a basic level of individual moral autonomy and (2) the development of a perception of self as a part of a larger political community. In short, our normative references can be identified as: (1) individual autonomy and (2) citizenship.

Starting from these normative references, we were able to identify a series of basic valuable functionings. Those related to individual autonomy are: the perception of oneself as a subject capable of making free choices without having to give in to the harsh need represented by the lack of basic material resources such as adequate food intake, decent shelter, healthcare, etc.; a sense (at least a nascent one) of becoming master of one's own life; the ability to take responsibility for one's own actions without having to obey inexorable mechanism of behavior imposed by material deprivation and by the immediate social milieu (in particular by husband and family); and finally, the capacity to care for oneself and one's family without depending on others individuals (i.e. freedom from interpersonal dependence). The basic valuable functionings related to citizenship are: the perception of being considered by the State as a real person whose needs cannot be satisfied individually; the awareness that policies of public assistance are not a sign of charity or personal favors but are due to a constitutionally protected right; and the awareness that one's vote is of worth and is relevant to determining one's life conditions.

The basic idea of an evaluation of public policies from a capabilities approach is (1) to identify capabilities necessary for achieving the valuable functionings and (2) to identify which resources (commodities, in Sen's language) ought to be distributed by the policy in question, taking into consideration the factors that turn these resources into the previously defined capabilities. This clarifies the methodological necessity to define the factors of conversion that represent the set of social conditions that influence how people convert goods which have been distributed into capabilities.

In the case of the BF, we are dealing with the distribution of just one good, namely, monetary income. This income leads to a set of capabilities that are necessary for achieving the functionings linked to personal autonomy and citizenship that were mentioned above. This transformation, however, depends on social conditions that are peculiar to the group of people who are the targets of our research, i.e. poor women living in economically disadvantaged, rural regions or in semi-rural neighborhoods on the periphery of urban centers. This gives rise to the need to go on to a phenomenological description of these women's' lives (see specifically Chaps. 3 and 4) in order to identify the conversion factors to be taken into consideration. We opted for a type of narrative that justifies the selection of the abovementioned normative references, the description of the capabilities and the conversion factors. Finally, it also explains how monetary income creates capabilities and also achieves valuable functionings, not in an isolated fashion but as part of a unified discourse made up of several elements that evoke others and thus form a homogenous fabric.

2.1 Poverty, Suffering, and Humiliation

It is traditional for utilitarians and others to use the satisfaction of individual preferences (which they sometimes call "happiness") as the criterion for measuring people's lifestyles. Amartya Sen criticizes this view for being overly abstract and distanced from reality:

> Consider a very deprived person who is poor, exploited, overworked and ill, but who has been made satisfied with his lot by social conditioning (through, say, religion, or political propaganda, or cultural pressure). Can we possibly believe that he is doing well just because he is happy and satisfied? Can the living standard of a person be high if the life that he or she leads is full of deprivation? The standard of life cannot be so detached from the nature of the life the person leads. (Sen 1987, 8)[4]

Happiness is not a good criterion for evaluating the life of a person for several reasons, two in particular. The first one deals with its subjective character: a person can be happy due to self-denial or to exterior conditioning (as Sen points out). The second refers to the impossibility of arriving at a universally accepted definition. In his analysis of the social causes of human suffering (Moore 1972, 1978), Barrington Moore states that we do not have at our disposal a generally accepted definition of happiness, while we do have several reliable definitions of suffering – especially socially avoidable suffering. With this statement, Moore speaks to suffering arising from human action rather than natural causes (he would exclude, e.g., aging, disease, natural disasters, etc.) and that related less to immediate personal interaction than to social relationships (in short, it does not relate to those acts that cause pain between individuals, such as romantic betrayal or physical violence between individuals, but to sources of suffering like war, poverty or exploitation, etc.). He focuses, therefore, on the social and avoidable nature of this type of suffering, which could be prevented if the originating actions and situations failed to take place. By pointing out the social nature of this suffering, it ought to be possible to attribute responsibilities for it to institutions or individuals so that the duty to make reparations might eventually come to pass.

Emmanuel Renault's concept of social suffering is particularly useful in this context (Renault 2004, 2008). This French scholar distinguishes between living through a situation of injustice and experiencing injustice: in the latter case, the experience is accompanied by the feeling of injustice (Renault 2004, 35). The experience of injustice is felt as a violation of a series of fundamental normative expectations and consists of a qualitative experience. What is at play here is not just the quantity of basic resources demanded by people who feel themselves to be victims of injustice, but a qualitative claim. It is not a greater quantity of resources that is demanded but the abolishment of the injustice itself (Renault 2004, 42 ss.). When the women we interviewed complained about the limited amounts of the BF, theirs was less a quantitative complaint rather than a qualitative one: it expressed the feeling that this amount did not sufficiently recognize their needs and their dignity. Therefore, the

[4] See more about this phenomenon called "adaptive preferences" in Burstin et al. (2010).

distributive paradigm of more traditional theories of justice (e.g. that of John Rawls) lacks the necessary scope to comprehend the situation of the BF grantees. The experience of injustice that they live through is related to a situation that is simply intolerable. However, as Renault reminds us, what is intolerable can be experienced, but it cannot be measured quantitatively (Renault 2004, 77). What is in play is having one's personal integrity violated, and one's individuality denied recognition. That is why Renault proposes the concept of social suffering, since it arises from social origins. The subjective side of this suffering means that it is a psychological pain that can be felt by the subject as intimate and personal. This means that subjects do not see its social nature and take on the responsibility for their situation (Renault 2004, 334). To tell the truth, we are dealing with a form of social pathology rather than an individual one. Individual therapeutic responses (i.e. such as in the medicalization of poverty that treats the depression of the poor as if its genesis was to be found merely in their individual biographies) are not appropriate; demanded is rather the "transformation of the social condition that give rise to the suffering" (Renault 2004, 344). Pierre Bourdieu, on the other hand, in his postscript to *The Weight of the World* speaks of the "moral suffering" produced by the "passive violence of economic and social structures" (Bourdieu 1999, 629). Serge Paugam points to the painful trials to which people in socially demeaning situations are subject: "the people who undergo this type of experience feel as they had been disqualified". They become progressively aware of the distance that separates them from the rest of the population and come to suppose that "their daily behavior is interpreted as a sign of the inferiority of their status, like a sort of social deficiency" (Paugam 1991, 6).

Renault calls our attention to the problematic role of liberalism that does not allow social suffering to reveal itself. As the preeminent social theory of modern times, liberalism focuses on the concept of rights, relegating to invisibility those life experiences grounded in domination and poverty: "Political liberalism, having excluded the questions of well-being and suffering from the domain of rights, has led to the political invisibility of problems related to poverty and misery" (Renault 2008, 105). One potential exception to this critique might be the position of Amartya Sen, whose liberalism not only fails to exclude such problems but brings them center stage. It is worth citing the words of Antoin Lousao:

> Amartya Sen is not content to reproduce the liberal political model, extending its access to a greater number of people. One of his critiques to some proposals for development and the eradication of poverty deals exactly with the insufficient nature of the amplification of the liberal model without putting its basic foundation to question[5]. If on the one hand, Amarty Sen has inherited some of the principles of traditional liberalism, his critical body of work approach does not limit itself to expanding the social reach of the model but offers a severe critique of its foundation. (Lousao 2010, s. p.)

[5] "Regarding this issue, we can cite an enlightening comment by Amartya Sen at a lecture given at the *Institut d'Etudes Politiques* in Paris (*Sciences Po*) in June 2007, about the model of micro-credit developed by Mohamed Yunus (who had given a lecture at the same location a few months previously). Sen situated himself, politically, to the left of M. Yunus, since the later did not question the basis of the liberal political model, rather limited his attention to expanding people's access to the model," (note by Antoine Lousao, Ibidem). Regarding micro-credit, see the discussion at the end of Sect. 5.4 of the current volume.

Returning to Renault's observations, it is worth pointing out that the elites of any society are generally able to impose their view of the world. They can deny that the suffering of the poor is dictated by the social and institutional structures that place them in a position of dominance. Therefore, they do not feel minimally responsible for said suffering. So, "ideological justification and psychological defense come together in the euphemizing of suffering and in the imputation of responsibility for it" onto the poor themselves (Renault 2008, 207). This discourse blames the poor for their own misery and condemns their irrationality, whether regarding their use of money (they are accused of drinking *cachaça*[6] and wasting money), whether in regard to their sexuality (the poor have more children than they can support). They are condemned as well for their immorality, their moral depravity, particularly regarding sex (precocious and promiscuous sexual activity), their tendency towards criminal activity, etc. Meanwhile, the irrationality and immorality of the elite that contributes to the phenomenon of poverty and to the suffering of so many people is ignored or even praised as examples of rationality and ethical correctness. In the case of the upper classes, sexual promiscuity is seen as a form of freedom. An exaggeratedly ostentatious and consumerist lifestyle is presented as a model to be followed. Criminal activity ranging from tax evasion, to the exploitation of workers (e.g. the refusal to offer labor contracts), to drug use is trivialized or considered acceptable.

Social suffering is seen as natural, or is ascribed to people's individual characteristics (the individual's personal characteristics make them poor; they are weak, they are childish, they are old, they are sick, they are handicapped, etc.). The elite appeal to economic laws that are presented as natural, immutable, and independent of human intervention.

At times the social causes of human suffering are not immediately observable and identifiable. They can be found in a time long past, so far back that the question of responsibility for the suffering is impossible to answer. It is possible that the causes may be deeply rooted in the structure of a society (like in the case of slavery in Brazil). In these cases, it can be argued that the suffering has been institutionalized. It is not the actions of specific individuals that have caused it but those of institutions. Here, the concept of a decent society of Avishai Margalit becomes useful (Margalit 1996).

Margalit distinguishes a decent society from a civilized one. In the former, society's institutions do not humiliate individuals. In the latter, the members of society do not humiliate each other. The concept of a decent society is, therefore, a macro-ethical one, since it refers to a society as a whole. That of civilized society, on the other hand, is a micro-ethical concept: it deals with private, interpersonal relationships. This distinction between macro and micro-ethics allows us to differentiate between many types and many increasing levels of solidarity. At the lowest level we can think of solidarity between the members of a family, or family solidarity. The community of solidarity, for its part, can be amplified to wider and wider circles

[6]Translator's note: *Cachaça* is a strong, alcoholic drink made from distilled sugar cane juice and that is popular with all social classes in Brazil.

which, however, still remain at the local level. This is surpassed by solidarity among citizens which can be called civic or citizen solidarity. Finally, there are two types of solidarity that extend past national borders. The first one can be found among members of transnational groups (that range from religious communities to groups that are defined by sexual orientation or by gender: a woman may, for example, feel solidarity for oppressed women worldwide). The second form can be called cosmopolitan solidarity, and it deals with that solidarity that can be felt with humans in general and that shows itself particularly when one tries to relieve the suffering of people in other countries (e.g. following natural disasters). In our case, we are dealing exclusively with civic solidarity.

Margalit defines humiliation as "any sort of behavior or condition that constitutes a sound reason for a person to consider his or her self-respect injured" (Margalit 1996, 9). He insists that it is irrelevant whether the person actually feels humiliated. What is relevant is the fact that the person has a sound reason for feeling humiliated. It is worth pointing out that the humiliation in question only becomes relevant when the circumstances behind it arise from the actions or omissions of other agents. This excludes other instances, such as one in which we humiliate ourselves or when we find ourselves in a situation which is perceived to be humiliating for external reasons (e.g. due to an illness or accident). Thus, the responsibility of the humiliation can be attributed to certain agents (individuals or institutions) and we can demand that they stop acting in such a way as to cause the humiliation. We can insist that they eliminate the humiliating circumstances.

Thanks to Margalit, we now have a negative criterion of justice (namely, that of non-humiliation) that allows us to develop a weak theory of social justice, according to which a society is unjust when it humiliates its members. Otherwise, it would be merely a decent society but not necessarily a just one in the strict sense of the world. That theoretical modesty must not mislead us regarding how ambitious the goal is of eliminating all the social circumstances that societal members have a sound reason for ing humiliated. If the theory is still limited in its pretentions, the corresponding praxis aims at highly ambitious ends.

The main goal of this modest theory should, firstly, be that of offering a more precise definition of "humiliation". Although Margalit struggles to avoid any attribution of social situations to individual psychological issues, it is not easy to understand exactly what the difference is between a mere subjective feeling of humiliation and the presence of "sound reasons" for having such a feeling. How can we objectively detect a case of humiliation?

2.2 Humiliation, Dignity and Autonomy

The phenomenon of humiliation is intimately linked to the feeling of shame and lack of self-respect experienced by people who have been humiliated. Richard Sennett analyzed the mechanisms which can lead to the lack of respect and the feeling itself, and highlighted the role of the social environment in this process. It is worth pointing out here a long citation from his work *Respect* (2003) in which he speaks of the three ways in which society contributes to people gaining or losing the respect for others and for themselves. It should be highlighted that the reasons that lead to gaining respect from others (due to certain qualities or actions) can simultaneously lead to the loss of respect on the part of others.

> The first way [in which people earn or fail to arouse respect] occurs through self-development, particularly through developing abilities and skills. The highly intelligent person who wastes a talent does not command respect; someone less gifted working to the limits of his or her ability does. Self-development becomes a source of social esteem just because society itself condemns waste, putting a premium on efficient use of resources in personal experience as much as in the economy.
>
> The second way lies in care of the self. In the ancient world, taking care of oneself meant learning how to regulate the body's pleasures and pains [...] Care of oneself can mean additionally not becoming a burden upon others, so that the needy adult incurs shame, the self-sufficient person earns respect. This way of earning respect derives from modern society's hatred of parasitism [...].
>
> The third way to earn respect is to give back to others [...]. Inequality plays a particular and decisive role in shaping this three character types. The unusual person who makes full use of his or her abilities can serve as a social icon, justifying inadequate provision of resources or regard for people who are not developing as fully; the celebration of self-sufficiency and fear of parasitism can serve as a way of denying the facts of social need; the compassion which lies behind the desire to give back can be deformed by social conditions into pity for the weak, pity which the receiver experiences as contempt. (Sennett 2003, 63f.)

The fear of parasitism is typical of modern capitalist societies, and it derives from the equivalence between work and respect which, however, is historically contingent, as the author emphasizes: "the absolute moral value put on work, the supremacy of work over leisure, the fear of wasting time, of being inproductive – this is a value which only takes hold of all of society, the rich as well as the poor, in the nineteenth century" (Sennett 2003, 109). This invites us to consider shameful the condition of unemployment and economic dependence. However, such a judgment is historically and culturally defined. The idea that those who receive something from the State ought to reciprocate with some sort of service is an expression of this type of cultural opinion. This same cultural, political and ideological attitude does not deem those who live from financial rent to be parasitic, although rentiers have just launched many supposedly developed countries into a grave economic and political crisis – one that threatens to destroy once and for all the huge gains in terms of social and democratic rights that entire generations have struggled to achieve. Likewise, conferring privilege on businesspeople is thought to be legitimate. In Brazil, for example, tax exemptions and incentives are offered; there are subsidies for setting up businesses; companies are regularly pardoned from paying social security taxes even though they have collected these amounts from their workers; there are amnesty programs for those who avoid paying their income taxes; entrepreneurs' debts to government banks are often forgiven.

The analysis of Sennett, as well as that of Veca mentioned in Chap. 1, points to the central aspect of the phenomena of humiliation and of shame. There is a tendency for the poor to internalize the negative images that society (or parts of society) has of them. People who have been humiliated by society are led to believe that they deserve that humiliation and that their situation derives from some fault of their own. They interpret their economic and social inferiority as one of intellect or of will. Thus, they accept their condition and imagine it to be the result of a personal weakness, rather than as something due to the socioeconomic structure. We will see in the following chapters how this actually takes place in Brazil. In general, we can say that this process of internalization is facilitated by the very mechanism of the market, which posits that economic success derives from personal merit (One of the most important scholars of the free market, Friedrich von Hayek, counters this view. Instead he points to the accidental and morally neutral nature of the process of the worldwide distribution of wealth and assets, since the market is totally independent of individual will, Hayek 1976). The very act of self-identifying as poor implies the self-imposition of a stigma, in a society that, as Nussbaum points out, considers poverty to be a shameful situation for which the poor themselves are to blame (Nussbaum 2004, 282ff.).

Generally speaking, people who are humiliated and embarrassed about their situation in the world are at risk of entering into total psychological collapse. Furthermore, such negative feelings are generally the greatest cause of the destruction of anydefensive mechanism and may lead to the introduction into people's subjectivity of a deep alienation relative to society and its norms (Nussbaum 2004, 263ff.). Adam Smith, the great theoretician of capitalism and the inventor of the metaphor of the "invisible hand" that supposedly regulates the market, observed:

> [A] coward, a man incapable either of defending or of revenging himself, evidently wants one of the most essential parts of the character of a man. He is as much mutilated and deformed in his mind as another is in his body [...]. A man without the proper use of the intellectual faculties of a man, is, if possible, more contemptible than even a coward, and seems to be mutilated and deformed in a still more essential part of the character of human nature. Though the state was to derive no advantage from the instruction of the inferior ranks of people, it would still deserve its attention that they should not be altogether uninstructed. The state, however, derives no inconsiderable advantage from their instruction. The more they are instructed, the less liable they are to the delusions of enthusiasm and superstition, which, among ignorant nations frequently occasion the most dreadful disorders. An instructed and intelligent people, besides, are always more decent and orderly than an ignorant and stupid one. They feel themselves, each individually, more respectable, and more likely to obtain the respect of their lawful superiors, and they are, therefore, more disposed to respect those superiors. They are more disposed to examine, and more capable of seeing through, the interested complaints of faction and sedition; and they are, upon that account, less apt to be misled into any wanton or unnecessary opposition to the measures of government. (Smith 1976, 787f.)

Thus, it can be concluded that a situation of severe material poverty generates feelings of humiliation, a lack of self-esteem and self-respect and, more generally speaking, a feeling of alienation towards the world. It can even lead to various types of psychological disturbances (obvious signs of depression were not at all uncommon among the women that we interviewed).

2.3 Autonomy and Gender

In order to analyze the relationship between autonomy and gender, we went back to the pioneering work of John Stuart Mill. The existence of control or the mere possibility of women's managing to wield any control over their own lives and to make decisions for themselves, is one of the most complex and difficult topics to be studied by sociological research. This is particularly so when, as in the current work, we are dealing with women who are extremely poor and subject to many different types of oppression. First and foremost they are subject to the appropriation of their subjectivity, as Mill observed in his essay *The subjection of Women* (Mill 1911).[7] He pointed out that, in its political manifestations, male domination of women presupposes cultural and social institutions that support and reproduce said domination. These institutions operate fundamentally on people's emotions and sentiments rather than through explicit oppressive actions. Mill stated that women are not only trained to serve men (husbands, fathers, older brothers, fathers-in law and brothers-in law). More than that, they are trained to "desire to serve them". To this extent, the subjugation of women is different than that of other individuals or social classes.

It is worth reiterating that for the means of the current argument, women worldwide arrived very late to the world of rights and citizenship. This, per se, has profound political consequences on democratic life in general. To date, insufficient study has been directed towards the negative effects of such a late introduction of women into the prerogatives of the world of citizenship and the lack of a public culture based on civil democratic and republican values for women. These are the same women who hold the responsibility for educating the younger generations.

It is certain that if first impressions of the world are transmitted to children by people devoid of any civic culture, this portends a profound lack of democratic culture in any society. The feminist movement laid this question bare: the education of women does not focus on forming republican and democratic citizens; the values transmitted, rather, revolve around the reproduction of private individuals. As women, their education is always, normatively, concentrated on private and domestic life. Even worse, this ethos of the intimate world of family is projected into public life.

There comes to mind a brief observation by Tocqueville written in his memoirs about the 1848 French revolution. He was speaking of a domestic incident that involved his sister-in-law and he described her in these terms: "She was the most respectable woman and the worst citizen one could find" (Tocqueville 1987, 40). The two descriptions of the same person and her respective actions could be antinomies.[8] Research by feminists has shown ad nauseam that this antinomy is still alive and well and active today, albeit in varying fashions in different societies. This leads to a grave lacuna in civic education in general.

[7] See more about this topic in Urbinati (2002), 172 ss.

[8] After all, Kant had stated that one could be a good citizen without being a good man (cf. Kant 2003, 23 [Ak. VIII, 366]).

As we have said above, the domestic life of women, independent of social class, is culturally centered on the idealization of the values and the virtues of private life, and lacking in contents related to the principles of moral autonomy and self-governance. This leads to a situation where they, in turn, educate people to be averse to public rights and duties. Their dynamics work opposite to any normative understanding of what it means to be a democratic citizen. The historical result is that, as is well known, the reproduction of people who have been molded for domination, in the case of the men, and for subservience, in the case of the women. Both of these subjectivities are shaped in a way that creates great difficulties for them when dealing with the democratic life that presupposes, among many other things, equalitarian relations between the sexes. All this necessarily is mirrored negatively in the public world.

For all these reasons, the path of citizenship for women has always taken alternate paths, exactly because there are many forms of exclusion from public life. The forms of marginalization overlap. Giovanna Zincone speaks of exclusion in the pre-political plane, referring to the economic and cultural domination undergone by women in families that, as noted above, brings grave consequences for democratic political life, since the first teachers of future adults tend to reproduce this formative pattern (Zincone 1992, 189). Nancy Fraser commented on the hybrid nature of exclusion that reaches many social classes, though she speaks explicitly of African Americans and women. Her thinking can be extrapolated to many situations withstood by other social, ethnic and cultural groups. She argues that these social classes constitute what she calls ambivalent collectives, i.e., those that carry double signs of exclusion, bringing a double marginalization to the wider range of life. That is why they demand policies of recognition that address the various dimensions of the economic, social and cultural injustices that hold them back. We have not yet had a chance to discuss here the issue of recognition which is key to citizenship. It is impossible to overlook, however, that the recognition of the rights to citizenship of women implies what Fraser highlighted so appropriately: the recognition of the double injustice that they face. To overcome this obstacle, public policies specifically targeted to citizenship must be put in place to act decisively on their underlying ambivalence as collectives. Such policies must be framed to work critically against the many kinds of stereotypes, biases, violence and social exclusion that such collectives must face. The injurious situations have many facets, for example: being a woman, being poor, and being black. Effectively, in these groups there are certain ambiances and certain mechanisms of social relationships that heighten the psychological and civil suffering of their members. It is exactly in these situations that policies of fair economic distribution are essential as are cultural and educational policies aimed at changing the value paradigms regarding these women. This would be the only way to make any substantive changes in the mindset of dominated people, providing them with opportunities to acquire new visions of themselves and to free them up from a structure of sentiment based on the internalization of the ideas that perpetuate the numerous instances of exclusion and marginalization that they have been subject to (Fraser 1999).

It is important to emphasize that it is both the cultural as well as the economic marginalization that act to hinder the full enjoyment of civil and political rights by these social actors. Limited experience of a life governed by rights, democratic prerogatives of expression, and the right to a voice in society significantly limit their training as actors who are politically enabled not only to formulate but to augment their civic demands.

Thus, the experience of women in public life most often entails the difficulty of putting to use their capacity for argumentation and persuasion. This functional deficit arises from a private life marked by the experience of domination and exploitation. One of the most glaring impediments, commented on by several scholars, is rooted in the historical incapacity of women to develop their "rhetorical skills", a necessary condition for full participation in public life. The lack of this skill represents a forceful way of silencing them. Along this line, Susan Moller Okin brings up another facet of the problem when she observes that public life is less separated from personal and domestic life for women than for men. What they experience in the former affects radically their chances in the latter and vice versa. "Because of the past and present division of labor between the sexes, for women especially the public and the domestic are in many ways not distinct, separate realms at all; The perception of a sharp dichotomy between them depends on the view of society from a traditional male perspective that tacitly assumes different natures and roles for men and women" (Okin 1987, 133).[9]

To this extent, it is argued that there exists for women a sort of vicious circle of a lack of rights, of non-citizenship and unequal participation in public life. Okin traces the causes of this inequality to a dominant public discourse that hides the fact that the family is also a political institution. This takes place for many reasons, but, most of all, because the institution of the family has the right to allocate roles and functions to its members, doing so in an invasive and totalitarian fashion that is legitimized by tradition and habits. It thereby shapes differing subjectivities for men and women, and, principally, denies the latter the rhetorical capacity to fully participate in public life (Okin 1989, 44). In fact, this deprivation is much broader, as John Stuart Mill observed in *The Subjection of Women*.[10]

---

[9] Also see Okin (1989).

[10] Urbinati commented about this point: "Despotism – as described in The Subjection of Women – is a form of total and absolute power because it operates on the emotions, not just on actions. The despot, unlike the tyrant, strikes with fear and love simultaneously. Subjects of the tyrant long to rebel; under the despot they become affectionate chattel slaves. In the first case of repression, potential freedom is always latent; in the other, a condition of total surrender and pacification defines 'complete abnegation.' Tyranny represses action and violates negative liberty. Despotism violates the individual's very determination to act, and robs her of her self-reliance. Much more perverse than tyranny, it induces its subjects to transfer their freedom to formulate choices and make decisions to their master, who eventually will be seen as a source of tutelage rather than of coercion. For this reason Mill argued that, because women are not merely forced to serve their masters but are trained to *desire* to serve them, the position of women differs from that of all other subjected classes. 'All womena are brought up from the very earliest years in the belief that their ideal of character' is 'not self-will, and government by self-control,' like men, but instead 'submission, and yielding to the control of others… to live for others; to make complete abnegation of themselves, and to have no life but in their affections.' " (URBINATI 2002, 175; the quote by Mill was taken from *The Collected Works of John Stuart Mill*. Ed. by J. M. Robson. Toronto & London: University of Toronto Press & Routledge, 1963–1991, vol. 21, pp. 271–272).

It follows from these arguments that personal liberty must be seen as the subjective autonomy of individuals. Despotism, as delineated by Mill, annihilates all freedom, including the preliminary freedom that is linked to financial independence, the first step towards achieving personal self-governance. The lack of this minimal level of autonomy acting at the deepest level of their subjectivity prevents people from acquiring the necessary conditions for becoming holders of rights, with a determined personality, as Georg Simmel said in his work *Philosophy of Money* (Simmel 2011). It deprives individuals from being able to demand their rights and justice. As a result these people also lack the capacity to respect collective agreements regarding civic participation, a gap which hinders the civilizatory effect of any economic development within a nation.

2.4 Ethical-Moral Autonomy, Freedom and Capability

The motivational and legitimizing basis of what is called the "project of modernity" (to use the Habermas's famous expression: see Habermas 1996) consists of the promise of autonomy (individual and collective) that can be summarized by the idea that "we can decide ourselves who we want to be and how we want to live" (Rosa 2009, 39). Such promise is at the foundation of the search for the political, legal and social freedoms that characterize modernity. It unlies as well the search for an ever-expanding material well being together with the hope for the proliferation of options in an increasing number of fields of human life (Rosa 2009, 40). Now, there is an apparent paradox. Capitalism is the economic system that characterizes modernity and is intended to be the principle factor promoting individual autonomy. However, together with its underlying social, political and legal structures, it produces, in fact, the opposite. It leads to the loss of autonomy for a greater or lesser portion of humanity. In other words, the promise of modernity has not been realized for reasons linked to the development of modernity itself, in particular to the development of the capitalistic means of production (we will return to this point in Sect. 2.6).

We are of the opinion that authors such as Sen and Nussbaum, etc., who have drawn attention to the importance of the material basis for the development of individual autonomy are pointing exactly to this very deficit in contemporary capitalistic society: promising autonomy for everyone yet not giving them the real conditions (rather than the merely formal ones) for developing it. Obviously, we do not intend to argue that there is no autonomy in such societies. It is undeniable that the members of contemporary western societies have in general far more freedom than their ancestors in ancient and pre-modern societies. However, this freedom has come at a price that is paid not only by those who are excluded from the fruit of this technical and economic progress (excluded people exist even in the wealthiest societies) but also by the very beneficiaries. The price paid takes the form, as well, of individual pathologies (e.g. depression and other psycho-pathologies that have become so prevalent in our times). The concept of social suffering as used by Renault, Paugam and others, refers to the fact that individual psychological suffering is socially produced. Now, this also results in a loss of autonomy and freedom, whose causes cannot be imputed to individuals, who are impotent before them. The objective truth of the social and economic world imposes itself in a coercive fashion on people, to the contrary of what is commonly claimed by a certain type of liberalism.

The complexity of the concept of autonomy requires special care in using it. To this end, we will firstly offer a relatively broad and normatively weak definition of the concept. We can attribute autonomy to a person if they are capable of working towards a personal life project (a project which, however, can be inspired by pre-existing models) and if they are able to see themselves and others as able to establish relationships based on rights and duties (in other words, as holders of rights and duties). This is what we can call a minimal level of autonomy, which, in turn, is a quality that people can have to a lesser or greater degree. A person's autonomy increases to the extent that (1) they build their own project of a good life independently of the models provided by their most immediate context (the family, the immediate social context, their culture, etc.) and (2) they impute (to themselves and to others) rights and duties on the basis of universal principles rather than local or social beliefs or custums. While in case one, attaining greater autonomy relates only to individuals, since it implies amplifying their possibilities of achieving a good life, in the second case, it becomes relevant for others as well. Thus, individuals who are capable of imagining models of life dispproved of by their immediate social context (for example a woman who comes from a traditional, sexist family and decides to live alone, by moving to another city) would increase their chances of living a good life. Individuals who begin to look upon others in a different manner than what their context does and affords them greater rights (e.g., a brother of the abovementioned woman who comes to find her choice of lifestyle morally legitimate and who come to attribute to women rights that the other members of his family deny them based on their sexist beliefs). This contributes to creating an atmosphere that is more favorable to these people and their life plans. Naturally, social institutions (such as families, clans, religious communities, churches, castes, and anti-liberal political groups) often represent the greatest obstacles to the development of both types of autonomy, the personal and the social. These institutions offer moral orientation by suggesting values and models which oftentimes imprison people in a strict and rigid view of the world and of what is considered to be either licit or illicit. Thus we can see how the conceptual category that best allows us to study the situation of the women we interviewed is that of capability as drawn up by Sen (among others, Sen 1992) and we will return to it below. One last barrier to the development of autonomy is represented by the lack of "primary goods" in the Rawlsian sense (Rawls 1971) and, primarily, of the essential material goods that guarantee individuals' physical survival and a life that is minimally healthy. A varied diet, decent housing and basic free medical care make up part of these essential material goods.

The concept of autonomy discussed above has characteristics peculiar to two types of autonomy: the ethical and the moral. It has an ethical dimension. As far as people's life choices are concerned, their view of what is good and their life plans has an ethical dimension (we use the term "ethics" to refer to questions of good life in an Aristotelian sense). Insofar as autonomy deals with the rights and duties relative to other people, it also has a moral component. Therefore, we can call it the ethical-moral autonomy.

Now, the question is: how can an individual, first of all, develop a minimal level of autonomy and, in second place, surpass that level? In order to answer this question, we will start by trying to better define the very notion of autonomy using the concept of "real freedom" by Philippe van Parijs and that of "freedom of choice" by Amartya Sen.

According to van Parijs, real freedom has three components: security, self-determination and opportunity, "in contrast to formal freedom, which only incorporates the first two" (Van Parijs 1995, 22 s.). In order to be truly free, individuals must have security, independence (in the sense of being their own master) and they must be able to conceive of and carry out a life plan – chances that van Parijs does not define solely from the objective and exterior point of view but also in terms of the skills and abilities to do something that is internal or subjective.

> Thus the conception of real freedom presented above does not merely refuse to confine freedom-restricting obstacles to coercion – whether defined as self-ownership-violation or as right-violation. It also refuses to confine them to obstacles external to the person concerned, or to obstacles that are produced deliberately, indeed produced at all and/or removable by other human beings. (Van Parijs 1995, 23)

There exist, therefore, obstacles to liberty that are not external, that are not linked to the violation of rights by others but that refer to the internal nature of the people themselves. "Personal abilities or talents are internal to the person, and it is therefore correct to say that it is possible for freedom, on this conception, to be restricted by internal as well as external obstacles" (Van Parijs 1995, 24). Naturally, this does not mean that each lack of a skill or ability can be considered a violation of someone's freedom. On the other hand, the fact of not having the conditions available that are needed for a healthy life, or not knowing how to read and write normally have terribly negative impacts on people's chances of living a good life. Normally the question of the relation between poverty and freedom is looked at from a perspective that considers just the first two aspects, that is, the presence of external obstacles to freedom (a lack of security and the lack of self-determination or the dependence on others). Were these obstacles to be eliminated (e.g. by health policies, better policing, financial assistance, etc.) the internal obstacles would not be automatically done away with. In order to elucidate the nature of the latter, we will refer to Sen's theory of capabilities.[11]

Sen differentiates between functioning and capability. An example of the first is riding a bicycle. It requires engaging in an activity (in this case by way of a tool, namely, a bike). Now, the interesting question is what leads cyclists to ride bikes. They might be using it to get to work, or for leisure. In the first case, they might do so because they do not want to use their cars due to ecological awareness or in order to avoid traffic, or maybe they do not have a car. In the latter case, they might use a

[11] For a more recent formulation of Sen's concept of justice, see Sen (2009).

bicycle because there is no system of public transport or because the system is insufficient or even because the bicyclist might not be able to afford the bus or train ticket. In summary, a rich executive with ecological awareness and a poor factory worker, both of whom ride a bike to work, are sharing the same functioning but for reasons and in contexts that are profoundly distinct. This leads Sen to introduce the idea of "freedom of *functioning*" (Sen 1992, 39ff.). In this respect, the rich executive has greater freedom than the factory worker, since he can choose between a wider range of options (of different functionings). If we consider that certain functionings (e.g. being in good physical shape) have intrinsic and independent value, we can say that people with a wider range of functionings at their disposal has achieved a greater level of freedom and, simultaneously, well being. Freedom and well being can, therefore, coexist, even though this does not always happen (see the analysis in Sen 1992, 56ff.).

Certain functionings, in order to be achieved, require a complex set of conditions that must be satisfied. Returning to the case mentioned above, a woman who moves to the city to escape the confines of her patriarchal family is practicing a functioning that involves various aspects beyond the mere geographical move to another location. She is freeing herself from certain ties and, at the same time, losing certain types of security. She may increase her chance of having a good life or she might condemn herself to a life of hard sacrifices and poorly paid work (especially if she is illiterate – which is likely the case for a woman coming from the context in question). The result of her move to the city depends on her *capabilities.*

According to Sen, we should not think of capability as something isolated but see it always in relationship to other capabilities. A person has a set of capabilities that permits them to carry out a certain set of functionings, but there is no necessary relationship between the first and the second: two people might have the same set of capabilities and choose different functionings or, on the contrary, they have different capabilities and share certain functionings (such as in the case of the executive and the factory worker who both ride a bicycle). Sen sees capabilities as chances or opportunities for functionings. They are not mere capacities: saying that someone has a capability to move freely to another city says nothing about their physical ability to physically move (or about their ability to move themselves), rather to the real options that they have to do so. In this sense the capabilities refer not only to skills and abilities but also to mental and other subjective states (such as state of health, literacy or illiteracy, etc.) and to external circumstances. Therefore, they can be seen only as a set and not as isolated characteristics. Might the woman in our example really have the option of moving to the city in the search for a better life? Sen would invite us to consider if this is a real option for her, taking into consideration everything that a move of this type entails: for example, she would have to leave behind the place where she was born, her family, her network of relationships and affection, a world whose symbolic code and whose values she understands and, at least in part, shares, a climate and a lifestyle she is accustomed to. At the same time, she would have to go to some unknown and hostile place where she would be alone, at least in the beginning. She will be marginalized for coming from a poor region and for being unable (in the sense of capacity, this time) to understand the code of the big city, etc.[12] It does not suffice, in summary, to say that a person has a capability to choose a certain functioning (in this case emigrate), if we do not account for all the other capabilities involved in this choice.

Going back to the definition of real freedom of van Parijs, we could say that an individual should develop a set of capabilities in order to be really free (so that they might take hold of what van Parijs calls "opportunities"). The capabilities will permit them to perform certain functionings, in other words, to be able to actually choose between a range of different functionings. In our example of the woman wanting to escape from her context and move to a better one, she should have at hand a set of capabilities that includes, among others: the courage to exchange the known for the unknown, the strength to face the difficulties presented by her new environment, a good dose of self-confidence, etc. The presence or absence of some capabilities will influence more or less strongly her chances of success in the city. Examples include: her educational level, her physical and emotional state, her ability to understand and to make use of new codes, etc.

Martha Nussbaum differentiates between internal capabilities, which are, on the one hand, conditions (physical, mental or of character) that enable individuals to choose between various functionings that they consider to be valuable and, on the other hand, external capabilities that deal with the material and social conditions that will open certain options up to them (Nussbaum 1990, 228). This leads her to conclude that capabilities have different levels of development: they range from mere potentialities to capabilities actually carried out within the corresponding functionality.

Sen also sets up categories of capabilities but does so in a different fashion. We will not analyze this classification here but will limit ourselves to commenting on one aspect of it: it is possible to classify capabilities and functionings, based on their importance. Some capabilities are prerequisites for others (physical and mental health, for example), while some functionings are more essential than others for the well-being of individuals. In this project, we are interested mainly in the concept of basic capabilities, which is to say the capabilities that individuals must develop in order to live a dignified life with self-respect. Nussbaum offers a non-definitive list, in which she does not intend to offer a metaphysical or essentialist view of people (thus she avoids speaking of "human nature"). This inventory has been drawn up based on common characteristics found in descriptions from a wide range of cultures of what a good life, or more modestly speaking, a normal life might be. Thus, it is a historical, empirical and rectifiable list that ranges from the minimum conditions of physical health and the meeting of basic necessities to the ability to conceive of an autonomous life plan and including the development of cognitive faculties (Nussbaum 1995, 76 ss.). Having these basic capabilities on hand, individuals can take responsibility for their own lives. There is a close relationship between the lack of these capabilities and humiliation: those who lack such capabilities have good reason to feel humiliated, as Margalit would argue. It is

[12] Such difficulties are described in an exemplary fashion the novel The Hour of the Star by Clarice Lispector (Lispector 1992).

worth pointing out that this state of humiliation cannot be blamed on these humble people; they are not responsible for their situations. In most cases, these people are born or are forced into this state of affairs by external circumstances that they do not control (e.g. the loss of a job, accidents that leave them disabled, the breakup of the family, etc.).

From this point of view, institutional humiliation is related to the following facts: (1) that the citizens of a state are not able to develop their basic capabilities; and (2) that the state institutions (2a) are either directly responsible for this situation or (2b) they neglect to change a situation that they could, in fact, change. This should be differentiated from the unconditional duties that a state has towards its citizens. A state should, for example, offer its citizens free, public primary education and must not leave its poorest citizens in a state of illiteracy that prevents them from escaping poverty. However, mere literacy is not enough to improve the social status of these people. In industrialized societies and those in the process of industrialization, in other words, in these societies where the job market seeks mostly qualified workers, the lack of education above the level of literacy means that the people in question are not only excluded from the job market but they also suffer social exclusion, as their situation either leads to long-term unemployment or the acceptance of non-qualified and poorly paid employment. These jobs merely guarantee survival and lead to a life of indignity and lack of respect and self-respect.[13] Now, while the literacy of the population is an unqualified duty of the state, the offer of qualified training is not always considered to be so. Can it be said that a state that does not help its citizens achieve their social condition by way of adequate education and training is humiliating them? It is obvious that such a state is not minimally interested in the capabilities of its citizens (or certain classes of citizens) and this represents a form of humiliation.

According to Nussbaum, "a decent society" should protect the dignity of its members not only negatively, i.e. avoiding acts that would humiliate them directly, but also positively. It should create an "environment" that facilitates the development of self-respect (Nussbaum 2004, 282). She gives the example of poverty, which is considered humiliating in all societies. This frequently leads to the moral condemnation of the poor themselves as if they were responsible for their situation – due to a lack of will, to laziness, to moral corruption, etc. Nassbaum believes that a decent society should equip its members with a minimum set of capabilities. She points out one in particular. Each individual should have "the social bases of self-respect and nonhumiliation; being able to be treated as a dignified being whose worth is equal to that of others" (Nussbaum 2004, 283). Since said set of capabilities has an economic base, this latter should be institutionally guaranteed, where it is not possible to satisfy individuals' basic needs in any other way. Potential measures include: economic aid, the introduction of a minimal basic income, or the implementation of governmental programs such as, for example, the Bolsa Familia. These initiatives

[13] See Sen's considerations cited above. However, we would like to call attention to the fact that professional qualification does not represent a guarantee for entry into the world of work, as is commonly stated.

should be seen as attempts to help individuals develop their capabilities when they are not able to do so autonomously. At the same time, such schemes represent attempts to help these individuals escape from the humiliation of extreme poverty. It is worth noting that there is a large range of reasons for supporting such measures. One could appeal to the interest of the state itself in having autonomous citizens who are able to assume their responsibilities and take their lives into their own hands. In this sense, such measures could be justified even from a neoliberal perspective. Alternatively, like Sen and Nussbaum, one could opt for another perspective that sees these measures as arising from the moral obligation to eliminate unfair and humiliating circumstances.

By developing the concept of capability, Sen and Nussbaum take up a question that has been tackled by both Aristotle and Marx, namely, the concern with the development of human functions, and, in this case, with the training and qualification of people to live the full range of life's meanings and, particularly, its humanization. The humanity of people is not merely a simple biological fact (in Greek *zoé*) but also a political and social construct (in Greek, *bíos*).[14]

Marx argued that the human functions that manifest themselves in sensation are entirely the product of social life, in other words, they are born of collective socialization. He saw the education of the senses to be, very clearly, the humanization of people. This is what we want to call attention to when we speak of the idea of capability, because it must be effectively implemented in order that rights be exercised, be enjoyed and that they might come to be expanded due to the conquest of new freedoms, thus amplifying the very sense of human development. It is in this context that we read Marx's words:

> The *forming* of the five senses is a labor of the entire history of the world down to the present. The *sense* caught up in crude practical need has only a *restricted* sense. For the starving man, it is not the human form of food that exists, but only its abstract being as food; it could just as well be there in its crudest form, and it would be impossible to say wherein this feeding-activity differs from that of animals. The care-burdened man in need has no sense for the finest play; the dealer in minerals sees only the mercantile value but not the beauty and the unique nature of the mineral: he has no mineralogical sense. Thus, the objectification of the human essence both in its theoretical and practical aspects is required to make man's *sense human,* as well as to create the *human sense* corresponding to the entire wealth of human and natural substance. (Marx 1988, 109)

Thus, undergoing a harsh and limited life of deprivation prevents people from developing their human functions and hinders their capacities to demand and enjoy rights – and not only this, which is limitation enough, but it also reduces their ability to become fully human. The expansion of their rights and their experience in building a personality and a life in general make people into humans who are more capacitated to express themselves and to act in the world. Poverty is not only the lack of money and material resources; it is also the lack of capacities and the failure to develop important human functions. And this makes the poor even poorer.

---

[14] For more about the distinction between *zoé* and *bíos* and their significance to contemporary politics, see Agamben (1998).

We would like now to add a more positive element to the negative one arising from Margalit's theory: a decent society should not merely eliminate humiliating actions or correct humiliating situations. Above all, it should actively nurture the self-respect of its members, by way of policies with twin objectives: it should, on the one hand, free its poorest citizens from misery and, on the other, offer them the minimum economic independence needed to develop self-respect.

The autonomy of individuals can, thus, be seen as depending on a set of capabilities that permits them to choose between a range of functionings, whose breadth depends on the capabilities that individuals have developed throughout their lives. Individuals develop their capabilities in an intersubjective fashion, i.e. within a social context. We are dealing with a form of autonomy that is not yet legal (although it may be guaranteed by legal means), nor are we referring to political, social or economic autonomy. Our emphasis is on a much more basic autonomy. Obviously, these other forms are interrelated, even if not necessarily (a person may never achieve economic autonomy, for example). What we want to emphasize is the fact that the process by which individuals achieve their identity and develop basic autonomy is a complex and ongoing one. It has been described in varying manners by different social-psychological theories. Here, we are making use of a classic rather than a cutting-edge theory, that of the interrelationship between the structure of character and institutions developed by Gerth and Mill. We do so not because we feel that it is the best but exactly because of its paradigmatic nature. Other theories might better explain how identify and personality autonomy arise.[15] For our purposes, however, the idea that personal identity is (at least in part, if not totally) the result of intersubjective relations and processes is sufficient. The theory of Gerth and Mill serves as an example of how theories of the formation of identity and individual autonomy by way of social relations can impact those of autonomy as real freedom (van Parijs) and freedom of functioning (Sen).

Gerth and Mill's theory can be summarized as follows: "Man as a person is a historical creation, and can most readily be understood in terms of the roles which he enacts and incorporates.[16] These roles are limited by the kind of social institutions in which he happens to be born and in which he matures into an adult" (Gerth and Mills 1953, 11). In other words, individuals' capabilities are determined by their social environment, particularly by their position in the same, and by the roles that they are called upon to undertake. According to these scholars, individuals form their self-concept by interiorizing the image of them that is presented by significant others (the generalized Other, as Gerth and Mills call it, harking back to the concept of Mead[17]) as well as by satisfying the expectations that these significant others have of them and certain socially defined roles. In order to be recognized as fully entitled members of a group (or of society), individuals must satisfy the expectations associated with roles. Their education as children, teens and young adults should yield

[15] For a more general view of these theories, see Martuccelli (2005).

[16] This idea is at the center of the dramaturgical model everyday life by Erwing Goffman. (See Goffman 1959). [Note A.P. and W.L.R.].

[17] See Mead (1934).

them the characteristics that guarantee them success in acting according to the predicted role (or roles). In words other than those of Gerth and Mills, they should be armed with the capabilities that their environment considers socially, morally, or religiously desirable. In relatively closed and static contexts, such as a patriarchal family in the *sertão*, individuals are called upon to assume roles that are clearly defined and the entire family education aims to create people who are able to fulfill those roles (cf. Gerth and Mills 1953, 91ff.). Individuals of this sort can achieve an elevated level of self-confidence and self-esteem, but, even then, they may lack the above-mentioned autonomy, i.e., the capacity to expand significantly the range of options from which to choose their life plan. To this end, they should develop capabilities that surpass those available in their immediate social context. They should benefit from access to alternatives to the model of the patriarchal family (e.g. by way of contact with more emancipated people or even by way of TV programs),[18] from the access to public education, and from receiving the attention of policies promoting change for individuals in poor regions, etc. We are of the opinion that a program like the BF is a perfect fit for this context and that its primary effect, in addition to ensuring immediate subsistence, is to supply the material basis necessary for individuals to begin developing greater autonomy. Throughout our research, we sought to understand these transformations in the women's lives and the increase in autonomy that was prompted by the BF. From the beginning, we realized that we could not understand a process like this unless we were able to situate it within a historical dimension: the novel experience of receiving a regular income did not coincide immediately with increased autonomy, but it marked the beginning of a transformation that was not only external (improved living conditions, changes in diet, etc.) but internal as well. As George Simmel warned in the work mentioned previously, such an experience, when it is something other than the product of mere charity, changes the "soul" of its grantee. In his words, "the medieval type of almsgiving […] bypassed internally, so to say, the poor" without changing their basic situation (Simmel 1965, 125).

2.5 Monetary Income and Civic and Political Autonomy

As we have already seen, Amartya Sen and Martha Nussbaum took up an old point: the material basis for developing ones' capabilities and, therefore, the need for individuals to have access to the material goods associated with such development. Analogous positions were found in Rawls and other scholars of social justice.[19] According to said theories, when the necessary resources are not readily available, individuals should receive support in achieving them. The question is: What

[18] In Brazil some *novelas* (soap operas) had a substantial effect in promoting acceptance for alternative life styles.

[19] Above all see Rawls (1971). A discussion of Rawls and Sen's critiques of his work are outside the scope of this piece. For this point we would refer reader to Vita 2008.

resources should be distributed to whom and by whom? Since many differing levels of freedom and autonomy are involved here, there is a range of answers to these questions. We offer a simple one related to the most basic level: the state ought to guarantee to all citizens a minimal qualified income in order that each one might achieve basic autonomy, which is to say, to ensure each citizen acquire a set of fundamental capacities that would permit them to consider themselves as minimally autonomous. This is not the same as an unconditional universal basic income although it might be considered a first step in this direction.[20] The main difference compared to policies of income distribution that focus on the most fragile groups due to their extreme poverty consists of the presence or absence of conditions. Basic universal income is not linked to the idea of social responsibility, which stipulates that individuals should contribute something in return to the community. On the contrary, it is worth pointing out that the BF does stipulate reciprocation, since the payment of the grant is dependent on children going to school and being vaccinated. We are of the opinion that these exchanges have a republican value and contribute to the process of forming citizens and individuals who assume responsibility towards their political community.

Any other system of distribution of monetary income can be considered as a form of assistentialism or even paternalism. Naturally, there may arise urgent situations where the direct distribution of material goods such as food, shelter, etc. may become necessary. However, apart from these specific cases, state intervention should be as impersonal as possible. Distributing monetary income to people aims precisely to emancipate them, not merely from misery or poverty, but also from a social environment that may cause additional suffering. Returning to our example: a woman who depends either on her husband or her patriarchal family, or on the fruit of her own labor (which condemns her to poorly paid jobs due to her lack of qualification) has no real possibility of escaping her social environment and seeking out another where she might gain greater autonomy. On the other hand, if she could count on a minimal monthly income, she might be able to take that first step to leave behind her state of dependency, humiliation and precariousness (see Zelizer 1989), even if other things are necessary for this end. It is obvious that we are not arguing that such income could or should replace a decent public education system, full legal protection, free legal counsel, etc. What we are saying is that money is a necessary component for building a material basis for autonomy (or the development of capabilities or real freedom, as Sen and van Parijs would say, respectively).

Georg Simmel in his *Philosophy of Money* (1900) called attention to the fact that the emergence of the ideas of autonomy and individual autonomy is a specific phenomenon peculiar to western modernity and linked to the first appearance of a mercantilist system, following on from the capitalistic society. Thus, the first hypothesis

---

[20] The idea of a Universal Basic Income is argued by van Parijs. In Brazil, it was first raised by Senator Eduardo Suplicy and is currently defended by an important group of intellectuals. We refer in particular to BIEN, whose 13th conference took place in São Paulo, in June/July of 2010, organized by the economist Lena Lavinas. More than 1000 people presented research about the need for Basic Universal Income. See (Vanderborght and Van Parijs 2006; Suplicy 2006).

is not particularly new. What is useful and important to us, in this context, is the distinction by Simmel between "non-dependence" and "independence" (Simmel 2011, 322). In pre-modern societies, people have duties characterized by personal ties (e.g. the liege lord and the subject) and they are imprisoned in a network of relations and personal commitments that leave them practically no freedom whatsoever. In a mercantile society, as well as in a capitalistic one, these duties are depersonalized. Instead of owing hours of free labor to the liege lord (called in French *corvées*) the subject pays taxes. Thus, the relationship becomes less personal and the liege lords appear not like the real people that they are but as impersonal entities to which one owes certain taxes. This makes people independent from one another, to the extent that their mutual interdependence (which continues to exist, of course) is linked not to a network of inescapable personal relations but to a network of impersonal ones. Individuals offer just one side of themselves: they are clients, competitors, suppliers, etc. Our relationship with them is monetary: we pay them (or they pay us) for certain services. By way of money, we buy our independence from any personal commitment or tie, even if we still remain dependent on other people in our life. The only people who do not depend on others are "the lonely settler of German or American forests" (Simmel 2011, 324). The average person, who lives in society with others, depends on them for their survival, yet they can remain independent in the sense mentioned above: they need not become a prisoner of a network of personal commitments and may, therefore, begin to plan their idea of a good life, independent of the positive or negative opinion of those whom they must deal with in order to satisfy their basic needs. In other words, they are independent of any role imposed by their immediate social environment. They become free to take on other roles (but not free from the need to take on roles, which would be impossible due to the fact that they live in society).

It is worth pointing out that for Simmel, independence (as well as the autonomy on which it is based) is not a characteristic of an individual, like in the case of physical strength, instead it depends on relationships that this person establishes with others. "Individual freedom is not a pure inner condition of an isolated subject, but rather a phenomenon of correlation which loses its meaning when its opposite is absent" (Simmel 2011, 322). The material independence granted by money is an essential component of said freedom and must, therefore, be considered a basic resource and a potential object of any public policy aimed at creating autonomous citizens.

Thus, it can be inferred that the monetization of social relationships brings about, even if in a contradictory manner, the beginnings of a process of individualization. This is because individuals armed with the universal form of wealth (which takes the form of money) are able to express their individuality. They become beings who interact (by way of the exchange of money for goods and services) as "free and equal". The assumption of this particular action resides in its intentional, explicit aspect – in the case of the women interviewed for this research – in the fact of "going to the market each week". Such an act contains within it an element of *individual* choice and determination that surpasses the mere purchase of the necessary food to provide material sustenance to their families. The BF card, in this case, is synonymous with a certain amount of money that is available for the purchase of goods precisely for that person. The card, therefore, plays the function of "personalized money". This situation is exactly the opposite of the Roman *servus*, or slave. Marx reminded us that, according to Roman law, slaves were not allowed to buy anything for themselves. Now, the life of people who hunt for food like animals because they are outside of the monetary economy due to their extreme misery is not so very different, or perhaps it is even worse than the life of the ancient Roman *servi*.

In the act of buying the specific goods needed for their survival, individuals take the first steps toward reproducing themselves as humans but, at the same time, they introduce themselves into wider social relationships, full of contradictions, but also potentially emancipatory. In other words, such social relationships intrinsically bring with them as much potential for freedom as they bring new forms of oppression, which, however, we will not be discussing here (cf. Marx 1993). For our ends, it suffices to point out the liberating potential that the access to monetary incomes opens up to these individuals.

The consequences of the situations described above are, without a doubt, paradoxical, as they can lead to a wide variety of functions. For example, they might lead to the dissolution both of traditional ties and of ties and structures of personal domination – a phenomenon that is especially common in the case of the poor women living in highly patriarchal regions like the Brazilian North and Northeast. They equally might lead to the dissolution of the ties of domination of the relationship with local powerful figures, the most visible expression of which is the patronage vote – a relationship that is based on the expropriation of the will of the other. Returning to Marx's views about the medieval relation of servitude, it can be seen as a form of economic coercion, but also by way of personal relations of domination and submission that exist within extra economic constraints (Marx 1964, 102ff.). The political, social and moral mechanisms that usurp the will of others prevent individuals from becoming their own masters, which is the primordial condition for making basic life decisions, even the most basic ones.

It is worth bringing to the debate the democratic and feminist theory of Carole Pateman with regard to the compelling need for basic universal income in order to attain truly democratic forms of relating (Pateman 2004). Such income represents the fundamental condition, not only for establishing a more democratic society in which each citizen's autonomy might be guaranteed, but also for increasing women's autonomy. Such income would contribute to untying the individual income from a job (female unemployment is traditionally higher than that of males) and it would break the vicious cycle between marriage, work and citizenship. Women would no longer depend on their husband's incomes but would have an independent source of money. Thus, Pateman argues, there are arguments in favor of basic income (rather than a mere minimal income), not only from the view point of a theory of social justice, but also starting from considerations about democracy, since this system depends on having autonomous citizens. Such autonomy (understood by Pateman as self-governance) is only possible, in the first place, as economic independence (which, in turn, becomes in current times, social independence from the family and the political situation). Pateman cites the abovementioned definition of a basic right offered by Henry Shue (a right is basic if its enjoyment is a condition for enjoying all the other rights). She then argues that there exists a basic right to an unconditional minimal income. Martha Nussbaum, as does Pateman, points out that "a person who is in a bad way through lack of nutrition or health care cannot participate as an equal in politics. An illiterate person is unlikely to be able to go to the police or to the courts for enforcement of other political and civil rights" (Nussbaum 2004, 285).

These remarks bring us to identifying a second level of autonomy that can be reached by subjects and that relates not only to a strictly individual dimension but to social and political life in general. Conditional basic monetary income, which the state should guarantee its citizens, is not limited to ensuring material life conditions and to providing people with ethical and moral autonomy. Upon their inclusion into the citizenry, these people gain a sense of identification with the nation, due to the recognition of their personhood by the political institutions of the state. Their needs become the object of rights whose defense can be demanded of the political power. In turn, these people are required to fulfill their duties relative to the political community and the state itself. Thus, a double learning process takes place with regard to what citizenship means: individuals learn to see themselves both as subject of rights and as subject of duties. These two dimensions are necessary for individuals to consider themselves citizens, i.e. active members of the body politic rather than mere clients that passively receive services offered by the state. This concept is applicable not only to basic social programs such as the BF but in relation to any state benefit. We bring up an example that is not destined to the poor but, on the contrary, shows the need to awaken civic awareness on the part of the middle and upper classes as well. Brazilian public universities train the country's best specialists: doctors, lawyers, engineers, etc. Paradoxically, this free education has been reserved, before the introduction of a quota system, almost exclusively to the middle and upper class youths who had the resources to better prepare for the university entry exams, called the *vestibular.* Once in the university, the studies are paid for by public funds: laboratories, libraries, teaching salaries, grants for studies and for internships. However, nothing is demanded in reciprocity regarding service to the country. Their professional training prepares them fundamentally for private success. Nothing encourages them to dedicate any time for the public good, in the form of services in areas where they country is in need of qualified professionals. Their obligation to the society is settled mostly by paying taxes (unless they practice tax evasion). Now, reducing one's own responsibility to the community to the mere paying of taxes suggests a worrisome lack of civic responsibility.

Thus, it is important to point out that conditional social programs such as the Bolsa Família may represent, at least for a little while, an important instrument of civic education. This leads us to take up the relationship between public policy and the nurture of citizenship.

2.6 Public Citizenship Policies and the Formation of Political Subjects

Contemporary legal literature about rightholders suggests great innovation. Fruit of a huge struggle for civilization, modern rights are subjective, i.e. they accrue to subjects, who, in order to hold them, must inevitably be able to act. However, in order to act in the wider world, individuals need to perform certain human functions, to be capacitated to do so.[21] In order to act as rightholders, they must learn certain things about how to enjoy their fundamental freedoms and how they should be able to respond, as citizens, for their actions. Nevertheless, the principle of reciprocity that underlies the very idea of subjective rights presupposes duties towards the pertinent political community, in other words, the existence of a certain consciousness that the enjoyment and the demand for rights give rise to duties, as much towards oneself as towards the greater political community, in this case, the country. Since the French Revolution, at least, a nation has come to be seen as a collective body (preceding any class or other divisions within the it). It evokes the existence of unifying political and symbolic forces, the centripetal forces that link people and the sentiment in each individual member of the political community. We are speaking of belonging to a "we": we, the Brazilians, we, the Argentines, etc.

Such a collective entity, which is totally shared among the poor and the extremely poor on the one hand and rich people with a strong culture of privilege[22] on the other, will find it difficult to create and establish bonds of solidarity and belonging. Instead, the social distance produced by asymmetric situations develops within a people centrifugal forces that create separations and divisions that are deeply rooted in their hearts, making the inhabitants of their territory strangers to each other, unable in any sense to see themselves as equals, except in the asymmetrical obligation to obey the same laws. We should not forget, as Habermas reminds us, that every legal order is also expression of a specific form of life and does not just mirror the universal content of some fundamental rights (Habermas 1996a).

We would add that the presence of internal divisions within a society irreparably undermines its democratic structures. The idea of equal rights to democratic participation that characterizes our democracies is based on an ethical principle, namely that of equal respect: each person has the same rights as the others with regard to participation in the political life of the community, because each one is worthy of the same attention and the same consideration (this is to say it is both individuals who deserve the same attention and consideration as well as their interests, their preferences, their needs, etc.: see Galeotti 2010). At times, however, this link between the right to participation and respect is lost for historical reasons. For

[21] For more about this, see the comments of Hannah Arendt: "With word and deed we insert ourselves into the human world, and this insertion is like a second birth, in which we confirm and take upon ourselves the naked fact of our original physical appearance" (Arendt 1958, 176 f.).

[22] See Sieyes (2003) for a better understanding of the notion of privilege and its incompatibility with the creation of a democratic and republican citizenry. For the mechanisms of the reproduction of the power of the elite, see the classics Pareto (1935), Mosca (1939) and Mills (1956).

example, in the USA after the Civil War, the Afro-Americans gained the same political rights as the white population, but in many cases, they failed to enjoy the same civil rights and they did not gain the respect of the white citizens. In this sense, we could make use of the distinction of Margalit between the decent and the civilized society and say that the USA in the post-Civil War period, was a decent society (at least in the case of those states that did not deny equal civil rights to the Afro-Americans) but it was not a civilized one. The same can be said about Brazil after the abolition of slavery in 1888: the formal non-discrimination did not correspond and, in part, it still fails to correspond to an attitude of respect on the part of a vast segment of the white population regarding the ex-slaves and their descendants. In the case of Brazil, however, the classic race-based discrimination (whose presence, banalized by any scholars and many common Brazilians, has been demonstrated by the classic studies of Florestan Fernandes[23]) has been accompanied by a true classism, which bases its discrimination of the Other on their belonging to a socially inferior class.

These brief considerations are merely intended to raise issues that were made obvious in the question about the human capacities and abilities that are necessary both in order to live a life in community but also to be able to act as the authors and the receivers of citizens' prerogatives. Some of the most ancient concerns of political thought arise here. They refer to the awareness that the capacity of a person to enjoy constitutionally guaranteed rights is linked to their ability to benefit from the liberties achieved. Marx liked to call attention to the fact that the freedom of the press, a fundamental achievement of civilization with its consequent contribution to human emancipation, was useless for the illiterate, as they lacked the ability to read and to debate and, therefore, to enjoy that right. To a certain extent, this type of discursive incapacity makes the freedom of the press useless for those who are illiterate. The life of rights, or, in the words of Habermas (1996a), their use value, depends on the civil and participative vitality of the political community. Since the time of the Greeks, it has been known that educating people for freedom, as well as for civic virtues in general, depends on the provision for minimal material needs. Misery and hunger are in and of themselves serious detriments to human freedom, in its deepest sense.

Social policies should not be compared to mere acts of public charity. They are rather instruments for promoting individual autonomy and creating a sense of community: in one word, they are instruments of citizenship. This is because their aim is to protect "the status of a person as a full member of the community" (Harris 1987, 30). At times, they are justified as a sort of compensation to people for having been left marginalized or excluded from the market system in which, if the system were different, they might have found themselves in a better position. Even if we accept the neoliberal idea that no one is personally responsible for the imbalance and the huge wealth gap created by the market, there is a collective responsibility of the community relative to all of its members, particularly when some of them are

[23] For more about the various branches of this discussion, see, among others, Souza (2003) and Hofbauer (2006). The classic study by Fernandes is, naturally, Fernandes (1965).

disadvantaged by a socioeconomic system that allows others to accumulate wealth. However, it is not necessary to resort to such debatable arguments to justify public social policies. The strongest argument appears to us to be linked to the social inclusion of the people who benefit from these policies.

David Harris offers the following thoughts about meeting people's basic needs as a fundamental condition for citizenship:

> Social policies should be directed toward guaranteeing a range of social chances to the citizens of a society. The relevant life chances are those required to protect the status of individuals as full members of the community. Their purpose is to offer material opportunities to participate in the way of life of the society. Needs, by implication, are defined as whatever is necessary to that end. An individual is 'in need' for the purposes of social policy to the extent that he lacks the resources to participate as a full member of society in its way of life. (Harris 1987, 101)

Elisabeth S. Anderson, upon presenting her theory of democratic equality and returning to the Rawlsian definition of society as a fair system of cooperation, points out the importance of guaranteeing to the members of the political community the conditions that allow them to participate equally in the system. She avails herself of the concept of capabilities and states: "Negatively, people are entitled to whatever capabilities are necessary to enable them to avoid or escape entanglement in oppressive social relationships. Positively, they are entitled to the capabilities necessary for functioning as an equal citizen in a democratic state" (Anderson 1999, 316). Anderson defines the idea of citizen equality in a broad sense, since she does not limit it to the political sphere. She identifies three levels at which individuals participate in the common life of a society. At each level individuals should be able to fulfill certain functionings, and therefore, to possess certain capabilities. The three levels are: (1) the most general in which people should "function" as humans, (2) that of the economic system and (3) that of political life. At the first level, people should have access to the means to guarantee their biological survival (from nutrition to medical care) but also the capabilities linked to their development of their autonomy as moral subjects. The second level demands actual access to the means of production and the education necessary to develop one's talents, as well as the freedom to choose one's profession and to enter into contracts, and the recognition of ones' contribution to the production of social wealth (recognition which is mainly but not only provided by receiving a salary that is appropriate to the job performed). The third level demands the capabilities needed to actively participate in the political life of the community, which has been mentioned above.

While describing the scope of the society in which individuals live their lives, Anderson calls our attention to the fact that this scope is much broader than one might think, since

> [i]ts institutions include public streets and parks, public accommodations such as restaurants, shops, theaters, buses and airlines, communications systems such as broadcasting, telephones, and the Internet, public libraries, hospitals, schools, and so forth. Enterprises engaged in production for the market are also part of civil society, because they sell their products to any customer and draw their employees from the general public. (Ibidem, 317)

Now, any individual or group that is excluded from participating in said institutions by a lack of capabilities (or by class or racial discrimination) is, in fact, relegated to second-class citizenship, so to speak.

Accordingly, no member of a society is an island. Their personalities, including their capacities and talents, can only be developed within the social context in which they find themselves. Nothing that is achieved is totally the fruit of their individual action but always depends on the maneuvering space that their social context confers. The practice of a profession, the development of a certain lifestyle, the nurturing of personal tastes, everything depends on the context. In daily life, it is common for people to forget this and think that it is an obvious or natural phenomenon, which, in fact, actually depends on the existence of a society and the fulfillment of certain tasks by other members of society. One of the greatest successes of the neoliberal ideology consists precisely in occulting these aspects, aggrandizing the myth of those individuals that are able to completely master their lives alone and who, therefore, are solely responsible for all that they have attained. In her critique of this image of the economy as a system peopled with so many self-sufficient Robinson Crusoes, Anderson sarcastically points out that the Wall Street tycoons would not have managed to win their millions if they had had to personally answer the telephones, or, we would add, to clean their offices, cook their food, take care of their children, walk to and fro from work instead of taking a car or subway, etc. From this point of view, their efficiency in performing their tasks depends on the efficiency of others carrying out their responsibilities, no matter how simple and apparently distinct from the activity of earning money on the stock exchange. The fact that society is based on a division of labor does not mean that there is no relation of mutual dependence between the different activities. No one produces alone what they need to survive, just as no one deserves to be born in the family they were born in and which, for better or worse, will define their chances in life. As Jossé Souza posited, in his critique of the neoliberal economic ideology, "the process of social competition does not begin at school […], but it is, in great part, decided in advance by the pre-school family socialization that is produced by the differing 'culture of social class'" (Souza 2009, 18).[24]

Gerald Cohen proposes a principle of interpersonal justification that insists that any argument regarding public policy must be translated into a statement about some member of society (Cohen 1995, 348). If we were to apply this principle of interpersonal justification in our context, it would be difficult to defend public policies that discriminate some members based on their social position or that do not guarantee them equal status as members of the community. (For example, it would be hard to support a position like the following; "We will spend two thirds of the education budget for fostering higher education to which only the middle class young people have access. We will then allocate one third to basic and secondary education which serves almost exclusively the lowest income young people"[25]). The

[24] For more about these issues, the pioneer work of Pierre Bourdieu (2010) is recommended, especially where it deals with the concept of "cultural capital".

[25] Nevertheless, this was the Brazilian government's policy for many decades.

principle of equal respect that is essential to all democracies, requires that we treat all citizens with equal respect, even those who carry out the least qualified and most humble tasks, or even those who carry out no social responsibilities at all, due to a lack of conditions (i.e. unemployment, illness or lack of qualification, etc.).

There exist, however, both a negative and a positive duty that society has towards its members. The negative one is not to discriminate, not to oppress, not to exploit. This duty should lie with the very institutions of the society as well as with each member. The positive duty is to create the conditions so that its members can participate as free and equal subjects (in the sense outlined above) of the system of socioeconomic cooperation that is society itself. Fulfilling this duty is the responsibility, first of all, of political institutions. However, it is also the duty of any citizens who would call themselves democratic to support any measure and public policy that contributes efficiently to such an end. In our opinion, the BF represents a basic contribution towards this goal.

Chapter 3
The Interviews

"I speak my truth."
"Dona Cássia, Piri-Piri (State of Piauí), July 2009"
To talk like this with a stranger,
who listens well and soon goes far away, has a second
advantage: it is as though I were talking
to myself. Stop and think: whatever is bad within people, they
always distort and rationalize
to rid themselves of it. Would that be
why people talk so much?
"Guimarães" Rosa

In the following chapter, we will tell the story of some of the interviews we carried out during our research. In doing so, we have chosen those excerpts that we consider to be more significant or emblematic. Each interview took, on average, half an hour, although some lasted more than an hour (and in some cases, we spent an entire afternoon talking to one or other of the women). Their speech has not been altered, so as to keep as close as possible to their own voice. Here, we present the interviews directly, without any evaluation or analysis based on our theoretical framework. The conclusions we reached based on the data collected will be presented in Chaps. 4 and 5.

The interview questions were of two types. The first dealt with family makeup (number and age of the family members, level of schooling, etc.). The second category looked into how the BF money was used, particularly, in relation to purchases of food, clothing, and school materials. One of our goals was to ascertain whether and to what extent the money and its regularity impacted the daily lives of these families. We were especially interested in any changes in the lives of these women, most of whom spoke of feeling greater freedom (the words they used were "more at ease") and less distressed about their ability to provide basic goods for their families. A third set of questions sought to elicit the women's opinions about the program and its effects on their lives (this time in a more direct fashion). Among other issues, these questions were intended to find out what the women thought about the fact that the card came in their names rather than that of their husbands and to

A. Pinzani, W. L. Rego, *Money, Autonomy and Citizenship*,
https://doi.org/10.1007/978-3-030-01361-5_3

discover if they thought the program was a governmental favor or a right (naturally, the question could not be formulated directly in these terms, since the concept of "rights" was almost totally absent from these women's vocabularies). Finally, a fourth group of questions dealt with the women's attitudes about politics and their exercise of the right to vote.

The questions were phrased differently from place to place and person to person. We relied on the support of four local contacts in order to take advantage of their familiarity with the linguistic codes (including the implicit ones) the women used. For example, it generally made no sense to ask a woman how much she usually spent at the market because her answer was usually a highly inaccurate estimate, not due to bad faith, rather than an inability to make such an abstract calculation about their experience. We had to ask what they bought at the market and then, with their help, add up how much she must have actually spent. It is our contention that the difference between the various linguistic codes showcases inevitable issues with the use of standardized quantitative surveys which do not take into sufficient account the particular nature of people's linguistic, expressive, and cultural habits.

The interviews presented below are either representative of the majority of the answers given or they represent the most interesting cases that we came into contact with.

In short, we can state that these women generally experienced important changes in their material well-being, although a significant number of them complained about the limited value of the grants (which many women described as a "help") and almost all of them stated that they would prefer to have a regular job. It is worth pointing out that, contrary to a widespread misconception, only 2 of 150 women interviewed said that they had quit working in order to live off of the BF. Both of them had worked as housemaids for middle-class families, and they received a "salary" of between R$ 150 and R$ 200 (to work either 6 or 6.5 days a week). Almost all of them thought it was better that the card came in their name rather than that of their husband (about 10% said that they were indifferent, while none of them said it would be better if the card came in their husband's name). In support they almost always said that the women were better at managing money, had a better idea of the family's needs, and were able to buy things more cheaply. There were many who said that their partners would use the money to drink, although, when asked directly, they almost always denied that their partners drank (we were not able to verify this information; in other words, we could not tell if they were just repeating a common opinion even if it was contradicted by their personal experience or if they were commenting on the drinking habits within their communities) A significant number (about 75%) said that the BF was a favor of the government or resulted from the fact that President Lula had been poor and, therefore, knew better what their lives were like than his predecessors. Only a few said that the government had the duty to help them, and only five used the word "right" (only two were able, when asked, to demonstrate an adequate notion of this concept, while the others did not appear to have a clear idea of what it meant. One mentioned "right" in the context of a "favor"). Almost all of them, however, recognized the fact that having voted for Lula and his election to the presidency president had changed their lives. In short, they perceived a change in the direction of the federal government.

3.1 State of Alagoas (2006, 2007, and 2011)

3.1.1 Maceió

In Maceió we got together with several academic colleagues: Golbery Lessa, of INCRA (the National Institute for Colonization and Agrarian Reform), who traveled to the *sertão* with us, and Luiz Sávio de Almeida and Cícero Péricles de Carvalho, both professors at UFAL (the Federal University of Alagoas) and specialists, respectively, in the history and economics of the state.

Our talks with Luiz Sávio were especially useful for penetrating into the mindset of the *sertanejo* world, which he knew intimately and about which he has published several works. He stressed the importance of taking the appropriate hermeneutic stance when interpreting the words of these women. This might appear trivial, but in the following days, we saw what he had been warning us about. He also taught us about the political situation in the region, where the traditional Brazilian system of political patronage called *coronelismo*[1] was still predominant, although it took different forms from place to place. However, in his opinion, the BF was freeing the grantees from the influence of the local *coronéis*, as the results of the previous presidential election had demonstrated. At the local level, though, we witnessed the continued strong presence of the traditional elites holding tight control of the small towns. From this, it can be concluded that those who received BF grants attributed this fact to the president of the time, Lula da Silva, and therefore voted for him without switching their local votes away from the local *coronel* or his front men, either out of fear or in hope of favors.

Cícero Péricles cited many statistics showing the growth in consumption in the state of Alagoas (in the previous 41 months, consumption had broken records) and the development of what he called an "economy of the poor, for the poor," such as the production of cheap furniture sold in installments without interest or the production of inexpensive, handmade clothes, etc. There was a series of other governmental programs including microcredit, the PRONAF (National Program for Enhancing Family Farming), and the Seguro Safra (Farm Insurance) that appeared to be helping local farmers and agricultural businessmen achieve a certain level of economic security. All of this led us to realize that the BF not only supported the families of grantees but that it provided them with a certain extras that enabled them to escape their current situation of a practical privation of all resources.

Cícero reminded us that there was practically no industry in the *sertão* of Alagoas, with the exception of a textile factory which had been founded by Delmiro Gouveia, and, at the time, provided almost 1000 jobs.[2] In short, without the money coming in from the federal government in the form of the BF, retirement pensions, etc., the

[1] Translator's note: *Coronelismo* refers to a peculiarly Brazilian form of patronage politics in which informal, extra-democratic local strong men hold the actual political power and trade favors, jobs, etc. for votes. *Coronel* (*coronéis*, in the plural) refers to the strongman himself.

[2] Delmiro Gouveia was murdered, according to legend, and even Brazilian novelist Graciliano Ramos (Ramos 1965), at the behest of English businessmen who did not want to lose their monopoly in the Brazilian market.

residents of this region would have survived exclusively on farming which is notoriously difficult in that part of the country, due to the extreme climate characterized by frequent droughts. In the places we visited in the depths of the *sertão*, large landholdings were not the norm, rather small and medium farms. Ranching predominated on the medium-sized properties, while subsistence farming was the most common on the small farms (corn, bean, and manioc were the most common crops and were grown almost exclusively for family use). In addition to the land use patterns, the precarious economy suffered from adverse climate conditions, due to droughts that threatened the harvests yearly. The grueling life has led many families to abandon the region and move to the cities (the state capital Macéio but also the largest Brazilian city, São Paulo) where they usually end up living in the shantytowns, or *favelas*. This situation is changing due to federal social programs, particularly the BF.[3]

3.1.2 Maragogi (2006 and 2007)

Our first interviews with BF grantees took place at Maragogi beach, on the north coast of the state of Alagoas. The trip to Maragogi passed through a region rich in sugarcane production. The cane fields had replaced the original *Mata Atlantica* (the Atlantic Rainforest) of which only the briefest glimpses still survived on the steepest hills. The ocean appeared between well-spaced lines of palm trees. The place looked like an authentic tropical paradise and has attracted many domestic and international investors who have built small and large hotels and luxury resorts. Wealthy foreign tourists traveling along the coastal road on the way to their five-star paradise had to drive through a purgatory of humble little towns and a hellish collection of straw or clay huts built on the shoulders of the roads, chock full of children who are naked, or nearly so. The huts were surrounded with scrawny dogs, countless cyclists and pedestrians, and dozens of impromptu sellers of chewing gum and cookies. From the comfort of their air-conditioned rental cars, they could not even feel the humid heat, the smells, or the noise. They might stop for a moment to take a picture of a picturesque woman carrying a plastic bucket on her head full of mussels before setting off again in the direction of their cabana, which was not built of straw but was equipped with all possible creature comforts and cable TV "facing the ocean."

Near Maragogi in Peroba, there was an extremely poor neighborhood with a few precarious houses and totally lacking in any urban services, neither waste disposal nor any other basic facilities for a healthy life. That was where we conducted two interviews. One of them we were not able to use, due to the woman's situation. She was still carrying the old blue Gas Aid card. In order to be eligible for the research,

[3]For more of the research of Cícero Péricles, see http://www.bancodocidadao.com.br/noticias/?vCod=212.

she would have had to be carrying a Citizen's Card,[4] the famous yellow card that would enable her to receive a BF grant. At that point in time, at least in Alagoas, this type of confusion about the color of the card was still frequent. The woman in question, for example, exclaimed "Oh! I haven't got a yellow card yet! But my neighbor's already got one. I don't know what the difference is yet." Generally, we always needed to explain that the objective of our research was to interview only those people who had the yellow card.

Early in the evening of our first day in Peroba, we got our first useful interview with Dona Ana,[5] a young woman of 25 and the mother of three children. Her house was very small and almost without any furnishings. In order to conduct the interview, we had to sit on the couple's bed. Immediately, the awkwardness of the situation could be felt, the shame of the poverty of the family situation, and the lack of even the most basic furniture for a family home. The husband, a black man, was unemployed. He appeared to be much older than Ana, a bricklayer's assistant; he lived from doing odd jobs that they called "beliscões." He was very talkative and intelligent and, like his wife, was a proud man with a strong personality. He told us about his life and about his parents who worked on the Pau Amarelo sugarcane plantation. Ana had gone to school until the fourth grade and then had gone to work on a farm until she was 11. She got married at 18, and in 2006, she had three daughters aged 6, 5, and 4. She told us that the city hall authorities had gone to her house to tell her how to enroll in the BF. Here is a short quote from the interview:

> "So, I went to try to sign up; it took almost a year to get it. Then I got to get it and until now I've been getting it. I get 80 reais."
>
> "Does the Bolsa Familia help?"
>
> "It's a lot of help. I spend the money on food."
>
> "Ana, the card is called the Citizen's Card. What do you think this means?"
>
> "Nobody's explained it to me yet."
>
> "Ana, so you think that this money you get is a right or a favor that the government does for you?"
>
> "I think it's a right. It's a right, of course."
>
> "Why do you think it's a right?"
>
> "Because we depend on a right from the government. It's not a favor because we pay taxes. We, for example, here, we don't pay for water but we're gonna start paying, so we depend on something from the government too!"
>
> "Is it a good program? What do you think of it?"
>
> "I think it's great. We can't buy everything because eighty reais is not enough to get by on for the month. If my husband doesn't happen to get work, sometimes he goes a whole month without working, we can't depend on eighty reais."
>
> "Is it hard to get work here?"
>
> "You bet it is."
>
> "Even cleaning in people's houses?"
>
> "Oh! It really is. Because this is a touristic area, there's only people from the outside. Sometimes there's a bit of work there but it's only for a few people."

[4] At this point in time, the yellow BF card was also called the Citizen's Card, a name which was later changed.

[5] The names of all the women were changed to protect their privacy. Translator's note: All the women's names are preceded by the honorific "Dona."

Another interview took place in the house of Benedita, 36. She was a community health agent, married with her husband unemployed. She had two children (one natural, another adopted). Her household also included her mother, who had other children, including a baby. There were ten people living in the house. This explained why she was receiving a grant, in spite of having a job. It was a poor, crowded house. Benedita was a lively and intelligent person. She was well-spoken and talked about her rights and the need to fine-tune the BF program. She repeated several times that it would be preferable for her if her husband and the other men, who are always unemployed and living off of odd jobs, had a job with a contract. She got together a group of women who agreed to be interviewed. As mentioned above, at that moment, April of 2006, in this region, the BF issue was still very confusing, especially regarding the cards. Few people in this area had received the card specifically for the program, the yellow card that at the time was called the Citizen's Card. Previous cards (Gas Aid and the School Aid) were still being merged into the BF and this led to many mismatches in the information they provided us.

In any case, the group interview was a friendly and lively in atmosphere. There were six women, who arrived one at a time. They were a bit suspicious at first, which always happens during fieldwork. Dona Cecília, 48, appeared to be much older. She was the mother of ten children (including Benedita) and she began talking about how hard it was to find work in the region. In fact, she had two sons, aged 16 and 17, who took up "little odd jobs here and there." When we asked her what happened when they could not find any work, she answered "They hang around waiting for the future!" All of them, men and women, had to take odd jobs. They worked as washerwomen and bricklayer's assistants, whatever came around.

The conversation was very high-spirited and hard to keep on course, since everybody talked at the same time. Several times we had to ask them to let the interviewee finish speaking.

We tried to listen to what each one of them had to say about the program. Then we asked the question, "Do you think the BF program is a duty of the government or is it a right of yours?" They exchanged glances and a vigorous discussion ensued. "It's a big favor," said first Dona Dejanira, mother of four children, who was receiving a grant of R$60/month, "because it's a help to those who don't have anything, right? If most people had it, it would be a real help but most people don't get the grant. When they do, it takes a long time to get here." We asked Elizete, 23, mother of three children born in Maragogi, whose husband worked odd jobs without a contract, what she thought of the program, and she said, "I think it's fantastic." Regarding the question of whether it was a favor or a right, she answered emphatically, "I've got two opinions. Sometimes, I think that it's a favor and sometimes I think it's their duty. But 90% I think it's their duty." Dejanira, a bit confused by Elizete's vehemence, said, "It's a good idea." We answered, "But what is a good idea?" She answered, "This, this thing of giving grants to the poor people." Wanting to know more about their lives, we asked them to tell us what they used to do before receiving the BF grants. Dejanira explained that they, in order to increase their income, or when they did not have regular money coming in, would work, and still worked, gathering (she said "digging" which is more accurate) *massunim* (a local mollusk that women gathered and sold to local restaurants). They are known as *maçunim* or as *berbigão* in southern Brazil. It is a sort of small clam that is said to be a great source of protein and is prized for its flavor. We asked how they gathered it and Dejanira went on to describe how they did it. They would walk into the sea to dig the mollusks from the sand, and it would be either hard or less so, depending on the tide. "If the tide is way down low, it's easy to dig them. But those times when the tide's high, you can't get anything." To dig them, they would tie a rope around themselves, and they gathered the mollusks into their bras, panties, or tied them up in the ropes. We asked them why they didn't use plastic bags. "It doesn't work!" Bags are useless, as it's also no use trying to hold them in your hands, because "the waves come and knock everything out of your hands." Dejanira went on describing, "Sometimes I dig them to sell, sometimes I do it to feed the folks at home, and that's how it is. When I can, I go dig. When he lets me. I go mostly at night. I even went last night, but he was sleeping...." It took us a while to realize that "he" was the mollusk itself which, in her opinion, could not be found in the normal location because "he was sleeping" (in another place, obviously).

Another "digger," Dona Francisca, told us in another interview that she knew where to look because she can see "its eye" referring to a little hole in the sand where the *maçunim* breathes the water to filter its nourishment. Generally, we had to expend a certain amount of hermeneutic energy to try and see the world through the eyes of these women and understand their speech. As professor Luiz Sávio had told us, "the ocean is a text that these women interpret in their own way." And we tried to interpret their interpretation.

Getting back to the women gathered at Dona Benedita's house, we asked what they thought about the Citizen's Card, in general, and what they thought it meant to be a citizen. The answer was always the same, "Oh! I have no idea. That's a hard one to answer." When we asked about the fact that the card was intended for the women, they once again all answered at once. With one or two differences of opinion, most of them said that the idea of putting the responsibility for the card in the hands of the women was good. We asked them why.

The most frequent answer (which we heard in almost all of the interviews, here in Alagoas, as well as in other locations) was always linked to the issue of the woman's responsibility for the family and the children. The women were better able to manage the money because they are more fully aware of the needs of the family. The topic of the independence of the women due to the existence of income is an issue that did not make any sense to them at that time.

When we insisted on the question, Dejanira answered, "I think that she is more independent when she is working. As for having the card or not, because it's so little, it doesn't stay around, because it's one thing today, tomorrow...." (she made a gesture signifying "Who knows?"). "But she didn't have anything earlier!" we replied. "And now the card is in her hand. Don't you think this has changed anything for the women?"

She answered, "I don't know. If her husband didn't smoke, didn't drink...."

Dona Gerusa entered into the conversation at this point and added, "And then when you get that little bit of money, you put it all inside the house, right? You buy clothes, you buy shoes, one thing or another for the kids, right? And the husbands no, when they get the money, they go straight to the bar to have a drink. So, that's how it is. It's got to go in the women's names, otherwise…." Her countenance took on the expression of one who doubted the destination of the money. She looked up and then to the sides.

We posed another question. "Do all of you think that there are women who hand the money over to their husbands?" Again, they all answered at once. "Oh! Yeah, there are. Many of them do hand it over. I wouldn't hand it over, no way."

We insisted, "Are there women who hand the money over?"

One of them answered, "Only if the husband is a bit rough." And then they told us a story where the woman handed over the password and the husband did the shopping. According to them, the wife did that because she was afraid of him. "Really heavy handed, you understand?"

In general, these women, even as they praised the BF, also complained that it was not enough. But they recognized that with the current amount, they were able to buy food for the family and that they felt fewer "necessities" (this term is used in their speech to speak of needs and privations). When we asked them why more women had not come to the interview, they all told us "They were afraid!"

One of them said, "People here are all afraid, and they say, 'I'm not gonna do it.' It's the fear, yeah? Sometimes people who don't get much, they are afraid. You show up and not everybody agrees to talk with you because they are afraid it'll be bad for them, got it? Sometimes I see people saying that it's not much and if you got more people together from one neighborhood, in the interior, in a quieter town, where not everybody's got a job, I mean, the people that live with that little bit of money, if it was more, wouldn't that be better?"

When we were leaving Benedita's house, we raised the question, "But without the income from the BF, how would you make do, or how do you still make do?"

Her mother answered, "We'd get by, you know? People got to survive with what they got, right? Those that got a lot, live with a lot. We who haven't got much, you know…What you can't pay for today, you can pay for tomorrow. If you can't pay, you wait a bit…."

In 2007, we went back to interview the *maçunim* diggers again. This time we also interviewed some women we ran into on the way. The choice of the *maçunim* diggers was due to the harshness of their work to try to increase the family income, as well as the tendency to look down on them and their work. They were obliged by the nature of their job to stay in the water, at low tide, kneeling and digging these little mollusks that they sell in the fairs and to hotels in the region. This was obviously seen as a humiliating job for desperate people.

One of the women interviewed in the city who did not work digging *maçunim* was Dona Isabel, 28, with two daughters, married and one of the only women whose husband was employed and *fichado* ("papered" as they say there to refer to someone who has a signed contract). She looked down on the others who worked "digging *maçunim*." When we asked her if she would resort to this work to increase her limited income, she answered in a contemptuous tone, "No, I've never sold *maçunim*. No. I would be ashamed. I think it's ugly. I've never needed to do this, no."

She used the income from the grant to eat better and buy some clothes and school supplies for her daughters and, sometimes, she told us in an embarrassed fashion, hair cream for herself. Isabel herself brought up that the BF has afforded her more freedom. “When I get it, I’ve got my own money. I go out and I buy things. I don’t like to keep asking him [her husband], not a bit. That’s why I work. I don’t like to keep asking my husband for anything.”

Despite the fact that Maragogi is a beautiful beach, full of hotels, small inns, and restaurants, these women cannot find jobs. It is thought that they lack the experience to work in these places, whose customers are normally from the upper-middle class. They have neither training nor experience, since most of them are illiterate or have very little schooling. Therefore, it is hard for them to get jobs in the hotels or restaurants that are there.

Dona Joana, an old *maçunim* digger, was a thin black woman, with her long, curly hair twisted into a thick braid, the tendons in her neck as thick as ropes, with large, lively, energetic eyes. She was a grandmother who received the grant due to the fact that her grandchildren lived with her. She said with all the force of her strong personality, “I prove my worth by digging mussels at low tide.” She spoke forcefully about the harshness of the work digging the mollusks, “When I get home (from the sea) I am completely broken. I can’t take it any more, no I can’t. You got to stay on your knees, the whole time until you fill the bucket, a big bucket, on your back. When I get home, I have this right here [she points at her back] …my back can’t take it. Today, I had to go dig, I had to get wet and I was so cold when I got home that I couldn’t stand the pain in my back.” She sold the *maçunim* at R$10/kilo, but sometimes she had to lower the price due to competition from other diggers. Her husband worked as a coconut picker, when he could get work. She was well-spoken, even though she had only gone to school through the second grade and only knew how to sign her name.

We asked her if the grant helped her to work less, and she answered, “It helps, for the girls.” In fact, it was obvious that the grant did not free her up from hard work. When we were leaving her house, she gave us as a present a round bread fruit (*Artocarpus altilis)* that was big and green, and she told us how to cook it.

Closer to the downtown of Maragogi, we met a woman called Dona Lourdes who was a representative case of the new economic processes that the state of Alagoas was undergoing following the strong and extensive implementation of the BF: the rapid rise in economic activity and the spread of small food factories making cookies or pasta, as well as small clothes manufacturers. These were businesses employing about five or six people and whose products were targeted for the masses.

Lourdes, 35, had three children, and her husband worked at odd jobs. She studied until the eighth grade and was relatively highly skilled. She worked at a small clothes factory as a seamstress. She was one of the few women who, when asked whether she considered the BF to be a favor of the government or a right, answered, “Neither a favor nor an obligation. People like us, who are citizens, we do have our rights. The politicians, they have conditions to live their lives, to live honestly and yet they don’t do it. So, this is how they live. So, the little bit that comes here to us,

I think that it makes no difference to those people, you know? So, you got to split it up. It's got to be balanced. I think it's got to be this way." That's how Lourdes saw the question of income distribution in Brazil.

We interviewed Dona Maria, 29 years of age, who was married and taking care of her stepdaughter, 9. She had gone to school until the seventh grade and gave us a surprising answer to the question about the women being the beneficiaries of the BF card. "Yeah, she gets more rights, right? Because we live with more rights. Since women haven't got anything, they don't work, so now they have this right, got it?"

Still in Maragogi, in the neighborhood of Carvão, in a bar, we interviewed Dona Neusa, a black woman, 36, a single mother of three children who had gone to school through the sixth grade. She answered our questions positively and enthusiastically about the BF grants coming in the name of the women. "We become more independent when you put the card in the name of the person herself."

We asked her, "But if it was in the name of the men?"

Her answer, "it would be fatal. The men are sneaky…." Then she burst out laughing. "Oh, my big mouth. I can't control myself."

In the other interviews, we could see the importance of the BF in these women's lives. This was manifest in several ways, from the generalized complaint of the grants insufficiency to guarantee them a better and more dignified life, to the grant's indispensability for them to continue living such a life. Everyone recognized that, if their lives were harsh, without the grants, they would be even more so. This recognition showed up in the form of comments such as, "Oh! I don't know what would happen to us poor people, without this grant!" Generally speaking, answers that involved any true consciousness of rights were rare. The figure of Lula da Silva, the President of the Republic at the time, was regularly referred to as "He." They would say that "He thinks about the poor" or "He does this for us." Such statements (or similar ones) were frequent.

3.1.3 Sertão de Alagoas (2006, 2007, and 2011)

The sertão of Alagoas was a brilliant green just after the rainy season. A crystalline blue sky was crisscrossed by huge white clouds that hung suspended over blue mountains that fell in regular waves like ripples on the water. It was hard to believe that, during the long summer, all of this green would disappear and this paradisiacal landscape would turn into a Dantesque hell. There would arise a scrubland of cactus and short thorny trees without leaves called *caatinga,* which in the indigenous language Tupi means "white forest" in reference to the white wood on the trunks and branches. The roads were unending straight shots that rose and fell according to the great folds in the terrain. They were all in a precarious state, full of potholes. They passed through poverty-stricken little towns peopled with children playing along the side of the road. Trucks drove by that have been turned into clandestine buses where people sat on improvised seats. Carts were pulled by oxen and driven by people from the *sertão* whose faces appeared to be made of the same leather as that of their typical hats.

3.1.3.1 Povoado da Cruz

Povoado da Cruz was the first place in the *sertão* where we conducted interviews. It is inhabited by *quilombolas*, people descended from runaway slaves,[6] and it was located within the city of Delmiro Gouveia. In the hamlet, there were rows of masonry houses like in the former living quarters of factories, with a small porch out front. It seemed to have been built for the workers of the famous textile factory of Delmiro Gouveia, but we were not able to confirm this version of the origin of the community. The women we interviewed did not live, however, in the masonry houses but in humble dwellings (huts, in fact) sprinkled about in a disorganized fashion. There are no streets but paths, where you could find dogs, free-ranging pigs, and many chickens. Vegetation was sparse and consisted– in addition to the grasses and the yards – of the low trees that were typical of the region.

It was a community of black people, with an origin myth that was still vividly alive. All of the current residents were said to have descended from a single slave couple who ran away in 1868 from a neighboring plantation, after they fell ill. The couple apparently had had ten children and founded that community. These supposed descendants appear to have an intense community spirit, to the point of not allowing their members to speak individually about anything. The women accompanied us on our visits to the various houses and participated in each interview. They had no respect for any communication difficulties (which were frequent among many of them), and they all spoke at once, which made the interviews almost impossible.

The women we interviewed lived in mud houses, with a very simple wooden frame. Some had poles sunk into the ground, with a few smaller poles crisscrossing them and with the empty spaces filled in with clay, where the rain constantly opened holes. Only one of the houses had plaster (albeit worn and falling apart in some places). It was painted blue and had a concrete floor. Others had a dirt floor, and one of the houses was missing one wall, which had been replaced with a black plastic tarp. Some families had pet sheep that they treated like dogs. Sometimes baby chickens wandered freely inside the houses. The children stared with avid curiosity at the tape recorder and tried to get our attention, pushing out in front while their mothers talked and laughed. They were beautiful boys and girls, but in that environment, they would age quickly, like their mothers who, although aged 22 and 25, already appeared to be old. The husbands, who normally were not present when we arrived or who preferred to go out during the interview, were all unemployed or at most worked at odd jobs on farms, in other words, working 1 or 2 days a week when they could find someone who needed their services (like at that point in time, which was the bean harvest). At that time, they earned R$10 for 8 hours of hard labor.

On our first visit, we were guided by an official from the social work department of the Delmiro Gouveia City Hall. We were taken to a large room where several of the residents of the community were waiting, including many men, who were

[6]Translator's note: *Quilombo* is the name that was given during the colonial period in Brazil to communities of runaway slaves. They were analogous to the *palenques* in Spanish-speaking Latin America.

attending a cooking class taught by a teacher, also black, who appeared to be an employee of the social work department of the city hall. She was lecturing precisely about the need to recover their identity and that of their *quilombo*. That was why she was "there to teach them their food" or in other words, the food from the *quilombo*. In fact, she was teaching them a recipe for cooking fish from the São Francisco River that ran nearby, one of those recipes that can be found on a package of ultra-pasteurized, long-life milk. There was a lot of confusion when we arrived. Everyone was laughing and talking at the same time. The teacher made a point of treating them like school children, reinforcing their childish behavior. Some of the older women and men began telling us, always in a lively fashion and with the help of the teacher, about the importance of prayers for curing illnesses, especially those caused by snakebite. The woman accompanying us explained our research and then we went to another large room. It was impossible to carry out individual interviews, but we tried anyway. We began with a woman who was introduced as being a BF grantee and she did in fact receive the grant. She was evidently ill, with serious mental and communicative challenges. Everyone, at the same time, tried to answer her questions, saying, "She is a fool. She doesn't know anything." And the poor woman laughed and tried to answer our questions. We asked her if she had ever been to school, but she said no; she was illiterate. In this rather chaotic atmosphere, we nevertheless managed to get in a quick interview with two women. One of them, Dona Adele, 46, had two children who were no longer eligible for the program[7] and an unemployed husband (occasional fisherman), and she received R$50, which was the minimum grant. She was able to tell us, "This has changed my life because I did not use to get anything. It's not much but it helps." Later we spoke to Dona Belmira, 40, and the mother of seven children. She got R$95: the basic grant of R$50 and, since she had three children who attended school (aged 4, 9, and 12), R$15/child. Her husband, like all the others in this hamlet, was unemployed. He was also an occasional fisherman. Both husband and wife were illiterate. Dona Belmira told us several times that she suffered many privations and that she would prefer to have a regular job with a contract.

Walking through the community, followed by a veritable and lively procession, we came to the house of Dona Claudineide. It was an extremely humble home that had been lent to her by a relative. Claudineide was a young woman of 25, mother of three children, 5, 3, and a 5-month-old baby. She was married and her husband was unemployed. She had been getting a R$65 grant since 2003. She complained a lot about her poverty and the difficulty of her situation and she easily volunteered that she would prefer her husband to have a job with a contract. The fact that the Citizen's Card was in her name made little difference to her. She said that it was the same for her if it was her name or her husband's. "For me it's the same. It would be the same thing if it was in his name." In this house, at this moment, we had the strong impression that the members of this household were deeply depressed. The faces of both Claudineide and her husband were marked with tremendous sadness. The husband sat to the side, his head hung low, and displayed tremendous humiliation. He spoke not a single word.

[7] At that point, the Pro-Youth program had not yet started.

When we went back in 2007, we were able to talk to Claudineide and two other grantees again, this time more quietly, although always accompanied by a small group of women and children. They all said that their grant was used to buy basic foodstuffs like rice, flour, beans, pasta, and chicken (the city hall has a program that distributed milk to the children). Claudineide told us that she had bought a package of cookies for her children for the first time. Another of the women told us with poorly concealed pride that she was now able to buy "spaghetti in a package", in other words, an entire package, rather than just a partial one (some shops in the region were willing to sell in quantities small than those of the package itself). None of the women were literate, except one who proudly announced that she could read and write. All of the children, however, were in school, as was required by the demands of the BF.

Claudineide was more bitter toward her husband, and she was surprised when we reminded her that the year before she had said that it was indifferent to her whether the BF card carried her name or her husband's. She claimed now that the card should really be in the name of the women. Her husband was still unemployed, and he came into the house wearing Bermuda shorts and tennis shoes and appeared to be much calmer than the previous year. Claudineide was still a strong young woman who was talkative and still complained about the amount of the grant and her husband's lack of a job. Her distinctive features and her forceful way of speaking made her one of the women who stuck out most clearly in our memories. She had a rather rascally tone of voice, and when we were saying goodbye, she said in a childlike voice, "Next time, bring me a present!"

The most difficult cases were those of Delia and Fernanda. The former was an illiterate woman who lived in a hovel that appeared to be more of a toolshed than a house, so small it was a room with nothing more than a bed, a small gas stove, an improvised shelf made out of planks, a small chest, and a bucket that probably served as a bedpan at night. Her grant had been suspended, she explained, and she did not know why. We asked if she had not received any justification, and she showed us a letter that the city hall had sent a few months earlier and that had called her in to renew her card. The problem is that Delia did not know how to read and her relations with the other women, among whom at least one could read, were not very good. According to the confusing story she told us, she was bringing in some sort of money, but it was not clear whether it was from doing odd jobs, cleaning houses, or prostitution.

A little later, we arrived at a house with one wall that consisted of a piece of black plastic tarpaulin that allowed wind and heavy rain to come in. A woman named Fernanda lived here. She obviously had serious mental handicaps, but she was able to tell us her name. She had eight children, who slept draped over two double beds in the one room of the house. It was almost impossible to interview her, whether because she sometimes did not understand many of the questions and was only able to laugh nervously or because the other women answered in her stead.

At times like these, we put the recorder and notebook aside because we knew the interview would be unusable and we would have an informal talk so as not to disappoint the woman who might have felt guilty if we went away without asking questions. There was tremendous commotion in Fernanda's hut. Children were jumping on the beds, the baby was crying, and all the women were talking loudly at once. Outside, night fell, and the darkness fell over pathways interrupted only occasionally by the weak light of isolated houses. The feeling of desolation was suffocating.

We came back to Povoado da Cruz in 2011. First, we sought out Claudineide. We found her house after asking around, for she was now living in another house: a brick house without plaster, but new, with a porch. That was where we caught sight of her, on the porch. We were surprised at her appearance. She was much fatter. She had aged and she appeared to be ill. For a few seconds, we were in doubt that it was her at all, due to the changes in her appearance. We asked her if she remembered us and she answered to Walquiria, "I remember, yes, you are the research lady." She invited us to sit down and brought out some old chairs that had been given to her, but we did not go in the house, as she did not wave us in. We found that strange, as it was normal for us to be invited in. We could make out in the main room of the house, just two mattresses lying on the floor and a small table where a TV was turned on. Her husband was lying on one of the mattresses watching some program. Claudineide's face looked sad, melancholy, and she told us that she was very ill, with high blood pressure and depression, but she was not able to tell us if she was getting medical treatment or not. We explained that we had come back to see how the BF grantees were getting along and that is how we began the conversation. Slowly she began to open up to us and she revealed her great personal hardships.

At times, she had to keep herself from crying. She mentioned more than once her depression and high blood pressure. It had been extremely high recently and more than once had gotten as high as 180/100. Her mother arrived at a certain point in our talk, and while the two of them were talking, we asked if any divorces or separations had happened in the community. They answered, "Ah! Five separations had taken place." There were various reasons. We asked if abusive behavior by husbands had been one of the reasons. We asked if the BF might have encouraged these women to react in ways they might not have been able to previously. They exchanged glances, and Claudineide said, "I think the BF has given us more courage." Meanwhile the mother stretched up her neck and pointed with her eyes at her son-in-law who continued lying down watching the TV in the living room. That is when we realized that Claudineide's marriage was going through a deep crisis and that her dejection was related to this. We decided to ask her, "Claudineide why don't you do what the others have done?" She looked at us sadly and did not answer, but we could tell that she was struggling to keep back tears. Walquiria asked her several times what she thought about seeking help from the CRAS (Social Assistance Reference Centers), but – as we always heard from the women when we mentioned this institution – she answered: "That's no use. They never come around to ask how we are doing and they have cars and everything." It is worth remembering that Povoado is located about 10 km from the city of Delmiro Gouveia, which is the seat of the city hall. There are school buses, but we did not see any being used by the local residents. At the end of the afternoon, when we were leaving the community, we could see a group of women walking with their hands full of their grocery shopping. This made us wonder whether this was due to the lack of transport services that might bring them from their neighborhood to the city. We visited the area three times and never saw any vestiges of regular transportation services.

Going back to the case of Claudineide, after complaining about CRAS and returning to the subject of her husband, she muttered with tears in her eyes, “He says he’s not leaving. He says it’s his house too. Besides, he lies a lot.” We asked if he abused her physically and we told her about the Women’s Protection Police Station. She said she was not familiar with it and thought that there was not one in Delmiro Gouveia. During our talk, she told us that, despite her personal distress, she could see that the BF had significantly improved the lives of women, especially after the recent increases and, particularly, the raise instituted by the new President Dilma Rousseff. She told us that she had found it wonderful to vote for a woman to be president. When we asked her how she had managed to build that house, she told us it had been with the help of the neighbors.

“And the money to buy the material?” we asked.

“Ah! My husband managed a bit of extra money for a few months, working in the state of Ceará and that made it possible to build the house.” Unfortunately, the work had not continued and they had not managed to finish the house. That is when the city hall of Delmiro had intervened, she explained, and had paid for the roof, but they had not contributed to plaster or to a bathroom. At that point in time, she described the precariousness of the installations that were intended to become a bathroom and her fear that the children might fall into the hole in the floor that they used for their necessities. When faced with her enormous sadness, we could tell that this topic of conversation made her even more melancholy. We even asked her if she wanted to wrap up the interview. She said, politely, “No. It is good to talk. It’s good. I need this.” When we asked her if there was not a risk of having more children, she said that the doctor in Delmiro Gouveia had “operated” her, in other words, that she had had her tubes tied, which was the dream of most of those women. The story of how she had managed to have the procedure done conveyed the desperation that the women feel when faced with unwanted pregnancies. She told me that she could not take the pill and that she was allergic to the latex in the condoms. So, she told us, the doctor had performed a cesarean during her last labor and had taken advantage of the situation to remove her tubes. She was smiling as she told us (and it was significant that this was the only time we saw her smile), “The doctor showed me the tubes she had pulled out. Now I’m not at risk of getting pregnant again, and I told the doctor – for the love of God, help me! I can’t have any more children.”

It had begun to get dark and we wound down the conversation. We left Povoado da Cruz shaken and moved by the situation of this young woman, who would be 30 at the end of that year. She carried so much suffering, and even worse, she saw no meaning in her future. In Delmiro Gouveia, we went to the city hall and asked to speak to the mayor. They called the chief of staff and through him set up a meeting with the mayor for the following day at 8:00 in the morning. We were very upset by the situation of Claudineide and wanted to ask him to improve the health and transportation services to Povoado, as well as, of course, to finish building Claudineide’s house and finish putting in the bathroom. It was useless, however. The next day we waited an hour, and we later found out that the mayor had arrived at the city hall long after the appointed hour of our meeting.

3.1.3.2 Inhapi

In addition to Povoado da Cruz, we visited a small town called Inhapi that was located some 40 km away from Delmiro Gouveia. On our first visit in 2006, we met a young man named Claudemir, who was riding a motorcycle, and we asked him for directions. We were lucky because he turned out to be the son of our local contact, Genivaldo "Geno" Vieira da Silva, one of the founders of the local MST, the Landless Workers' Movement. His father had later broken off from the movement and became extremely critical of some of its practices, at least as they had been carried out in the *sertão* of Alagoas. Geno was a man of great experience, who was at that time active in the struggles of the local small farmers.

Claudemir took us to the homes of some BF grantees. The first of which was the house of the family called the Caras Pretas [a nickname of the family that translates as the Black Faces]. They were a very nice and highly politicized family. They soon told us that their nickname was due to the fact that they were members of the Workers' Party, the PT, the party of former President Lula da Silva, during whose administration the BF had been set up.

We asked them, "But why the name Caras Pretas [Black Faces]?"

The father, a distinguished-looking gentleman of an advancing age, solemnly told us, "It was the Oropas who gave us this name."

We asked who the Oropas were.

The father answered, "You don't know? They are the African bees, who have a terrible sting. It's so strong it can kill you." We then understood that he was talking about their political enemies and the local *mandachuvas*.[8] They told us several stories about the arbitrary nature of the local power schemes. The older man told us at a certain point, "Here, the political parties are real booby traps." Claudemir told us that the BF deposited R$250,000 each month in the city of Inhapi and that this had led to a total revolution in the local economy. It had attracted business and had brought new life to the community.

That is when Dona Graciele, 26, and the mother of four small children, joined the conversation. She was the daughter-in-law of the owner of the house. She was getting a grant of R$95 (the basic grant for mothers of three children). She gave us two important pieces of information. Firstly, the money made it possible for her to buy cookies for the children and sometimes even a package of pasta. She explained that she spent about R$20–30 per week at the market. She bought all of the essential foodstuffs for the family. The second important piece of information related to the fact that several women had overrun their BF grants and the shop owners had confiscated their cards. Some women had even handed over their passwords. We discussed this among all the people present, and we expressed our concern with this habit, and we argued that its continuation or its potential for expansion would put the women under the power of the shop owners and that it was a way of destroying the small bit of independence that the BF had afforded these women. Someone immediately suggested that we should take this information to the government, to the responsible Ministry because the risk of this practice becoming a perverse habit was immanent.

[8] Translator's note: *Mandachuvas*, or rainmakers, is the name of local power brokers.

Our second interview in this community in the countryside, where the houses were crowded close together and normally housed by members of a single family, was with Dona Luisa, 36. She was the mother of seven children, the oldest of which was 15 years old and who had fathered a child of his own. She got R$95/month, since she had four children at school.

When we asked her about her own schooling, she answered, "I went, but I quickly gave up. Then it was onto the farm."

"Did you learn to read and write?"

"No."

"Dona Luisa, what do you think about this BF program?"

"I think, Ave Maria, I think it's really good. Because it's a real help to us. And to many people out there that need it. It was really good for us to get this money. If they do away with it, there'll be no way for us to get by in this world, you know? It's a great help, it is. [...]"

"Dona Luisa, has it come to your attention the fact that the card comes in your name and not that of your husband?

"Yeah, it has. I think that's great!"

"Why do you think that's great?"

"Because the women always know how to do things right, you hear? The men are more…."

"More what?"

"More unruly and go out and buy things that are more expensive."

"Dona Luis, did you know, for example, that other women think that the fact that the card comes in their name, that they feel freer, or more at ease?"

"Around here," she answered, "many women feel like that because they don't have to depend on their husbands any more."

"So, for example, if she wants to separate from her husband, because he drinks or because he beats her?"

"But no, not that."

"That doesn't happen around here?"

"No. That doesn't happen, no."

"So even if the husband drinks and beats her, she'll stay with him," we asked.

"She'll stay with her husband."

The issue of conjugal relations came up in a dramatic fashion when we interviewed Dona Madalena, 34 years of age with three school-aged children. She could read (she had studied until the fifth grade, which was unusual in the region). This was a dramatic interview. She answered the questions laconically. When she was asked if she knew of women who had managed to leave irresponsible or violent husbands, she began to cry and said,

"I don't want to talk about this anymore."

We could tell we had touched a nerve, and we apologized and thanked her for the interview.

In the rural community of Inhapi, we could tell that the family lives were much improved if there was the presence of a mother or a mother-in-law who had a retirement pension from the federal system. Retired women, always more common than male retirees, were generally strong, outspoken, and bossy. They were aware of the fact that they guaranteed the well-being of their relatives – they were the de facto heads of the family. The men, as we have said above, were almost all unemployed or living from odd jobs (where they got at most R$10/day, which summed up to around R$30–40/month). They were mostly illiterate. In the sertão de Alagoas, at least where we were, there were no jobs for these men, due to a lack of both private business and of public policies intended to build the infrastructure needed to attract investment.

Some statements showed that the region, despite the achievement of a certain level of autonomy relative to the local political bosses, was still under the heavy hand of patronage. Problems would come up at registration, when the risk of fraud was great (at the time of writing, the book registration had become stricter). The enrollment of grantees was carried out by officials of the city halls or the Federal Savings Bank. These officials were always fully entwined in the local systems of political power. In general, we think that the biggest problems in managing the implementation of the BF took place at the local level, whether they arose from the pressure of patronage and of local party politics or due to pure incompetence on the part of the officials chosen by local mayors to take these positions of trust.

We went back to Inhapi in 2007, when the father of Claudemir, Genivaldo, or Geno as he was known by all accompanied us on our interviews. As we returned to the same places and the same women interviewed in 2006 in order to see what changes had taken place in the various dimensions of their lives, we found them in the same poverty in which they had always lived. The most evident outer aspects were the precarious housing, the poor clothing, and the profound sense of shame and humiliation. This feeling was mostly manifest in the form of a great awkwardness to have us come into their houses, which were normally without furnishings, oftentimes even without a chair for us to sit on. However, it is not fair to say that nothing had changed in the lives of these women and their families following the state grants. Our attention was attuned precisely to discovering the fine distinctions in the new situation afforded by receiving regular monthly income. These differences could be perceived, at times, by the women's new forms of self-recognition of their abilities to manage family business and their responsibilities to their families and the state. An increase in the self-esteem of these women was, in sum, revealed which pointed to minimal increases in autonomy regarding their management of their lives in general. Some of them (very few, in fact) had taken difficult moral decisions, such as managing to get out of unhappy marriages. Touching on these subjects was, however, a very delicate proposition in this region.

We went back to see Dona Graciele, who was now 27. She still recognized the tremendous help that the BF had brought into her life and reminded us that she now earned more than her husband, when he was able to find work. Nevertheless, she complained, "But I'm thinking that for four children, it's not very much."

Her house now sported a TV that was on, thanks to the "Light for All" program of the federal government.[9] Graciele said that she really enjoyed watching football. "I most like to see games, the kids like to see Pica-pau and Zorro and the Power Rangers."

[9]Translator's note: The goal of the program was to bring electric power to isolated houses or communities.

When we asked what she thought about the BF card coming in the name of the women, she answered, "I think it's good." Questioned about what the differences would be if it came in her husband's name, she offered what was a classic answer in the local circumstances. "No, he would take the money and drink *cachaça.*[10]" The children watching the interview would occasionally join the conversation and give opinions similar to this one about their father, "Every Sunday, he goes to play football. Then, sometimes, when he comes home…." They were clearly making reference to the fact that their dad sometimes arrived drunk. When we asked about what her life was before the BF and if anything had changed, Graciele's answer was immediate, "Ah! I think my life has changed. I didn't use to have anything. My mother helped. So did my mother-in-law."

Then we went to the house of Dona Madalena who was now 35. We found her working her bean plants on her miniscule farm. She approached us with a smile on her face. She was very different than the year before, when we had found her to be laconic, serious, often bursting into tears at a certain point in the interview. We took her picture together with her children, and at that moment, she made a point of telling us that we had found her the year before at one of the most difficult points in her life, as she was wanting to leave her husband. Now she had managed to separate and life had improved greatly. We asked her how much she was getting from the BF, and she happily said, "I am getting $R112 with the small recent increase." She told us that she had to buy something worth R$5 at the place where she withdrew her money because the Caixa Econômica was located inside a shop. Genio explained that this strange practice of some shop owners was quite common in the region.

When asked what had changed in her life after joining the BF program, Madalena said, "I love it because I don't know what my life would be without it, you know? It would be really hard, with three children. I think it's great, great, because if it wasn't for the BF, I don't know what would happen to this poor family."

From the point of view of the women interviewed, their desire to secure a better future for their children was immediately obvious. You could almost say that this was their only hope in the world: to make them into people less devoid of capabilities than they are, in other words, to equip them better so that they may find another fate.

At the end of our visit, Madalena invited us in to her cousin's house to see his paintings. He was a 47-year-old man, "sick in the head" as she told us who drew in charcoal little figures on the bare walls of his absolutely primitive hut (there were only three stones, serving as a fireplace, a pot, and a bedspread that served as a bed). They were fantastic drawings, inspired most probably by newspaper pictures, with airplanes, helicopters, portraits, fighter jets, cars, ambulances, houses, and churches. It was like the work of a Basquiat from the *sertão*, illiterate and crazy. He could hardly remember his own name and he insisted that he was called Zé da Mangueira. Geno said that he did not carry an identity card, as was the case of many people in the sertão (which explained, sometimes, why some people were

[10]Translator's note: *Cachaça* is the most popular distilled alcohol in Brazil which is made from fermented sugarcane juice.

not eligible for the BF). However, these people without an identity can get a voter's registration card, since the *coroneis* or their henchmen who want their votes can manage to get them a work permit with a photo.

We returned to Inhapi in 2011. We first went to Dona Luisa's house. She was now 41 years old and the mother of eight children. This time she had become a grandmother of a baby of two (her daughter was 18 when she got pregnant and was lucky enough to marry the baby's father). When we got there, Luisa showed up, laughing, the baby she was carrying in her arms (her eighth child) and said, "One more gift from God." The improvement in her life was visible. The house was painted, there were three covered sofas in the living room, and, of course, there was the regal presence of the TV. We could sit down comfortably, very differently than had been the case at the first interview when we had barely been able to fit, much to her chagrin. Her grant had now reached R$160, and her husband, a bricklayer's assistant, was doing odd jobs. This had been fundamental in helping with the improvements to the house. The children were wearing Bermuda shorts and tennis shoes, and as always, they stayed in the living room, curious about our presence. Dona Luisa, to the contrary of Claudineide, spoke happily about the improvements that the BF had brought to her life: She and her family were eating better, and in fact, life had improved significantly. They had not yet managed to buy a refrigerator because the installments were too expensive, but she told us happily how she was going to go about getting new mattresses. She had saved every penny, without telling anybody, and then suddenly she bought a mattress and then, following the same method, she had bought the others as well. She looked very happy with herself especially due to the fact that they now all slept on "real beds." The house and the family looked poor, but they had seen an enormous increase in their dignity, which was manifest in their gestures and the way they spoke about the improvements on their house and in their diets.

We said goodbye to Dona Luisa and went to speak to Dona Madalena, who was by then 39 years old and who, as we mentioned above, had separated from her alcoholic husband in 2007. We were surprised when she told us she had gotten back together with him because of the children, but that she now wanted to separate again, as he was still drinking. She made a hand gesture to indicate the act of drinking. Her husband, who was unemployed, was lying in the bed, and we could tell that Madalena was afraid he would hear our conversation. The house had changed for the better. It had been painted. She had gotten from her retired mother a used refrigerator and she had bought new furniture for the living room. She told us that they were living better, that the children were eating better, and that, in fact, their lives had improved significantly. At a certain point in the conversation, seeing her excitement, we asked if she did not want more children. She told us, "Thank God, I've had the operation. I won't be having more children. Now I need to settle things with my husband." When we asked if her husband got violent when he drank, she answered, "He gets aggressive, but he's never hit me."

We asked all the women that we interviewed in the rural community of Inhapi if the city hall gave them any support. They said no. One of them said, "The Mayor of Inhapi is no use at all. He's invisible." The children laughed and echoed her, saying

"Ah! He's invisible!" We later found out the reason for this expression as the Mayor lives in Maceió and only comes occasionally to the city. According to the women, it is not unusual for him to take up to 3 months between visits.

3.2 Vale do Jequitinhonha, State of Minas Gerais (2008)

3.2.1 Pasmadinho

The city of Araçuaí served as our base for our trip to the Jequitinhonha Valley, one of the poorest regions of Brazil. It is the largest town in the center of the Jequitinhonha Valley. As always, we needed the support of local social workers, who, on the one hand, helped us find the families receiving BF grants and, on the other, established a climate of trust, reassuring the women and vouching for our intentions. We always had to explain that we were not sent by the government but were just researchers. We had to reassure the women that their answers could in no way affect their grants. Generally, the women were very suspicious and afraid of people who were new to their world. There was a lot of fear that they might lose their grants, and this meant we had to explain the goals of our research and reassure them that we had no power to either raise or lower the amount of their payments. They did not always understand us, and the mistrustful look sometimes lasted throughout the interview. That is why it was so important to have someone they trusted with us. In this case, two nuns helped us, sisters Ana and Sandra, who worked in the Migrant Pastoral Program[11] of the Catholic Church and other social work programs.

We began the interviews in the little community of Pasmadinho, a few kilometers from Araçuaí. The poverty of the surrounding environment was marked, starting with the precarious nature of the roads. For example, the one that linked Araçuaí to Diamantina and Belo Horizonte was a dirt road, full of holes and very hazardous, which made the trip long and unpleasant. The physical isolation translated into economic isolation, since none of the region's businesses would invest in regions that are so hard to get to and with so little infrastructure. But there were other sorts of difficulties as well, since the people who lived in these locales had no access to the bigger cities where hospitals, institutions of higher education, etc. were located. In other words, the geographical isolation corresponded to a loss of freedom and quality of life which were not unrelated and that could reach dramatic proportions (due to the terrible road conditions, e.g., a person who suffered a heart attack would not be able to reach quickly a hospital capable of helping them). Pasmadinho revealed its poverty by way of the conditions of the homes of its residents who were BF grantees. They were very poor houses, uncomfortable, and normally full of people.

[11] The Jequitinhonha Valley suffered from considerable emigration by the men who went to work in the cane fields of the state of São Paulo or other places. This constituted a serious social and psychological drain on the women and children who stayed behind, without fathers and husbands for many months of the year.

Most of the women were young and had many children. The husbands were either away cutting sugarcane in other states, especially São Paulo, or they were doing occasional odd jobs for which they got R$20–30/month. Generally, they were unemployed and, like their wives, had had very little formal schooling. Functional illiteracy was still very high.

Their precarious houses lacked every kind of comfort, but, worse of all, they lacked any privacy for the members of the families, since in many cases all the family members slept together, almost always in two double beds that were set out in the one room where they cooked, ate, and watched television. Few houses had more than one room. The houses were either owned by the families or lent to them by the couple's parents, in-laws, or other relatives.

In Pasmadinho, we began at the home of Dona Amélia. She was 41 years of age and the mother of ten children. Her husband was unemployed and did odd jobs when he could find them. One of the children had died at the age of 17 ("I had an older son who died at the school gate. They killed him at the gate of the school. He was about to graduate. He was 17 years old. It was the last day of school. A man showed up who was high on drugs and started shooting. And when they shoot, they shoot, you know?"). She had had her tubes tied to prevent getting pregnant again.

In 2008, she was receiving R$172/month. As was the case with almost all the women interviewed, Dona Amélia complained about the insufficiency of the amount of the grant ("For me, it's helping, you know, but it's very little, it is. There're a lot of children, you know? When you go to buy school materials, sometimes it's not enough. We spend more than we earn. Lots of times, I go to pay the grocer's and I can't pay for everything. I got to negotiate my debt [with the shop owner]". But she described the BF as "a good thing that we got in our pocket," and she pointed out that the family no longer went hungry. ("At times, I didn't use to have anything for dinner, or for lunch. So, now, it's better, you know? Even if we still lack stuff, that's how things are. I'm thinking it's great.") We always asked if receiving the income had changed the harshness of her life. Dona Amélia answered yes, "because we have more freedom in the money."

"Why more freedom?"

"Because we can buy what we want, you know? Because my husband has freedom too, but if he goes shopping, he buys what he wants, and if I go, I buy what I want."

We noticed she had an inhaler in the house. We asked if anyone in the house suffered from asthma. She said there was, yes, one of the boys. And she told us that due to the BF, she had been able to buy the inhaler and that this had reduced the boy's suffering considerably during his asthmatic episodes. She told us that one of the girls had "serious anemia" but that there was a lack of milk and greens (the children got milk through a state program but only 2 liters per week). We asked if she could not plant a garden in the yard, and she answered, "No, because there isn't enough water. We've only got water two hours per day, just. [..] So, it's not enough to water the plants. Can't plant a garden, it wouldn't work, because it uses too much water. And now that we're gonna have potable water, you can't use potable to water the garden."

"Potable? So, you can't pay for the water, is that it?"

"We can't pay for it."

When we asked, as we always did, if the grant was a favor or a duty of the government, she answered "a duty of the government" because she helped the government with her vote.

Next, we went to the house of Dona Viviane, 24, married (she said *amigada* or "friendly with"), mother of five children (she was planning to have her tubes tied soon), who was able to read and write. Her husband made wooden spoons that he sold on the street. Thanks to the BF there had been some improvement in their family diet, for example, the purchase of yogurt for the children. She said that the kids were getting the flu frequently due to the dry climate and all the dust ("because of the terribly dry air and all this damned dust!"). She thought the program was a duty of the government "because we are citizens."

"What does it mean to you to be a citizen?"

"It means having rights, right? Being equal. For me, that what I think it means."

"Why do you think that?"

"I watch the news every day on the TV and I think about things. [...] When they talk about this inflation now, I don't know why he is doing this, because those who suffer are always the poor. Those that don't have any wages at all. They go to think about this. How is it that we're going to buy things? How is it that we are going to survive? To eat? It's just to eat. Because we go to the supermarket and we can't buy anything. And sometimes I get what I'm needing and I have to return it because I don't have enough money. So, I don't know where we're gonna end up at this rate, I don't."

"Do you think that the rich people are interested in raising the prices?"

"They are, right? Because they are the ones that are profiting from this situation."

You can tell from this statement that her frustration arose from her inability to meet her basic needs, even after finally getting a regular monthly income. Can you image the discomfiture and the sense of humiliation of entering into a supermarket to buy essential things and not being able to complete the purchase, no matter how modest, for a lack of income?

We went to the house of Dona Zulmira, 30, who was married with two children. When we asked her about the program, she answered, "I think it's a really good program. Because I live from it, you know? Because we work on the *roça*.[12] I plant the farm but it happens that sometimes it's a good year, and the farm brings in stuff, other times, the next year isn't any good, right? So, the BF helps me a lot because I can buy food for my children." When we asked her if the program was a favor or a duty of the government, she answered by identifying the government with the figure of President Lula, as did many of the women, "I don't know, as a President, he saw that we were in a really hard situation before, you know? Many people were suffering, I'm not a bit embarrassed to say, there were points in my life that I had some rice and some beans in my house but I didn't have any pasta or anything else to feed

[12] Translator's note: A tiny piece of land destined for subsistence farming.

my daughters. It's sad when you wake up in the morning and can't find even any bread to give you child to eat. You look down and you don't see anything. So, I think that he is doing us a favor, right? It's not everybody who gets where he's gotten who would do the same, you know? Everybody thinks different. Does different. That's what I think. I really, really liked it when Lula got in, that he did this, because we didn't have this before."

3.2.2 Itinga

We carried out more interviews in this small town that was cut in two by the Jequitinhonha River. Until a few years previously, there had not even been a bridge linking the two banks of the river. Now there was one, built by the federal government, and a rustic statue of a ferryman was the only reminder of the time when you had to cross the river by boat.

We interviewed Dona Evelina, 58 years old, married with three children aged 19, 16, and 15. Her husband was unemployed. Dona Evelina was almost totally lacking in any ability to speak or express herself. Nevertheless, she said that the grant was the government's duty. To the same question, Dona Aparecida, 53, separated and mother of nine children, three of whom lived with her, answered, "I think that it is… It can be the two things, right? It's a favor, since they are helping people and it's a duty as well, because of the children's studies, because they want our children to go to school, as they say, because today there are many things people can give, and it's the studies. People say that the parents have to struggle for their children to get an education, right? To know how to survive in the future. Nobody knows what tomorrow is going to bring, right? Sometimes, from now to then, I'm not gonna see it but they are going to know how to direct their lives."

One of the most disturbing interviews was with Dona Nilza. She was 50 years old, but she looked about 15 years older. She was married and had 12 children (just 10 still alive). When we asked how many of them lived with her, she had to stop and count, since occasionally one of the children would go to another state to cut sugarcane. Her husband, an unemployed bricklayer, had respiratory problems and had had a lung operation. One of her sons had a heart problem. A daughter suffered from renal illness. In addition to being a diabetic, Dona Nilza also had circulatory and heart problems. She was illiterate and did not know how to read the medical information leaflets for the medications she was supposed to take. This meant she sometimes took the wrong medicine (e.g., a sleeping pill instead of high blood pressure medication), and she got ill. We asked why she didn't ask for any help, from a neighbor, for example, but we could tell that she was embarrassed to do so. She said she voted because she was afraid to lose her voter's registration and did not know if she might lose her retirement pension or have to pay a fine.

In Itinga, there was a community bakery funded by the federal government. It was a cooperative of women who mostly produced *biscoitos de polvilho*[13] (of excellent quality, by the way). It was there in the headquarters of the community bakery that our first meeting took place, organized by Sister Ana. There were almost 50 women present, some of them accompanied by their husbands. The predominant topic of the meeting was complaining about the manager of the program, a woman. The complaints ranged from accusations of harassment against certain people due to their not having been included on the roll of grantees, to more subtle insinuations. We could tell that there was a certain animosity, not only toward the local manager and the local politicians but also among the grantees. The most common questions were, for instance: "Why does that woman get more than I, since I have more kids?" and "Why does that person get her grant before me if we enrolled at the same time?" We asked if there was not a women's council, like there was in other cities, and we suggested that they set one up. From that moment on, the discussion took on a more constructive note, and the women began to think about different ways of taking their problems to the management.

3.2.3 *Araçuaí*

We did interviews in two neighborhoods of the city of Araçuai, the first called Canoeiro. We visited hovels with bare brick walls and dirt floors, plastic chairs, couches without covers, and bare walls, with the exception of a few religious images (always the same: Christ with his eyes pointed up at the heavens, Virgin Marys with their hearts in flames, guardian angels with arms extended to protect children who were crossing a bridge in ruins). The streets and the houses were full of hungry dogs, chickens with necks thinner than your finger, baby chicks the size of humming birds, and skeletal cats. The suffering was not limited to the people but extended to the animals and the objects as well.

The houses were found in dusty neighborhoods, with streets that were little more than paths, in which the wind raised dust devils reminiscent of the dust storms in the Sahara. The children almost all suffered as a result of the dry air and the dust: Asthma, bronchitis, and pneumonia were common illnesses that sometimes led to premature death.

We went to the house of Dona Helena, 31, an unemployed, single mother of four. She told us that she had previously lived on a *roça* and that life there had been very hard. She told us that they had moved to Araçuaí so that her nephew could continue studying since he had shown great interest in doing so. "So, I grabbed him and I said, Ah! My son. You already missed one year of school but next year, I…even if I have to…I'm going to help you, so I moved here."

[13] Translator's note: *Biscoitos de polvilho* are very light and airy donut-shaped crackers made of water, milk, oil, and cassava flour.

To our question about her opinion of the BF, she answered: "It's really good, it's like they say: it saved our life because before this grant, we were really needy, to tell the truth, because it's hard. I don't have a husband, and I've got this bunch of kids, to take care of them all with the farm…, this BF was worrying me, but after it came out, I was relieved. It helped me buy their school supplies, buy them shoes."

> "Do you think that if you hadn't gotten this grant, you would have suffered?"
> "I would have had hardships, I would have kept on suffering."
> "What do you think about the fact that it comes in the women's names and not that of the men? Do you think that's good or bad?"
> "It's good because if it was in the man's names, if they got ahold of it, I think they wouldn't let the kids suffer for want of anything but, I don't know, we wouldn't have the privilege of them taking care of the money. Even when the husband works, they don't ever put the money in the women's hands…I don't know, they like to look powerful. I'm gonna buy this. It's my money, I'm the one who worked for it. I'm the one that earned the money, it's in my name. So, I don't know. Sometimes they might avoid buying something like a pair of sandals for his kids, so that, I don't know, he could buy something else. Because men, not all of the, but most of them have a weak head. They take the money and they go to the bar to have fun."

About voting, she said, "I don't much like voting, no. But I like to participate. It's interesting. I don't know if we make good choices but we're always trying to help those that leave here."

"Do you think your vote helps you," we asked. "Does it change anything or not?"

"Not just for me, it changes things for everybody, but the vote helps, right? Because choosing, it's just that we don't know how to choose. Sometimes I vote for a candidate thinking that he's good but he turns out to be the worst candidate possible. But I think that it helps, yeah."

We interviewed Dona Palmira, 33, who was unemployed, with three children. She had gone to school until the third grade, and then "my dad pulled me out to work on the farm," she said. She told her story in this way:

> It was like this. I came from Belo Horizonte, in a hurry to set up a little spot, because my family is from here. I went there, found a man, a real treat: He left, I got myself these three kids, so my life is long. I left and went there. I got this treat here on the farm. I took him there. I got myself these kids. He showed up there and got into crime. Ay! I said to myself: I'm not gonna live my life this way. I saved up some money working in Belo Horizonte, I brought this money and I bought these two small rooms. […] so my life is big, with these kids".

We asked her what she thought of the BF.

"It's really good because otherwise I'd have died of hunger with my kids. I would have just starved to death with them, happy. Because what we earn here is really little, I work 3 days a week to earn R$25."

"You work in what?"

"As a maid, doing just about anything."

"R$25?"

"For 3 days, my boss pays me. Three days without crying. I do the washing. I cook on the 3 days I go. I iron. I clean the house. You can do the math there and figure out how much I earn a day."

"Less than R$9."

"Not even R$9…."

"She [the employer] told me that was what she could afford to pay. I said, 'I'll take it.' So, it's R$25. So, I said, so, I'll go so as not to sit around doing nothing. I don't like not having anything to do, no way. The boy wakes up early in the morning. He wants some bread. What am I gonna do? I can't buy it. The father doesn't help. He disappeared off the map, the father of these three. So, what is it that I'm gonna do? Work to earn R$25, and if she says like this: I'm gonna give you R$9, will you come today to wash some clothes? I'll be there."

The second neighborhood was called Nova Esperança [New Hope]. Despite the name, it was an area of dirt roads and bare brick houses, with a wind that carried a fine dust that got into the pores of your skin and in your nostrils that clogged up your throat and your lungs. We spent the afternoon and the night coughing.

We visited the house of Dona Maria, 27, with a daughter of seven. She was married and her husband was unemployed and did odd jobs. The house, like the others, was very simple. In the kitchen/living room, there was a stove, a small refrigerator, and a table with three chairs. The light had been cut off because the family couldn't pay the bill. The interview was hard because Dona Maria answered in clipped answers, looking around as if she were afraid of something. We thought it was because she thought that we were with the government, at first, but her reaction to the question about what she thought about the card coming in the woman's name led us to suspect that her discomfort had another cause. We asked her if her husband drank.

"Sometimes."

"Is he violent?

"He is."

Then she told us that she was afraid to separate because she knew that her husband would never leave her alone. "He wouldn't let me stay quietly here. I'd have to move far away."

She confessed that he beat her when he got drunk and that their daughter got scared watching the violent scenes.

We asked if we could take her picture and she accepted. She stood up and went to a corner of the kitchen behind the table putting her daughter in front of her like a shield her eyes open with an expression of fear blended with sadness.

Even heavier, if possible, was the atmosphere in the house of Dona Quitéria, 44, a widow, with six children and a granddaughter. The house was built of bare bricks. The kitchen had a stove in a corner and a table in the other. There were not any windows; the only light came from the door. Dona Quitéria had an unspeakably sad expression, with her gaze fixed on something long gone (a happy past or perhaps a less rotten one than her present?). She sat as if she felt tremendously exhausted, as if she were completely worn out. As soon as we started the interview, she began to give vent to her feelings, telling us the story of one of the boys, the 17-year-old, who had given up school after being beaten up by the doorman.

> I went to complain to the teachers' counsel and they didn't do anything. I made an official complaint but nothing happened. You have to go first to the teachers' counsel and nothing happened. Here we are, he's wanting to study and I can't pay for private school and he complains. That's how it is. I've taken him to the doctor and he's depressed because of this. Now, the other ones are studying. The little girl, 7 years old, she doesn't miss a day. Even on holidays, she wants to go to school. Now the others all want to go to school. They said that they are going to cut my school grant [evidently Quitéria was confusing the former *Bolsa Escola* or School Grant with the *Bolsa Família* or Family Grant] because this one here [she pointed at another child] is sort of…because he's got a problem, since he was little, a problem with his hand, and when his hand swells up…his hand swells with a sore that nobody can figure out. The doctors here have never figured out what it is. They think it's syphilis. They asked me if I had had it when I was pregnant with him. I said I didn't know. So, his hand swells up and gets full of sores and he can't even pick up a pencil. I went over there to talk to the principal and she turned to me and she said that I had to bring her a justification from the doctor. And I took it to her, but, I don't know, the justifications, you know. She said that they had taken his name off the School Grant and so I just had two kids, just two on the School Grant. When his hands get like this, his hands and his feet, they get full of sores and they begin to ooze and then when they start to dry out, it takes a few months, you know, when it starts to dry up, it smells. Ay, the kids laugh at him at school. I went over there to complain. So, he came home one day and talked to me and said he didn't want to go to school anymore because the director had hit him. I went over there and they said it was a lie. Nobody knows who to believe because I wasn't there. He said that the gym teacher had hit him. When I said I was going to the teachers' counsel, while I was on my way, there they came up to me and said that I shouldn't go over there, I shouldn't. They went and gave the boy a ball, so that we wouldn't go and complain."

Quitéria sometimes used her grant money to buy medication for the boy: One injection costs R$70. "I quit buying food for myself, I stopped just for me, because I couldn't afford to buy [the shots]. The doctor came from out of town and told me that in order to get rid of it [the boy's problem] I had to buy the injections, get them in Belo Horizonte and have them sent here, to give him the shot."

The house had not had water for almost a year because Dona Quitéria could not pay the bill, which had risen to almost R$500. She diverted water from the neighbors' houses. And the same thing happened with electricity. She hooked up to the neighbors' line. In general, without the help of their neighbors, the family would not have been able to survive. Dona Quitéria could not take a regular job because she could not leave the children alone at home. She did odd jobs for the neighbors: She collected firework and fetched water from the well.

Dona Quitéria's case was representative: It showcased how several types of suffering were interconnected. The lack of access to public health services turned any illness into a sort of biblical plague that could have serious implication for the life of the person (in this case, the child) and the whole family: The shame caused by the illness and the humiliation inflicted by the schoolmates and the adults ran the child out of the school and led the family to lose that grant. These cascading consequences, in turn, deepened the suffering and the sense of injustice even more. The lack of state services obliged these families to spend their money buying medication or paying light and water bills that they could not afford.

3.3 State of Piauí (2009)

3.3.1 Teresina

Piauí is traditionally known as the poorest state in Brazil. The impression that we got on our trip, however, was that the region was undergoing profound change. Our impressions were very different than those of the neighboring state of Maranhão.

In Teresina, we spoke with the head of the Services for Social Work and Citizenship (SASC). We were told that the state government prioritized their efforts against poverty in the semiarid regions of the state (on the border with neighboring states of Pernambuco and Bahia). SASC had created a support service for BF grantees by way of a free telephone number (0800) and organized training for the local managers. Nevertheless, they had to face problems that arose when previous mayors lost elections and, before leaving office, had either stolen or destroyed government property (some had stolen computers or vandalized property, etc.). This had created tremendous obstacles for their successors or had even prevented them from working. Government workers from other parts of the state swore the same thing had taken place there. This illustrated the deep roots of a patrimonialist view of political power: Elected officials saw themselves as the owners of public property that they had been called upon to administer and they treated it as if it were their private property. From this point of view, our attention was drawn to a common phenomenon in this region, namely, the fact that the local social policies were typically coordinated and managed by the first ladies (i.e., the wives of mayors), who had almost never had the necessary knowledge or training to carry out these responsibilities. Equally, it was not rare that the local managers were chosen using arbitrary criteria, such as personal or political affinity with the mayor, rather than based on objective measures of competence (after all, these were political appointments).

3.3.2 Demerval Lobão

The first phase of our Teresina research took place in Demerval Lobão, a city of about 13,000 inhabitants. 1906 families received BF grants and more than 513 had met the criteria but had not yet received aid (in 2009). At that point in time, there was a long gap between enrolling and receiving the grant, according to reports of many of the women interviewed. This time lag often caused distress in the people who were waiting. However, the figures we received from the city manager Jean Teixeira da Costa were not up to date at that moment. According to his information, it was the current mayor who had set up the Social Assistance Reference Center (CRAS) in the city. SASC was located in a humble building, typical of most of the buildings in the city. The manager worked in a small, stuffy office. He showed us a bookcase full of documentation. It held the user records which had been digitalized, since the previous clerks, after the electoral defeat, had disconfigured the electronic systems, obligating them to start over from scratch (in addition Jean complained that 250 bad checks had been issued by the previous mayor and 20 civil service positions had been given out to friends and relatives 10 days prior to the election).

We first interviewed Dona Iracema, 43, married with two children (13 and 11). She could read and write (and was studying at home to finish high school), and she received a grant of R$102 per month. "When I get the money, I go to the market. I do my monthly shopping," she said. The money was enough for the entire month because her husband worked in another city and was only home 2 days a week. "When he comes, he gives me R$30 or R$50 and that complements things," she explained. Now she was able to decide what to buy. Before, she said, "That was impossible, completely, impossible." The house belonged to her father who had passed away, but Dona Iracema split the house with her ten brothers. She thought it was good that the BF card came in the woman's name, because in some cases, the husband, if he got the money, would use it to drink *cachaça*. She thought that the BF was "a kindness from him [President Lula] to the people, because many people needed it," and that "the people deserve it because they go there and voted and put him [President Lula] into office." She said that she liked voting and thought it was "important that the people have the right to choose those who are going to govern for four years, the right to see their platform, to really choose," and "if they aren't any good, we can't blame anyone else because we are the ones that picked them".

The second interview was with Inês, 30, separated, with two children aged 12 and 8. She had finished high school. She got $R102/month. She was a pretty woman with a sad face, but she spoke vivaciously and with conviction. She lived off the grant (which she said was enough to eat off for 2 weeks) and from odd jobs such as a street vendor or a home hairdresser. She bought rice, flour, and *mistura*[14] (such as chicken, sausages, eggs, sardines, and canned meats). She also bought greens from a truck that would come from Teresina selling the leftovers from the market for R$1/kilo. "Cassava is expensive," she said, as she spoke of the difficulties in buying vegetables for a good price.

She said the grant "helps me get to the end of the month. It's been a blessing to me, because it makes it possible to buy something for the kids, but you have to know how to manage it." In her opinion, the women were better at managing the money and the fact that the card came in their names gave them more freedom ("I feel more at ease"). When she began to get the BF, the owner of the market gave her credit. "This person trusted me. This [the card] brought me credit." She said emphatically, "My card, lady, was the only thing that has brought me credit in my life. Before this I didn't have anything. It's not much, though, because I'd like to have a better life." As she spoke, her voice was strong and full of emotion. It expressed clearly her indignation and dissatisfaction with the amount of her income. She was indignant about her own poverty.

[14] Translator's note: *Mistura* indicates the food that goes along with the ever-present rice and beans. Normally is some protein (meat, egg, fish, etc.).

She told us that she only voted because she was obligated "but I don't like it at all" because every mayor was just like the last one and did not bring in any jobs, or if they did, they gave them out to their friends and family. "Only the name changes: António, José Francisco, you know." However, her fear was that when President Lula left office, the program would be abandoned. "Look, what we want, the change we want, is to have a better life. What I'd really like would be to sweat for my salary, that I would have to work, every mother wants this for her children, her family, her home." She stressed the value of money to bring you anything what you need or want to do: "Everything that you want to do in life is with money. It's by paying." The money from the grant "doesn't shut up those who are in need. Need is not only not having anything to eat, it's not. It's wanting to eat something better and not having it, and not to be able to. It's wanting to wear something better and not being able to. To go to an ice cream shop with your child and not being able to. It's seeing a toy in the bakery and not being able to buy it for your kid."

At this point in the interview, she began to cry and thanked God for the help that Lula has offered. "It's money that is blessed by God." When we asked her if it hadn't been the government that created the program, she answered, "Yes, it was the President, but it was God who put him in office." When we asked if she was Catholic, she answered, "No. I'm a Believer," which meant that she was a Protestant. During the interview, one of the children was watching while eating a guava and wiping his mouth on the curtain that separated the "living room" from the kitchen. The other child was playing with a puppy on the porch of the house (a rundown house with the plaster falling off the walls).

According to Inês, poor people have to have someone on their side to help them, since "the world is made like this. There has to be the support of somebody who can afford it. It's like this. That's how it is in society, in our house, at school, at church, those places." She thought that the BF was allowing the government to repay what "we pay in taxes," but she recognized that the government of Lula was the first to do this, because, she said, "our President, he is poor, isn't he? How many times didn't he struggle to become President. He knows what I am going through. He knows what I'm feeling. He used to know. If he runs a thousand times, I will vote for him one thousand times. Do you know why? He was the only person who saw me, who I am. The only politician who still knows what poverty is, that can feel what I feel."

At the end of the interview, she asked what the reason behind the research was. She was one of the few women who did this during the whole period.

The words of Dona Inês illustrate a great complexity of emotion and moral intuition. On the one hand, she demonstrated a capacity, uncommon among the women interviewed, to feel indignation at her situation, which she judged to be unfair. Her sense of justice led her to look at the causes of her poverty as resulting from institutional, social, and political organization, rather than from random chance, destiny, or divine will. On the other hand, from her words there arose a huge disenchantment with the possibility of change in her life without the support of more powerful individuals. Inês would make a wonderful spokesperson to publicize the cases and the needs of the women who received BF grants in her city. This did not take place due to the blindness of the institutions and the local public officials who, here as in almost all of the places we visited, did little or nothing to encourage the BF grantees to organize and participate in the management of the program, so that they might let their voices be heard.

The third interview in Demerval Lobão was that with Dona Zélia, 23, married with two daughters (of 6 and 2 years of age). She was getting R$102/month. Her husband did odd jobs on a daily basis and earned “R$20 when he can find work.” The house belonged to her father, who was retired and lived in the countryside and who helped them “when we’re in the red.” The only reliable source of income in the family, in sum, was the BF grant, without taking into consideration the fact that the card allowed her to get credit in the market. Like Inês, she complained that it was almost impossible to find work. “Here you can only get a job if it’s through the City Hall and the City Hall can’t hire everybody.” Regarding the grant, she thought that, “according to the constitution, it was our right but it had never been respected until now. Now it’s shown up.”

3.3.3 Santa Cruz dos Milagres

The second city we visited in Piauí was Santa Cruz dos Milagres, which was famous for a miraculous natural spring and, moreover, for an equally miraculous wooden cross that was kept in a church located on a hill near the entrance into the city. At a certain time of the year, there was a large pilgrimage that brought a lot of money into the city and filled the steep streets with people. Beside the church, there were several little chapels with ex-votos, votive offering given in thanks for requests granted: rustic wooden statues representing heads, legs, hands, breast, internal organs, or even whole human figures.

In the preceding municipal elections, the city underwent a true revolution with the election of the poor, black candidate João Paulo de Assis Neto, of the PDT (the Democratic Labour Party). João Paulo managed to defeat the traditional large land-owning elite, despite his lack of resources. He had spent part of his life working as a *garimpeiro*[15] at the mines at Serra Pelada, before returning to Santa Cruz. He told us that when campaigning he had crossed the broad area covered by the city limits by motorcycle and he arrived home “with his throat inflamed because we went by motorcycle and they [his opponents] went by fancy cars.” He tried to convince the voters (most of whom were black and poor, like himself) to vote for him. “People were afraid. They told me, ‘You haven’t got a car. You haven’t got money. You are black. You’ll never win.’” But he had won, and now he was trying to implement a series of social policies: setting up a free public notary service; expanding the Popular Pharmacy (subsidized by the government); hiring more doctors for the health center to guarantee medical assistance every day of the week; purchasing of

[15] Translator’s note: A *garimpeiro* is a gold miner, most of whom work in subhuman conditions. Their situation was brought to international awareness thanks to the photojournalistic work of Sebastião Salgado.

a tractor for the poorest of the city's farmers; and renting a house so that young people from Santa Cruz would have a place to live if they went to the state capital, Teresina, to either the federal university, UFPI, or the state one, UESPI. He told us about the debts and the vandalism left behind by the previous administration before leaving office. He thanked God every third sentence and told stories about the poverty of his fellow citizens.

> It hurts me to see a pregnant mother suffering from hunger with a baby in her belly. Once I arrived at a house and I saw a child grabbing onto her mother's skirts, begging for food, saying, 'Momma, I'm hungry.' And I got out and I was streaming with tears inside, because that is a scene that I never want to see again.

There were no job opportunities outside the civil service, because the large landholdings were mostly cattle ranches that did not need much labor. Most of the people lived in poverty. In Santa Cruz there were 390 families, nearly 4000 inhabitants, that received BF grants, but another 808 had been enrolled for meeting the program's criteria.

The women we interviewed lived in extremely humble, stuffy houses with cement floors. Most had no windows and only had doors to let in light and air, while the sun beat mercilessly down on the rooftops. The furniture was poor: a bed made out of four planks and a half-rotten mattress. Oftentimes there were no walls between the rooms but only old, dirty curtains, full of holes. From the rectangle of the door, we could catch a glimpse of a dusty backyard, with dirt and grass, a clay brick wall, the roof of another house, and an incessant blue in which the little white clouds were no more than stage props. Often there were domesticated animals wandering through the rooms: dogs, chickens, and chicks.

First, we interviewed Dona Marta. She was 38, single, with three children (7-year-old twins and a 2-year-old). She lived in a house belonging to her father, who had a pension from the National Social Security Institute (INSS), and she got R$122/month. She thought well of the BF because "it helps to buy a few things" so that she could "feel a bit more at ease" since the fathers of the children did not help support them. She did not like voting: She only participated in elections to avoid losing her voter's registration. She had no opinion about whether the BF was a right or a favor.

The second woman interviewed was Dona Sueli. She was 28 years old and had three children (8 months old and 4 and 5 years). She had a high school education. Her husband did odd jobs as a painter. She got a grant of R$112, but she spent R$200 just on food. She said that the program "isn't terrible," but she would have preferred to have a regular job, even though, she said, no one in Santa Cruz earned the minimum wage, since there were so few jobs with contracts. She thought it was great that the card came in the woman's name, since the women took better care of the children. "Everything that I want and that I do is focused on my children. This is what it's like to be a mother." In her opinion, the BF was a help from the government. At the same time, she said she had a right to this help, "because I vote and I pay taxes." The house was a complete mess with toys and clothes strewn all over the floor. On a small table, there was a pile of Bibles.

3.3.4 *Piripiri*

In the city of Piripiri, we first spoke to the First Lady Maria do Socorro Brito Cavalcanti e Menezes, who was responsible for managing the BF. The program had covered almost 8,000 families, but there were 10,000 enrolled. Dona Socorro complained about problems with registration. The problems were various: difficulties in getting in contact with all the families who would have the right to the grant, lack of documents, and contradictory information due to mobility (this is a common phenomenon in the region, many people when they have economic problems, move in with family members in other cities but are still registered in their home city). The local government (the mayor was from the PSDB or the centrist Brazilian Social Democracy Party that formed the opposition to the government) was trying to solve these problems by sending task forces into the countryside to update the documents of people who were warned in advance by community radio stations that were very popular in the area. In addition to professional courses and literacy programs (the later had been canceled due to a lack of interest on the part of the target audience), the city hall also organized university entry exam preparation for the young people from grantee families. In fact, later, during the interviews, we noticed a situation in which the parents were illiterate and the daughter was studying at the State University of Piauí (UESPI). There was a jump from illiteracy to a university degree in just one generation.

Contact with grantee families was made by way of health agents. There were associations of residents but not of BF grantees. The manager commented that in the counseling meetings, she often heard expressions such as "I was graced with this grant" or "I haven't been lucky enough to get a grant" which served as testimony to a half-fatalistic attitude and a lack of awareness of the fact that the grant was a right that was tied to fulfilling certain conditions.

In the company of health agents, we visited several neighborhoods in the city: Floresta, Recreio, Vista Alegre, and Fonte dos Matos. In one case, the interview took place in the presence of the husband, who strongly influenced the woman's answers with gestures and comments. That interview was excluded from the data pool.

We interviewed Dona Rita, mother of four children (3, 4, 7, and 10 years of age). She could read (she had had 6 years of schooling) and she received R$112. The husband did odd jobs, delivering groceries for a small store. With the money she would buy medicine, school supplies, and clothes for the children. Before the program, "it was only possible to eat" because she lived with her father, who was retired and who helped her. The BF enabled her to move out and live alone, at first. Even now that she lived with her husband, she was happy to get the money in her name, because "when I have my own, it's even better." She voted because it was obligatory, saying "I mean, what can I do?" However, she thought that "all politicians were cheats." However, she said that she would vote for anyone who would keep the BF and not for a politician who wanted to cancel the program. In her opinion, the implementation of the program is a duty of the government, as "there are many people who go hungry in this world."

Dona Cássia, 55, separated, lived with several grandchildren, but she only registered the grandson of 17, so she only received R$82. It was enough, however, to get her credit at the stores. Her daughter was working and helped out. She was attending literacy classes (which she liked so much that she missed them during school breaks) because as a child she had worked on a farm and later as a washerwoman ("Ay! If these arms could talk!" she said showing the hands stiffened by so much work). Before telling us the story of her life, she set up her conditions: "I'll tell my truth." She thought that it was better that the BF card came in the name of the women. She "really" liked voting, due to the excitement on election day. She thought that it was the duty of the government to guarantee the BF because "there are many people here going hungry." If the BF were taken away, "children would go out into the streets to beg" instead of going to school. She gave great importance to the education of the children.

Dona Marinilda was totally illiterate (she could not even sign her name). She was married, with children 17 and 20 years old. She received R$92 for herself and the 17-year-old. She used the money to buy food and school supplies. Her husband did odd jobs selling homemade popsicles, but he worked very irregularly and brought in about $R100/month. She would often earn a little money washing clothes for people. She thought it was very good that the card came in the name of the woman, since she thought they knew better what the household needed. She called the BF a "blessing" and "a duty" of the government because there were many people without food. She was always afraid that the grant would end. "When I go to collect, I'm afraid that it might have been cancelled." She liked voting "despite the fact that these politicians don't do anything." She wanted "to keep her son in school to give him what I never had." She used to live in a mud house, and, thanks to the BF, she and her husband had managed to save enough money to buy construction material, and they had built a very simple brick house.

Dona Diva, 21, single and without children, lived in a family of six, with her mother (a housecleaner) and her stepfather (illiterate, who worked occasionally as a metalworker). She received R$62 that she used to buy food and clothing. She thought of the BF as a help ("neither a favor nor a right; it's a help") and she always voted because it was her duty. She stated that there were "few rights that we can fulfill" and that voting was one of them. It's a "power within my hands" and "it can change things in politics." While speaking about the lack of using her rights, by way of example, she mentioned a situation in which "there are people living under bridges" and that there are "many people who don't work and just lie around." She demanded her rights "as a human being" and argued that the most important one is to receive education so as to understand and to carry out her very rights "as a citizen, as human beings." She was attending the college entry exam preparation of the city hall and hoped to study pedagogy.

3.4 State of Maranhão (2009)

3.4.1 São Luís

In São Luís, we approached the City Secretariat for Social Development, where the city's BF program was coordinated. We were met by the secretary, who granted us an interesting interview. She spoke about local struggles against poverty, but she admitted that the BF was the main initiative "because it confers dignity and citizenship on the women." She politely told us about the poorer neighborhoods in the city and the cities within roughly 100 km of São Luís, such as Rosário, where there was immense poverty. We found out that several grantees had managed to even buy a cell phone on installments. This was news to us.

Traveling through the neighborhoods of São Luís, we headed for Anjo da Guarda, which is known to be one of the poorest in the city. In fact, the poverty was shocking: open sewers; dirty streets full of little, unhealthy houses; children playing in the streets beside the sewer ditches; and rats running every which way. We finally arrived at our first interview. As always, it took place in a poor house. We found a talkative woman, Dona Júlia, 41, a widow and mother of 11 children. Seven of the children lived with her and were young people between the ages of 11 and 17. She was getting R$150 at that moment, but she owned her own house and she also got a widow's pension. She liked the program and said that she used it to buy school supplies.

We conducted several interviews in this neighborhood. One of them was with Dona Carmen. She was 62 years of age, but she looked to be at least 70, due to the fact that she only had one tooth in her mouth. She could read. She had 11 children, 2 of whom had already died. Three of them lived with her, together with a grandson of 16. She got the basic amount of 62R$, due to having made a mistake upon enrolment (a common occurrence, due to a lack of information, the lack of literacy, and lack of preparation of many of the local public officials). She used the money from her grant to pay for drawing school for her grandson, who was talented (according to many people, she said). Her dream was that he could have a career as a painter, selling paintings. Some of the paintings were hung on the walls, and, in fact, they suggested that the boy had both good technical potential and a strong artistic personality. "Those who don't study are worse than animals," Dona Carmen exclaimed. According to her, the card should come in the woman's name since "the woman takes care of everything in the family." She thought that voting was important because it made a difference and she was of the opinion that "people are too complacent" and that they should take the initiative to get together and complain about things when they do not work, since "Unity is strength", as she vehemently pointed out.

We also interviewed Dona Fátima, separated, 60 years old, and mother of six children. In 2009, she lived with a son who was 14 and two grandchildren of 5 and 7. She got R$82 from the BF, probably due to a mistake during enrollment. Even though she was illiterate, she had a strong and vivacious personality and she was able to express herself in an original way. About President Lula, she said, "God gave us this son of God. He's great!" When she was asked what she thought of the fact that the BF came in money and how she dealt with this fact, she answered, emphatically, "Look. This money is mine. Lula gave it to me to take care of my kids and grandchildren. So, should I go and give it to my husband? I'm not gonna give it up!" About this subject, she emphatically stated, "The men might cheat you. There are a lot of scoundrels. Women are mothers. Just the word 'mother' is enough to explain it." She thought that the grant was simultaneously a favor and a duty. In her opinion, with any other president, there would not have been a BF, but Lula "is a poor. He knows what it's like to be poor. If he were the son of a rich man, he wouldn't be interested in us."

Her neighbor, Dona Rosangela, was 54, a widow, and the mother of two sons of 14. She received R$82, and she said, "The grant changed my life a lot. Look. It was great!" We asked her what she felt about now having some regular money, and she answered, "Oh! It was the first time that this happened to me! And and it's right like this, because women are more careful with money than men." We heard again that BF was carried out by President Lula because "he understands poverty. He used to be poor."

3.4.2 Rosário

This city is almost 100 km from São Luis. It is extremely poor, with holes in the dirt roads and also with open air sewers. Searching through the neediest neighborhoods for BF grantees, we arrived at Santa Luzia which, as we had been warned, was shockingly poor, unhealthy, and smelly. We conducted several interviews in this neighborhood. One of them was with Dona Sandra, 29. She was the mother of three children aged 13, 11, and 2. Illiterate, she received R$122/month as her grant. She told us that before getting the grant, she used to work as a maid in a middle-class family that paid her R$150/month, without a contract, nor did they pay her social security taxes. For this amount she worked 7 days a week, with just Sunday afternoon off. This was the first of two cases, in 5 years of interviewing, that we came across a woman who gave up her job after getting a grant. To the contrary of what is often claimed by critics of the program, it is rare for a grantee to give up her job and live only off of a BF grant. This can be explained by the low value of the grant which certainly cannot replace a fixed salary. Let us remind you that the maximum value of a grant in 2013 was R$242 (according to the MDS), while the legal minimum wage was R$545. Before criticizing the supposed laziness of the BF grantees, people should question the miserly actions of those who exploit workers by offering starvation wages.

The following interview took place in another neighborhood with the same characteristics described above. We came to the house of Dona Silvia, 28, who was married with two children, 8 and 3 years of age. She could read and she was getting R$60/month. There were nine people living in her house, and she appeared to be guided by her mother, who, we suspected, received a pension and who was, in fact, responsible for the house and the children. Sílvia was extremely depressed and could hardly express herself and could not explain why she only received the basic BF grant, if she had two small children. Her mother spoke for her, because she was a talkative sort with categorical opinions. Sílvia, when answering the question about whether the BF was a right or a favor, answered that she thought it was a duty of the government. The question about her opinion of voting, she answered, "I like to vote because it's a right," and she said that she chose her candidates based on "the proposals they make."

Her mother joined the conversation and gave several opinions about the improvements that the grant had brought to people's lives. She finished up saying, "It could only be Lula who would do this for us." When we asked why he was the only one, she lifed her hands and exclaimed, "Ah, lady! Because he came from eating beans!"[16]

3.5 Recife, State of Pernambuco (2011)

The neighborhood of Manguba is located in the city of São Lourenço in the vicinity of the city of Recife. When we asked our contacts where BF grantees lived, we were told that in the surroundings of the cities in the Brazilian northeast, the program was omnipresent. The women, still in 2011, complained about the time lag between registration and the arrival of the grants. We went to the house of Dona Maria das Graças, a married woman of 25, with an 8-year-old son. She worked as a home cosmetics saleswoman. She, just like her husband, a bricklayer's assistant, received an income that sometimes reached as much as R$200 but in a very irregular fashion. The irregularity had entitled them to enroll in the BF program. Their house, however, was a good one that they had built over the years, and it had a certain level of comfort, something which was unusual in these situations. Maria das Graças had been in the program since 2008. However, she told us that she had waited 3 years between registering and receiving the grant. She really liked the program, and, like almost all of the women interviewed, she complained about the inefficiency and inefficacy of CRAS as the institution of support. In her case, she would have liked to study or even finish high school and said that CRAS was of no help. When she was asked if there were any meeting places or any associations, she answered, as almost all of the women did, that the only place to meet people was at church (she was protestant). Maria das Graças stood out among all the hundreds of women that we interviewed. She dressed well and styled her hair. She was wearing light makeup when she received us. Her mother-in-law, during the interview, made comments while she cooked lunch. A protestant as well, she called upon Jesus several times during the interview. Her husband came in and greeted us, and we saw that he was doing maintenance on the house, as it was Sunday. We quickly finished off the interview because we could tell that it was almost dinner time. The house was well

[16] Translator's note: He was so poor that all he ate as a child was beans.

equipped with appliances. In other words, it was a very different household from that of other grantees, in that it had a certain coziness, a very rare trait in the houses of the other women interviewed.

We said goodbye to this family and went to the home of Dona Marina, 26, married, mother of four children, 10, 8, 6, and 3 years of age. She received a grant of R$162 and her husband was also a bricklayer's assistant. She had gone to school through the fifth grade and had worked as a maid in a family. She immediately told us, "I much prefer getting a grant, rather than going back to work for a family." They had built the house themselves, but it looked good and clean with a certain level of comfort. Marina was opinionated and told us that she thought the grant was a huge favor that the government had done for the poor. When asked if this was a right, she told us, "I don't know about that, but nobody had thought about this before, so I think that those who have done this the way it works now, has done us a favor because it's a great help. I can stay at home and take care of my kids while they are young. I'm still young. I hope to go back to school. I'd like to know more."

We asked her, "But won't you have anymore children?"

She immediately said, "No, because I've been operated on. I've had my tubes tied." During our talk, the conversation inevitably touched on the issue of the government and politics. In this context, she exclaimed, "I loved voting for a woman[17]! I voted for Dilma and, I was proud of it. I had never been so proud to vote as I was this time." Her eyes sparkled as she told us, "Oh! Now you're going to see how capable women are!"

---

[17] After serving two terms of office, the highly popular President Lula da Silva could not run for a third term in office. His chief of staff, Dilma Rousseff, ran on their common Workers' Party ticket and won the election in a runoff against a center-right candidate.

Chapter 4
Poverty: A Pluridimensional Concept

The fundamental objectives of the Federative Republic of Brazil are:

I – to build a free, just and solidary society;
II – to guarantee national development;
III – to eradicate poverty and substandard living conditions and to reduce social and regional inequalities;
IV – to promote the well-being of all, without prejudice as to origin, race, sex, color, age and any other forms of discrimination.

Constitution of the Federative Republic of Brazil (1988)
Article 3[1]

4.1 Poverty and its Non-economic Characteristics

As Amartya Sen has pointed out, "poverty should be seen as a privation of basic capabilities instead of merely a limited level of income, which has been the traditional criterion for identifying poverty." However, Sen himself recognizes that "a lack of income is one of the principal causes of poverty, so that the lack of income may be the primordial reason for the lack of capabilities," (Sen 1999, 109). Thus, even if the study of poverty cannot be limited to a mere analysis of inequality, this phenomenon is always associated with insufficient income. This means that it is essential to take income into account when studying poverty. Sen suggests two steps to be taken when defining poverty. Firstly, we should identify the poor people among the general population. Secondly, we should identify the characteristics these people share so that we can arrive at an evaluation of the level of poverty of the community in question (Sen 1997, 164 s.). In the first step, we should draw a "poverty line" which might vary considerably from community to community. Sen points out that identifying who is poor does not necessarily imply per se a legal right

[1] http://english.tse.jus.br/arquivos/federal-constitution

A. Pinzani, W. L. Rego, *Money, Autonomy and Citizenship*,
https://doi.org/10.1007/978-3-030-01361-5_4

to public assistance (Ibid., 167), since this may depend on the state's actual capacity to fulfill its duties to these people. In the case of impoverished states, such as, for example, Ethiopia or Eritrea, the state may find it impossible to adopt anti-poverty policies. However, the situation changes when the state in question has the necessary resources to at least guarantee a minimal level of aid (such as in the case of Brazil). The state sometimes draws a second line between those poor who have a right to public assistance and those that do not. In the case of Brazil, the BF is granted to nuclear families whose members have a monthly income per capital less than R$ 70, although people earning between R$ 80 and R$ 100 may be considered poor in the context of Brazilian society. Various political and pragmatic factors come into play when setting the line in question and identifying who has the right to public assistance. It is important to emphasize that a shocking number of poor people in the population co-exist with an immense wealth of resources. Furthermore, there is striking hostility on the part of the media and the so-called public opinion against public programs that combat poverty. This hostility expresses the position of the upper-middle classes who, although numerically limited, are incredibly powerful. Furthermore, Brazil has one of the highest levels of income concentration in the world. Its grossly unfair distribution is well known.

The problem of assessing poverty based merely on the criterion of income is that the latter does not express everything about people's well-being. For example, if the state has a highly developed level of well-being and offers almost everything freely to its citizens (education, health care, unemployment insurance, housing subsidies, etc.), a low income does not necessarily imply a life without comfort, in which the basic necessities are not met. On the other hand, if the state does not guarantee the aforementioned services, even a relatively high level of income might not be sufficient to protect individuals against risks normally associated with poverty (for example, in the U.S.A., the health care system is such that an illness might lead even a middle-class person into bankruptcy, since there is practically no free public health care). The presence of stable income does not, therefore, constitute an absolute guarantee against problems of poverty. These issues are resolved by way of public policies intended to provide basic necessities, whether directly (via the provision of basic services) or indirectly (via the creation of conditions for people to meet their own basic needs).

Thus, a distinction is traditionally made between primary and secondary poverty.[2] Primary poverty is defined as the difficulty or impossibility of meeting one's basic needs such as nutrition and housing by way of income. Secondary poverty is defined as when, even if their earnings are sufficient to meet their basic needs, the poor cannot do so for reasons other than those linked to income. If for example, due to living in a certain region of the country, people suffer illnesses that put at risk their ability to feed themselves adequately (for example, if their body is infected with parasites), the fact that they can buy food does not protect them from mal- or undernourishment. In a similar fashion, one can be mal- or undernourished either due to a lack of education that makes one incapable of nourishing oneself adequately, or due to a lack of foodstuffs in the market which are necessary for a healthy diet,

[2] This distinction was first drawn by Seebohm Rowntree (Rowntree 1901).

etc. (Sen would include all of these circumstances under the concept of capabilities, as we have seen). Therefore, the traditional criteria for measuring poverty based on income or on the distribution of wealth should be complemented, at a second stage, by considering other factors including: "a high level of unemployment (whose effects greatly surpass that of low incomes which is a direct consequence), the availability of healthcare, the presence of gender discrimination in the distribution of resources within families, etc." (Sen 1997, 214) Illiteracy and poor education, in general, can be added to the list of factors, in addition to social and cultural discrimination (factors that are determinant, as well, in getting a job and thus achieving a source of autonomous income).

In addition to income, there are at least two types of factors that help to define poverty and the poor. On the one hand, there are objective issues related to people's position in the world. Paul Streeten lists some of these objective measures that can help us decide who is poor in Brazil (Streeten 1995, 29 and ss.). One criterion is, naturally, social and economic class: we are speaking of landless farm workers, unqualified factory workers, farmers whose land is extremely infertile, drought-ridden and lacking in irrigation, such as that in the Brazilian *sertão*. Another is place of residence: the urban poor face different problems than those in the rural areas. Various geographical regions have different types of need. In the Brazilian case, the areas with the greatest needs are those that have been under the political control of powerful local oligarchies for centuries and are subsumed within a culture of violence, whim, and privilege. Finally, we must consider the fact of living in regions that are isolated and traditionally abandoned by the central state. These factors have permitted political arrangements in the National Congress, which, for many years, have allowed a series of Presidents of the Republic to maintain a certain level of "governability". Consequently, the people of Amazonia, of the *sertão* and other regions have become people *without a state,* by which we mean a significant lack of access to basic services and adequate infrastructure. One of the most brutal consequences of this type of widespread neglect and expropriation is the lack of human capital: the poor are generally people without education or professional training. They are obliged to work in jobs that are poorly paid and poorly qualified. Other objective criteria to be considered in the search for a definition of who is poor in Brazil include ethnicity or skin color (indigenous or black), gender, age, and family composition and structure. Finally, we must point out the issues of time, in other words, the chronic nature of unpredictable work and income. As Streeten points out "the income of the poor tends to vary considerably from year to year and season to season within 1 year, depending on the weather and other accidents" (Ibid., 30). Moreover, the temporal aspect is also relevant when looking at the effects of poverty on people: the lack or absolute absence of any hope of changing their situation in the future can lead to resignation or violence. All of this increases their vulnerability to becoming people devoid of rights and, consequently, more likely to be subjected to all the types of exploitation known to man.[3]

---

[3] Jonathan Wolff and Avner De-Shalit place the concept of risk at the center of their deliberations on poverty (Wolff and De-Shalit 2007, 63 and ss.). See the important work about poverty and social exclusion by Lena Lavinas (Lavinas 1996, 2002 and 2007).

This last consideration brings us to the subjective features of poverty. Streeten warns us not to "try to simplify the medication of poverty by resorting to just one indicator, especially those related to income or consumption" and not to "rely solely on quantitative indicators." He concludes that, "Whatever attempt to understand poverty must include the way in which the poor themselves perceive their situation." Therefore, he lists "intangible benefits or those difficult to measure" that are frequently "considered by the poor to be much more valuable than any material or measurable improvement." In fact, the list includes elements frequently mentioned by the women we interviewed, including:

> Good working conditions; freedom to choose your work and the way to support yourself; self-determination, safety and self-respect; a lack of persecution, not being humiliated; not fearing violence and not being exploited; the affirmation of religious or traditional cultural values [often the only thing the poor can affirm A.P. e W.L.R.]; empowerment and recognition; having enough time for leisure and satisfactory ways of using it; a feeling that your life and your work have meaning; the opportunity to participate actively in volunteer groups and social activities in a pluralistic civil society. [...] No lawmaker can guarantee that all of these aspirations (or even most of them) are met, yet public policy can create the opportunities for their realization. (Ibid., 50 s.)

In short, it can be stated that poverty should be looked at not merely from the economic perspective dealing with the lack or insufficiency of income. Other aspects of poverty are those we can call the ethical features that deal with self-respect, capabilities and growing autonomy. However, the economic aspect linked to the presence of regular income remains an indispensable condition for the escape from misery, including its ethical elements (see Chap. 5).

While dealing with the same distinction between the economic and ethical aspects of poverty, Mexican philosopher Paulette Dieterlen lists several elements of the question that are left aside when one looks at the issue purely from the economic point of view. Citing F. Vélez, she differentiates moderate from extreme poverty:

> The extreme poor are those persons who have an inadequate level of nutrition, resulting in a deficient level of physical and mental performance, which in turn prevents them from participating in the labor market or in intellectual activities such as education. The condition of extreme poverty also practically rules out any social mobility; the extreme poor are born and die generally in the same situation. The moderate poor, on the other hand, are those who, due to the degree of development of a country at a particular moment in time are not able to cover what they would regard as their basic needs. They differ from the extreme poor in having the capacity, but not the opportunities, to participate in economic and intellectual activities [...] Inhabitants in extreme poverty require immediate measures in order to leave their marginalization behind and to reduce their weakness and their vulnerability to the average. (F. Vélez apud Dieterlen 2005, 19)

Therefore, seen both from an economic and an ethical point of view, from an objective and a subjective perspective, extreme poverty is characterized by several aspects which can be listed as follows:

1. A lack of basic conditions for a healthy life
2. No or irregular access to income from a regular job

3. Child labor and dropping out of school
4. High birth rates
5. Accidents
6. Lack of access to credit
7. Invisibility and muteness
8. Inequality within families
9. Shame
10. Culture of resignation
11. Exclusion from citizenship

These different aspects will be analyzed in Sect. 4.4 and tied in with general theoretical considerations and empirical data from our interviews with BF grantees. The objective of this analysis is to describe the situation of the Brazilian poor before the implementation of the program for combating poverty introduced in recent years, particularly during the two mandates of President Luiz Inácio da Silva.[4]

4.2 Poverty in Brazil: Some Considerations

We do not intend to analyze the historical or structural causes of poverty in Brazil. There is a huge amount of literature on this topic, and we would prefer to refer our readers to some of it.[5] We will limit ourselves to a brief mention, merely in order to better tie our narrative together.

It is worth remembering the origins of the problem which, albeit distant, still influence the situation today. In the first place, the institution of slavery lasted for many centuries[6] and left a legacy not of only social, political and economic practices but also of moral attitudes towards the suffering of those who are excluded and subject to domination. This resulted in a society that is lacking in moral and civic

[4] Some writers call attention to the fact that the BF was born of programs instituted during the mandate of President Fernando Henrique Cardoso (namely the School Grant and Gas Aid). However, the BF is not merely an "expansion and consolidation of the social assistance program inherited from the Cardoso government" (Bichir 2010, 119). It represents, a qualitative rather than just a quantitative leap relative to the public policies of previous governments. In addition to unifying existing federal, state and municipal programs, it positioned itself as a program that aimed to promote social and economic inclusion, as well as citizenship, on the part of an overwhelming percentage of the Brazilian population, not only as support to people at school age (such as the case of the School Grant) or help with household expenses (such as the case of the Gas Aid). The monetary income profoundly changed the relationship between these poor people and society.

[5] See in more recent years Sales 1992, Diniz 1994, Souza 2003, 2006 and 2009. It would be impossible to list all the national, local, and regional publications within Brazil dealing with the centuries old poverty of the country, its causes, dynamics, and regional differences, etc.

[6] Translator's note: Brazil was the last country in the Western hemisphere to abolish slavery, in 1888.

solidarity.[7] Secondly, a history of authoritarian Catholicism legitimized inequality for centuries (including slavery itself). The church only briefly and never totally openly engaged in any decisive struggle against the causes of poverty. It limited itself to merely attempting to alleviate the resulting needs. The exception was the brief period when the so-called Liberation Theology emerged; however it quickly died due to the pressure from the conservative echelons of the Vatican, especially those of the popes John Paul II and Benedict XVI. The concentration of income (one of the highest in the world), which characterizes the history of the country from the colonial period, to the Empire, and then on to the Republic, originates precisely from slavery. It relies, for its legitimacy, on most of our liberal politicians,[8] as well as the Catholic Church. This combination of factors, such as the very nature of slavery and, in the Brazilian case, its wide extent, social pervasiveness and duration over time, led to the emergence of a "culture of submission" which can still be felt today, despite the changes that have arisen with democratization. The level of inequality in the distribution of income and wealth in Brazil corresponds to an economic, social and political chasm between the social classes. On the one hand, a rich minority enjoys high levels of consumption and the instruments to reproduce the existing social relationships (e.g., access to higher education), while remaining indifferent to the fate of their fellow citizens. On the other hand, the vast majority of Brazilians are condemned to a life of need, suffering, and sacrifice.

In the 1950s and 60s, the rates of economic growth in Brazil were among the highest in the world. This expansion, however, far from increasing the general standard of living, only intensified the inequality and exploitation. The Brazilian government, at the same time as it was modernizing, was privatized by a small elite and never developed any serious income distribution policies. The military coup of 1964 revealed the true interests of the dominant classes regarding this issue. The result of this process means that the words of the Conservative Prime Minister of Britain, Benjamin Disraeli can be applied to Brazil. Writing about nineteenth century England, his novel *Sybil* (1845) described:

> Two nations between whom there is no intercourse and no sympathy, who are as ignorant of each other's habit, thoughts, and feelings, as if they were dwellers in different zones, or inhabitants of different planets, who are formed by a different breeding, are fed by a different food, are ordered by different manners and are not governed by the same laws. (Disraeli 1845, I 149)

With this, we are not supporting Jacques Lambert's thesis of the "two Brazils" which posits a lack of a unifying principle in Brazil (Lambert 1967). Disraeli's

[7] "The slave interests enabled the maintenance of the vast Brazilian territory, as it was also slavery that determined the unique way of life of the freemen in Brazil," (Souza 2003, 103). Other works about this question include the classic studies by Florestan Fernandes (Fernandes 1965), Fernando Henrique Cardoso (Cardoso 1977), Otavio Ianni (Ianni 1962) and Maria Sylvia Carvalho Franco (Franco 1969). Regarding hunger and its impact on the body and lives of Brazilians subjected to it over centuries, see the classic studies by Jesué de Castro (Castro 1961).

[8] Translator's note: The word "liberal" is used here to refer to classical liberalism that evolved in Europe from the nineteenth century onwards, not (as in the US) as synonymous with "left-wing".

allegory of a separated nation cannot hide the fact that the division is the fruit of political construction. In our case, it is a political construction that is peculiar to Brazil, or to capitalism as a historical formation. Capitalism creates centers and peripheries within diverse societies, mixing archaic forms with modern ones.[9] The correction or improvement of these disparities are carried out by democratic policies, understood in the broadest sense, in other words, as a collective construction. This can be understood as the construction of a nation of citizens. What distinguishes Brazil is the systematic cancellation of any attempt at substantive democratization of the country, as indicated by the historical dearth of any cultural policies of integration, any serious public policies for education, in short of any true policies of citizenship.

Thus, it is worth pointing out that there is an ideological mechanism designed to make Brazilian poverty seem natural. The idea is that it is an immutable, natural phenomenon that it is useless to combat, and this notion masks many things, beyond, of course, the interest in maintaining the social, political and economic status quo. These ideological operations that serve to make poverty seem natural are openly contradictory. While, on the one hand, it is emphasized that the poor are almost anthropologically different from the rest of the population, on the other hand, the country's supposed "racial democracy" is extolled (as in Gilberto Freyre's works).[10]

The use of the latter term, rather the view of the country it expresses, has become the object of an active consensus and, thus, it constituted an excellent way to prevent, or at least postpone for many years to come, the emergence and the organization of a black power movement that might demand substantial as opposed to merely formal rights. Another example of the introduction of ideologically constructed terms and linguistic figures that have acted and still act as "structures of opacity" that veil the inhumane relationships between the rich and the poor and between blacks, mulatos and whites in Brazil was the affirmation of the friendly nature of the Brazilian (an idea harshly criticized by Sérgio Buarque de Holanda [1936]). The transformation of such ideological constructions into a stock phrase, or even common sense (as Gramsci uses the term), is evidenced by the insistence on the part of most of the Brazilian public on denying the existence of racism in Brazil, even while they widely practice the same.

---

[9]Throughout our field work, we witnessed this several times (in the infrastructures, in the hotel sector, etc.) but one of the most extreme examples of the coexistence of the archaic and the modern is that of the Fábrica da Pedra in the city of Delmiro Gouveia that employs up to 800 people, using ultramodern technology, while the surrounding city is filled with impoverished neighborhoods like Povoado da Cruz and most of the population is unemployed and illiterate.

[10]Translator's note: Gilberto Freyre (1900–1987) was a Brazilian sociologist who introduced the idea that Brazil was a racial democracy, because it has managed to reach a high level of miscegenation among "whites" and "blacks". What this idea tends to obliterate is the fact that miscegenation was more often than not the result of sexual abuse of female slaves by their masters. Of course, the elite continued to be made up of the descendants of the former masters, while the descendant of the slaves remained poor.

Regarding the nature of the endemic violence in the country, the media, which exerts a strong influence on the middle class, reduces the problem to drug trafficking, gang wars and micro-criminality, omitting the question of the centuries-old, day-to-day violence against the excluded, the poor, the blacks, women and children, as well as the super-exploitation of work, low salaries, and so on. The fact that most of the middle class, and the elites in general, identify the violence against people and property as the most serious problem in Brazil rather than the violence of poverty that afflicts the overwhelming majority of the population, demonstrates once again, the existence of interests and perceptions in the country that set up profound oppositions between "the two nations". It is as if the so-called 'public opinion' that is expressed by the media and coincides greatly with the middle class, did not live in the same country as the poor, even though they often live side by side. It is worth wondering if a country in which a portion of the population is systematically excluded and marginalized can commit to the ideal of democratic values. Jessé Souza calls attention to the "great historical drama of Brazilian society" that consists exactly of the "continual reproduction of a society that normalizes inequality and accepts the production of 'people' on the one hand and 'sub-people' on the other" (Souza 2009, 24). This is equal to the dehumanization of that part of the population who is considered to be less than human by the others (which is evident in the scandalous differential treatment that is accorded by the justice system to the middle classes rather than the poor). This is Souza's bitter conclusion:

> In Brazil, we do not see the classic division between workers and the bourgeoisie. Instead, in this peripherally modern society, our social and political 'central conflict', which surpasses all others in importance, is the opposition between the class that is excluded from all material and symbolic opportunities of social recognition and that of all the other social classes that are, even if differentially, included. (Souza 2009, 25)

Thus, we would like to point out once again that the situation of the people we interviewed is not one of natural need, nor one of general external circumstances (due to being underdeveloped, or from the periphery, etc.), rather it arises from the production of certain set of social situations that has been and that still is the result of political choices made by our dominant classes. The privatization of the state and its principal institutions, which has taken place throughout our governmental history, has left us the legacy of political, economic and administrative customs that are indicative of a grave negligence on the part of the state vis à vis its citizens, especially those who are poor. The people we are talking about and the women we interviewed are impoverished individuals, whose entire existence has been permeated by extreme need. As stated above, for many years, the Brazilian state has not guaranteed them the right to life and security, neglecting, thereby, the primordial function of a governmental body.[11] These people have never had access to the

[11] The idea that the state should at least guarantee life and security to its citizens can be found in the origins of modern political thought, starting with Hobbes.

resources that are indispensable for reproducing life. Many of them have undergone the humiliating experience of having had to 'hunt for food' as the animals do. Thus, we can include them as a part of that huge number of people that Hannah Arendt called "the stateless people" (Arendt 1968, 269ff.).[12] This having been said, it can be argued that the Brazilian state has for many years decreed, again paraphrasing Arendt, their expulsion from humanity. The absence of a state that might confer and guarantee rights leads to a situation of people without "the right to have rights" (to use once again Arendt's terms, Arendt 1968, 296 f.). In this fashion, the Brazilian state has condemned them to *civil death*. These people have, thus, been muted because their right to a public voice does not exist. They have been deprived of their basic civil rights since in this situation they lack conditions and institutional channels for expression and movement. There are millions of Brazilians with practically no schooling, who are completely lacking in qualifications and studies that would qualify them for any job that might require, for example, reading and writing. Nor are they able to follow more detailed orders. This puts into question the nature of the economic growth in Brazil from the 1930s to the 1970s. This process of economic modernization lacked any substantive democratic project. In this case, the high levels of ongoing poverty point to the profound inadequacy of growth as a mechanism for including the inhabitants of a country in the world of rights and the civilizing heritage of humanity. A similar situation clearly reveals the essentially exclusionary nature of market mechanisms. Therefore, and confirming in its starkness the discoveries of Karl Marx and Karl Polanyi, the capitalistic market has demonstrated once again that its mechanisms incessantly produce and reproduce social, economic, and political inequality with its resulting extreme injustice (what Polanyi refers to as the "satanic mill").[13] We would like to provoke debate by saying that this issue inevitably brings up the inescapable question of the need and the objectivity for a democratic policy that assumes its distributive responsibility as the only way to transform the meaning of economic processes and not leave them completely in the power of the blind forces of private interests. Karl Polanyi reminds us that "The richer, deeper and more multifaceted the structures of democracy, the more real this responsibility becomes," (Polanyi 1932).

---

[12] The expression 'stateless peoples' is used by Hannah Arendt in her book *The Origins of Totalitarianism*, to refer to the experience of people who have remained and still remain at the margins of society, who were not included in the body of the many nations due to ethnic or religious reasons, and who, worst of all, were the victims of great prejudice and numerous stereotypes. She speaks particularly about the Jews. The author states, therefore, that many of these people make up what are called 'refugees, or stateless people, since they have been abandoned by everything and everyone but especially by the nation states who deny them rights and do not carry out policies of political or social inclusion. These 'stateless people' are, thus, people devoid of rights.

[13] See Karl Polanyi's classic, *The Great Transformation* (Polanyi 1944), as well as several of his articles published between 1920 and 1930 in Polanyi 1987 (particularly the articles "Economia e Democrazia" and "La libertà"). There is today an abundance of literature replete with empirical data confirming and enriching with new information these classic theses about this question.

4.3 Fighting Poverty in the Light of the Brazilian 1988 Constitution

There is a legislative imperative of the democratic state to combat poverty. This is enshrined in the Brazilian Federal Constitution of 1988, which was drawn up following more than two decades of democratic struggle against a military dictatorship. With all of its possible limitations, this constitution creates the legal space to develop policies to enforce the rule of law in the country. It opened the door to public policies aiming to, for example, implement minimal social justice, as stipulated in the preamble where it says that the democratic state has the "purpose of ensuring the exercise of social and individual rights, liberty, security, well-being, development, equality and justice as supreme values of a fraternal, pluralist and unprejudiced society". Moreover, in Article I, item III, it asserts that the Brazilian state is founded on, among others, "the dignity of the human person", and in Article III, The fundamental objectives of the Federative Republic of Brazil are: I – to build a free, just and solidary society; II – to guarantee national development; III – to eradicate poverty and substandard living conditions and to reduce social and regional inequalities; IV – to promote the well-being of all, without prejudice as to origin, race, sex, color, age and any other forms of discrimination. Article 170 also sets out that "The economic order, founded on the appreciation of the value of human work and on free enterprise, is intended to ensure everyone a life with dignity, in accordance with the dictates of social justice." Furthermore, in Article 193, it is stated that "The social order is based on the primacy of work and aimed at social well-being and justice." It is also worth mentioning the Constitutional Amendment 31 of December 14, 2000, that modified the temporary constitutional Provisions Act and introduced articles that created the Fund to Combat and Eradicate Poverty, which, however, was only actually intended to function until 2010.

However, as history has demonstrated, none of the rights written into a constitution will be respected without collective action and without struggles to achieve the resources to ensure the respect for and enforcement of what is on paper (see Honneth 2003). The Brazilian Constitution is a directive one, in other words, a document that announces a plan for the country and for society and which aims to change reality by way of law. According to Gilberto Bercovici:

> For the Theory of the Directive Constitution, the Constitution is not only a guarantee of what exists but also a plan for the future. By providing guidelines political action without replacing it, it emphasizes the interdependence between the state and society [...] The meaning, the goal, of the directive constitution is to provide the strength and the legal underpinning for social change. A directive constitution is an action plan for changing society [...] The Brazilian Constitution of 1988 stipulates a vast program of inclusive and distributive public policies by way of its "transformative clauses". The "transformative clauses", such as Article 3 of the Constitution of 1988, explains the contrast between the cruel social reality and the need to eliminate it. Thus, it avoids that the constitution should consider achieved what has yet to be achieved, and it confers on the state the obligation to promote the transformation of the social-economic structure. Its realization does not signify the immediate demand for concrete action by the state but its positive, ongoing and diligent attitude. (Bercovici 2009, 273, our translation)

Thus, it is important to recall the text of the 1988 Constitution. This recollection speaks to our history of social hope and the struggles that are reflected in the document. At that moment in time, the goal was to establish and to regulate the rights and duties of citizens and their relationship to the state. It is worth mentioning here a speech given 150 years ago by the German Social Democratic leader Ferdinand Lassalle, "On the Essence of Constitutions". He argued something that we know but that is always worth remembering. We should think sociologically about a Constitution and its role in social transformation: what is its most intimate nature and what are its methods for acting within society? It is the Basic Law of a country. However, it is essentially based on certain grounds which are set out as normative goals; they do not deal with random or temporary issues of social life peculiar to a country. On the contrary, they refer to deep, long lasting and structural aspects of life in society. So, the potential longevity of a constitution and its appropriateness for a determined nation depend intimately on its capacity to mirror what Lassalle called "actual relations of force." He argues, "*The actual relation of forces* in a given society constitutes the actively operating force which determines all laws and juridical institutions of this society in such a way that they cannot be other than what they are in their essential characteristics." (Lassalle 1942).

Political sociology teaches us that the social forces only turn into actual relations of force when they are subject to metamorphosis by politically organized forces with tactics and strategies that are more or less clear and with a certain uniformity of political goals. This relation can be projected in many ways within society, especially in the production and the enforcement of Law as a body of regulations ready to promote, in the case in question, citizenship and to guarantee its full practice.

Once these assumptions are brought up, we can think about the limits and the reach of constitutions, such as the Brazilian Constitution of 1988. However, in order to understand it, we do not feel it is going too far to argue that the analyst cannot escape from mentioning Lasalle's paradigm, especially the issue of the actual relation of forces that provide the constitution with its political and moral grounds to shape its regulative framework. Constitutions written in times of great social change (and they almost always are) embody and express moral sentiment, political plans and hopes for justice, but they also express relations of power. Many constituents of the period remind us of the magnitude of the plans and the democratic political ambitions that were not able to win over the anachronistic and authoritarian forces at work in at the heart of the Constituent Assembly.

There is a recurrent phenomenon at these moments in history, whether revolutionary or not: the constituent act mobilizes the best political energies of a country, because, to a certain extent, they are focused on founding something new, a potentially new and better form of civil intercourse (see Arendt 1963). These moments are always preceded by great discord and huge social struggles as mentioned above. The struggles, to a certain extent, are translated and inscribed within the legal document: the constitutions are born out of conflict and by way of conflict. Our constitution of 1988 followed exactly the same rule. Thus, the production of regulations that arose from that document can be seen as an attempt at a legal synthesis of the conflict and as a way of healing the wounds that were still open. Its destiny was to break through obstacles and open avenues into the future. Piero Calamandrei was a brilliant and important Italian lawyer, member of the 1947 Constituent Assembly, a *partigiano* (i.e. he fought with the resistance against the Fascists). A famous quote of his will reinforce our message. When he saw the final version of the Constitution of the Italian Republic of 1948, he declared (Calamandrei 2010):

> How much blood, how much sorrow to get to this Constitution! Behind each article of this Constitution, oh young people, you must see young people like yourselves who died fighting, shot, hung, tortured, starved to death in concentration camps, dead in Russia, dead in Africa, dead in the streets of Milan, in the streets of Florence, who gave their lives so that freedom and justice could be written on this paper.

There is a second way in which constitutions incorporate decisions and that is that they serve to indicate the fundamental structures of a national community. This is why a constitution is not merely a legal text, it is also a political plan, precisely a directive constitution. These days, we cannot fail to demand loyalty to a system of universally valid democratic values, i.e. political democracy with free and fair elections, which must not mar the representation of the sovereign people. The democratic rule of law is based on and must be a permanent source of distributional fairness. In fact, we should recall that this is an old debate. We should mention some emblematic discussions of this issue in the twentieth century. Firstly, an event took place during the Weimar Constituent Assembly, and repeated itself on various occasions and in several countries, such as during the post WWII Italian Constituent Assembly. At both moments, the Weimar and the Italian, despite their differences, a very interesting legal and political reformulation took place, whose spirit it is worth recalling. The concept prevailed that a constitution should establish a legal system in which distributive justice would become a binding element throughout the regulatory system. Back in 1945, the Italian professor of Law, Guido Calogero, stated the following: "Legal norms participate in this supreme value which is the distribution of wealth, all the more so as they appear to be intended for this end. These norms are established as the sacred tables of the Original Legislators, as the Constitutions and Statutes, as the social contracts and the declarations of independence, and the people observe them and venerate them as did Socrates in *Críton*. And I fear that any harm to them means the ruin of civilization" (Calogero 1945, 14, own translation from the Portuguese).

We would like to point out a third aspect that is always present in this era of constitutions: it deals with the founding or refounding of a "we", a political people. In contemporary history, at least since the North American and French Revolutions, the constitution of a "we," a people ("we, the people" begins the preamble to the United States Constitution) is established as one of their most fertile processes, whose legacy has enriched western political thought until today. In the French case, the people positioned themselves as the central actors of political transformation, to such an extent that it was impossible to erase them from the process of the foundation of a Republic based on liberty, equality and fraternity. Why are we bringing this up? Our goal is to remind readers that all constitutions throughout a broad range of different historical contexts, have had one common purpose. They set out the ways in which political life should be organized. They establish how power should be distributed, which rights can be allocated and what the conditions are for benefitting from those rights, as well as the legal guarantees to their exercise and enjoyment by citizens who hold rights and prerogatives. After all, the constitution defines and redefines the objectives of the state. This has always been the ultimate goal of new constituent assemblies. These are weighty moments fraught with political and moral demands to bring about radical improvements to the current state of affairs by way of a pact of civic coexistence which is manifest in the form of a constitution. These moments are also propitious for establishing fertile political myths replete with evocative power for our lives. Why is this possible? Why can we not forget that a constitution is a program for the rights and duties of citizens? As Habermas reminds us, rights cannot exist in the absence of duties (Habermas 1996). To this extent, a constitution as a political program suggests avenues for defining the identity of a people as a political and democratic body centered within a sovereign nation and that is understood and expected to be a community of citizens. Another point that we would like to briefly raise is that of the process of implementing a constitution. To the extent that they are born from the power delegated by the people to the constituent assembly, the rights set out in the constitution must be effectively implemented and this depends on ongoing political participation and social struggle, which calls for and even demands the realization and amplification of the rights of citizens. This brings us to the notion that democracy and the rule of law are by definition incomplete works. They are political structures undergoing constant construction. Norberto Bobbio said that a constitution cannot be a mask of peace that hides a face full of rancor and resentment. It must be, rather, a living document that reflects the real conflicts extant within society. The nature of this process brings with it certain social and political conditions that ensure that such processes be carried out. Of utmost importance is the practice of open public debate that reflects the inherent conflicts within society and the social struggle for rights and recognition. The constitution must stipulate channels for the basic, free expression of the people's right to a voice. This is the only way to build that democratic voice that is necessary for the permanent reconfiguration of a "we, the people". Thus, the norms set down at the time of the constitution must be able to withstand potential ongoing self-creation, in order to better capture the needs and new desires that constantly emerge in large majorities. For this reason, the historical context that is almost always expressed by the Constituent Assembly has brought forth an institutional space for political discussion. This enables the legislative body to make progress towards the ideals set out in the constitution: the construction of a democratic rule of law based on principles of fair distribution which are indispensable for enhancing democracy.

We would like to remind readers that there was a tremendous amount of social struggle that predated the constituent assembly. The work of the assembly was accompanied by intense participation of a broad swath of the Brazilian people who flocked to Brasilia in order to offer proposals and to try to exert as much influence as possible on the legal norms set down in our supreme law. The Brazilian people made it clear that they intended to be a central player in their own history. We must not forget the closing words of Ulysses Guimarães, National President of the Constituent Assembly, as he presented to the nation what he called a citizen's constitution:

> There is, therefore, a representative and vitalized clamor coming from the people from the streets, the markets, the favelas and the factories, from the workers, cooks, underprivileged children, from Indians, from squatters, from business people, from students, pensioners, from civil servants and soldiers, all of whom are giving witness to the advanced and socially authentic nature of this document that now is coming into effect. Like a conch it will always remember the roar of the waves of the suffering, the hopes and the demands that gave rise to it.

Paraphrasing the President of the Constituent Assembly, in this research we have tried to showcase the suffering, the hopes of millions of Brazilians who even today still lack a voice but whose cries of pain and suffering were guarded within the text of the constitution, in hopes of transformative public policy.

Against this background we can state that a governmental program like that of the BF that transfers income to poor women makes up part of an incipient public policy for citizenship. These efforts are still insufficient. However, we cannot be allowed to ignore its potential to be transformed into a consistent policy of educating citizens. Such a policy should, in turn, be complemented by a much broader range of measures aimed at achieving the goals set out in the 1988 constitution. To this end, the BF begins with the most elementary of all of the prerogatives of citizenship, because it relates to the most basic right, namely, the right to life.

An Aside: The Failure of Economic Development

In 1955, the economist Simon Kuznets published a classic article where he presented the hypothesis that, in the short term, rapid economic growth would increase social and economic inequality but would reduce poverty in the long term. Despite its weak empirical basis (the writer himself recognized that the article was "perhaps 5 per cent empirical information and 95 per cent speculation, some of it possibly tainted by wishful thinking" (Kuznets 1955, 26), this hypothesis has come to be seen as almost dogma by generations of politicians and economists, although no empirical evidence has been found in the years following. On the contrary, an important study of the 1970s carried out in 43 developing countries proved that there was no direct relationship between economic growth and falling poverty. Instead, the effects of the former accrue almost exclusively to the middle and upper classes.[14] However, as has already been mentioned, this did not prevent governments and international institutions like the World Bank and the International

[14] Curiously, the authors cite the Brazilian case in their conclusion, according to which the development achieved had not functioned in the desired fashion, "During the 1960s, for example, the GDP/capital in Brazil grew, in real terms 2.5% annually. However, the percentage of national income received by the 40% poorest fell from 10% in 1960 to 8% in 1980, while the portion of the 5% richest grew from 29% to 38%. There is no evidence of a rise in political participation. On the contrary, there was a marked fall in participation between the early 1960s when the left under Quadros and Goulart was in the ascendancy to the early 1970s, when the military dictatorship held absolute power." (Adelman and Taft Morris 1973, 1).

Monetary Fund from making (in the first case) or demanding (in the second) policies intended to increase the GDP in the belief that those measures were the most effective for eliminating poverty.

The underdeveloped nations were therefore obligated by the above mentioned institutions to take a series of measures designed to guarantee economic growth such as: privatizing public companies and even services that were traditionally guaranteed by public power, facilitating free commerce, renouncing or strongly reducing import duties and subsidies to national agricultural, industrial or mining production (while industrialized countries continued to practice said subsidies and duties); trying to stabilize national budgets, etc. These measures, in fact, increased poverty levels as numerous writers have pointed out,[15] while they failed to produce the desired growth. In many cases, there was, instead, zero growth.[16] Therefore, it can be argued that the policies suggested or even imposed by such institutions have foundered. The anti-poverty 'recipes' of the international institutions revealed themselves to be either wrong or inadequate. However, this does not absolve the elites and local governments of their responsibilities, either in maintaining the status quo or in having critically accepted these theories and their subsequent initiatives. Thus, a certain economics based approach to development found that the growing misery of part of the population was a necessary and inevitable phase of a country's 'progress'. Justice must be served and we must remind readers that Latin American economists such as Celso Furtado and Raúl Prebisch never accepted the view that economic development must necessarily pass through a period of rising poverty. Instead, they denounced the ideological construction that legitimated social inequality. For them, development was not limited to economic growth but involved profound transformations in the social and economic structures (see Furtado 1961, 1962, 1962a, 1964, 1966, 1967, 1992 and Prebisch 1949 and 1950). Today, many economists recognize the ideological basis of this economic development approach (see Chang 2002 and 2010). This line of thinking, which Jessé Souza calls hyper economistic, posits that "all resolution of conflicts and contradictions is expected to come from a unilateral effort toward economic progress, including the basic social elements such as the spread of the type of people who are suited to the demands of the state and the market" (Souza 2003, 101, own translation).

The coup of 1964 aligned itself deeply with economic interests (internal and external ones, such as in the case of the United States) that were contrary to the social and political demands at the time that were calling for the improvement in the standard of living of a large part of the population. However, in the political grammar of Brazilian developmentalism, the concept of citizenship was not present: the preoccupation was, rather, with the above-mentioned improvement of the standard of living. The only one to speak of citizenship was, perhaps, Florestan Fernandes,

[15] In the words of one American economist "These actions might have helped underdeveloped countries to pay off part of their loans and thereby solving the debt crisis on the part of private banks in developed countries but, invariably, they have reduced the standard of living of the urban and rural poor" (Todaro 1994, 600).

[16] See the figures cited in Easterly 2001.

who spoke about human rights. In a well-known essay of 1986, a group of researchers surrounding the Chilean economist Manfred Max-Neef criticized financial Neoliberalism for leading to economic growth but not true development. They pointed out that this approach did not take into consideration the situation of Latin American countries. "It is impossible to eliminate poverty by liberalizing a market that excludes the poor".[17] They said it favored speculative instead of productive economic activity, since Latin American markets are in fact oligarchies and the groups of economic power cannot find subjects strong enough to control these entrenched groups (Max-Neef 1986). It appears to us that these conclusions are still valid 25 years later.

4.4 Poverty in Brazil: Phenomenological Characteristics

In the following sections, we will describe the situation in which our participants lived and which are representative of millions of Brazilians who are living in a state of poverty. To this end, we will use the criteria listed above (see Sect. 4.1). Chapter 5 will discuss the changes brought above by the BF.

1. *A lack of basic conditions for a healthy life.* Among the negative factors, the following stand out: poor nutrition (whether in the form of a lack of food, or that of an unhealthy diet), precarious housing, a lack of basic health care, and lack of access to many medications, etc. In the case of the women interviewed, access to the Unified Health System (SUS) and the medications by way of the Popular Pharmacies greatly depends on local circumstances (e.g., how far they live from the city, whether their mayor hires enough physicians and ensures services 7 days a week, etc.). Poor nutrition is not necessarily linked to the absence of food but also the lack of nutritional education – a phenomenon that was mentioned by a pioneering researcher of famine in Brazil, Josué de Castro, in his 1946 book, *Geografia da Fome. O dilema brasileiro: pão ou aço* [The Geography of Hunger. The Brazilian Dilemma: Bread or Steel] (Castro 1961, vol. I, 132 ss.). Castro speaks of a "hidden hunger, in which, due to the permanent lack of certain elements of nutrition in people's daily diets, entire groups of inhabitants are allowed to slowly starve, despite eating every day" (Castro 1961, vol. I, 22, our translation). The effect may be less drastic today, but it is not less important. In addition to traditional undernourishment, there is a shocking lack of nutritional information. In the families we interviewed, there was often a lack of foods that provide vitamins and minerals (such as fruit and vegetables) and protein (red meat) which were replaced by high calorie foods with an excess of fat and carbohydrates (rice, sausage, pasta). This poor nutrition represents an obstacle to the development of personal autonomy in various ways. The most obvious are

[17] This observation has become current as well in countries which, in the 1980s, seemed to be immune to crises of the magnitude that are affecting them today.

that it does not provide for a healthy life (physically or mentally) and it makes people more subject to disease. At the same time, it reduces their physical and mental capacity for work, condemning them to even more misery (see Dieterlen 2005, 25). Moreover, empirical studies have proven that there is a direct relationship between under- or malnutrition in childhood and the development of basic cognitive abilities and intelligence. For example, a diet lacking in iron limits children's ability to concentrate (see Brown 1993). In short, we are facing a series of poor functionings linked to the lack of the corresponding capabilities.

The reasons that have caused this diet are objective and do not solely depend on the lack of nutritional information. As some of the interviews demonstrated, it is not always a lack of awareness of the importance of eating fruit and vegetables. However, the women often cannot find such products at their local markets at affordable prices (see, for example, the interview with Dona Inês in Demerval Lobão, Piauí). They cannot grow such foodstuffs due to a lack of water or because they would have to resort to potable water which is unbearably expensive (see, for example, the interview with Dona Amélia in Pasmadinho, in the Jequitinhonha Valley). Similar remarks can be made about the possibility of buying red meat or other sources of quality proteins: the prices are incompatible with the income these women receive. A possible institutional response might be to grant strong tax relief to the most basic popular foodstuffs, or a program of nutritional education with the distribution of fresh fruit and vegetables in places where private enterprise does not provide them. Of particular importance is the designof school menus. These measures would create capabilities and allow access to basic functionings that, as we saw above, are linked not only to the intake of appropriate numbers of calories but also the development of physical and intellectual abilities.

It is important to mention that, in a situation of poverty, the individual differences such as level of education, personal experience, family structure, skills and talents become even more decisive in the administration of the available financial resources and, even more, in the management of scarcity. It is not our intention to blame people for the struggles they face. On the contrary, their potential incapacity to manage their situations of scarcity depends on a multifaceted social context. The lack of education, in the broad sense (e.g. correct guidance about the functioning of their bodies, about sexuality, nutrition, and personal hygiene), marks the quality of these people's lives profoundly. The life of two of the women is representative of this situation: Claudineide (Povoado da Cruz), mother of three, and Graciele (Inhapí), mother of four. The former is almost obese. She immediately complained about the insufficient amount of the grant, telling us that it is only enough to buy 2 weeks' worth of food. Graciele had a different situation. She told us that she was able to feed her family for the entire month, even though she had one more child than Claudineide. How can we explain this difference? Since we did not delve into their life histories, we cannot give a satisfactory answer because we do not know how to explain the differences in their personalities. We only want to mention that the differences in individual biographies regarding education, family structure, place of residence, and the social environment that surrounded them were reflected in the ways they managed their grants and their day-to-day lives. In the case of these two women, as can be deduced from their interviews, there was a marked difference in the family and social environment that had an important influence on their personalities and capabilities.

2. *Little or no access to income derived from regular work.* The people in question were subject to chronic or almost chronic unemployment. In the case of the women, the great majority had never had a job, due to having married and to having children at a young age. At the most, they and their husbands get occasional odd jobs that are temporary, very harsh and poorly paid (e.g., they might earn R$10 for 8 h of farm work, according to several women in Inhapi). They live in a constant state of uncertainty relative to the future. In some cases, the husbands work in the sugar cane harvest and in other places or even in other states and they leave the families behind for several months of the year (especially in the Jequitinhonha Valley). These sporadic and informal jobs rarely guarantee enough income to sustain a family for the whole year. The desire for a full-time job with a contract was repeated several times in the interviews. When people have the possibility to work autonomously (as was the case with small landowners engaged in subsistence farming), the scarcity of material resources, malnutrition, little or no formal schooling and the lack of information about their work represent insurmountable obstacles, to the extent that the results of their labor are disproportionately low in relation to the energy extended. Moreover, there is the risk that the harvest might be destroyed or harmed by natural causes. Several interviews pointed out the importance of governmental programs like the Garantia-Safra (Insured Harvest) or the creation of the so-called Territórios da Cidadania (Territories for Citizenship).[18] Faced with this situation, it is worth quoting the words of Luiz Eduardo Wanderley about this:

> *Poverty* has its own laws that are different from those of formal unemployment and the creation of jobs is not enough to solve the problem; *poverty constitutes a system that is parallel to the formal one,* however with relationships of mutual feedback. It should not be confused with the informal economy that exploits the poor [...]. (Wanderley 2007, 186; emphasis added)

According to Wanderley, poverty cannot be erased by mechanisms of economic distribution or by creating jobs because such a situation, due to its multifaceted nature, demands interventions at many levels that can only be carried out by political institutions, such as the state.

Thus, our research revealed and reiterated once more the situation that scholars and politicians such as Celso Furtado, Josué de Castro, Caio Prado Jr., Florestan Fernandes and so many others disclosed in their seminal works in the decades of

[18] For information about Seguro-Safra see: http://www.mda.gov.br/portal/noticias/item?item_id=3589624; and about Territórios da Cidadania see: http://www.territoriosdacidadania.gov.br/dotlrn/clubs/territriosrurais/one-community?page_num=0

the 1940s, 50s, and 60s.[19] They drew attention most of all to the gap between the rates of Brazilian economic growth throughout 30 years and the permanent and almost untouched specter of inequality and extreme poverty. Socially produced wealth did not reach the life of the poor, especially not that of the rural poor who were totally excluded from any social rights by the pact of the former president Getúlio Vargas.[20] We were fully aware of the deeply entrenched historical and structural processes that have translated into the enormous misery encountered when one travels across regions like the Vale do Jequitinhonha and the upper sertão of Alagoas. An issue jumps out at us. Poverty cannot be resolved without broad-ranging, state intervention acting on multiple fronts such as education and professional training. Moreover, mechanisms of business support tailored to meet to the needs of most of the population are needed, which provide incentives for types of work that are more suited to the local culture. One should remember that our poverty has not arisen by chance but is deeply rooted in our history and in the way that we politically implement state decisions.

Nevertheless, something has started up in these regions. For example, in the Vale do Jequitinhonha, we came across at least two examples of community experiences linked to the local traditional handcrafts: a community bakery in Itinga specialized in producing local cookies and a women's artisan's cooperative producing clay pieces and figurines (some of which were highly artistic) in the city of Santana do Araçuaí. Their craftwork, however, does not bring in enough income to lead people out of poverty. It would be necessary that public authorities promoted and encouraged initiatives of this type in addition to the more traditional forms of jobs creation and economic development stimuli, such as: building roads and health centers, general and vocational schools, irrigation and reservoirs, where necessary. In this case, such policies would not only target the economic development of the region but would also create access to the capabilities needed for basic functioning, namely, the ability to guarantee people's survival and their family's well-being.

However, even taking into consideration such policies from the perspective of the mere economic development of a nation, it is worth remembering that the latter is also a social process linked to regulated demands. In other words, it must have clear goals and objectives that should be discussed publicly. It is not and it has never in history been a natural, arbitrary process devoid of purpose. As Amartya Sen has said, the goal of development should be human freedom (Sen 1999; see also Chang 2002).

[19] As Celso Furtado warned in his 1962 book *A pré-revolução brasileira*, 1962: "We must, however, recognize that a movement of this size and transcendence can only take place if led by the national government itself. It is with a governmental program that we should be able to conceive of a movement on such a scale...]" (Furtado 1962, 116). See also Castro 1961.

[20] During the second mandate of President Vargas, a Project called the Statutes of the Rural Worker was sent to Congress. It augmented the application of labor regulations to the farms. This proposal, however, was only approved in 1963 during the government of João Goulart, [Translator's note: a leftist leaning President who was deposed by a military coup in 1964].

It is imperative to say that these women, as well as their men, want much more from life than mere survival. They never missed out on an opportunity to tell us so: they have a high regard for work that brings income, and they want a permanent job. We often heard sad, melancholic laments such as "I wasn't able to go to school. It was too far from home," or "My father pulled us out of school because he needed us to work." The culture of a wage based society as well as that of the 'work ethic' weighed and weighs heavy upon them. On the other hand, they know that they have not been trained for more qualified tasks and that a good, regular job is not easy for people like them to find. As we mentioned earlier in a footnote, a visible example of this can be seen in the city of Delmiro Gouveia (AL), where the Fábrica da Pedra that uses high tech to produce linens and tablecloths only has 800 workers. The poor women and their husbands that live in the surroundings know that they will never be able to work there, due to their lack of the requisite training, skills, and abilities. They know that they are excluded from the best jobs. What they do not know is that their fate was decided years ago by the ceaseless production of the inequality of distribution in Brazilian society. Formal schooling in these regions is the privilege of a few, and it is, therefore, a privilege to find skilled jobs.

The lack of training is joined with the sad awareness, based on their personal experience, of how hard and painful it is, especially for the women, to find a job and to commit to it. Yet, the prejudice and stereotypes against the poor, and especially against poor women, reproduce themselves incessantly. In fact, it is an essential part of the strategies of political, cultural and social domination that have been so frequently analyzed by sociology and feminist theory (see, for example, Okin 1987).

3. *Child labor and school dropouts.* Participation in economic life begins very early: daughters and sons of poor households begin working at a very young age, often while they are still children. They might help around the house (taking care of younger brothers and sisters, helping their mothers cook dinner, gathering firework for the kitchen, taking care of domestic animals in the backyard, etc.). Alternatively, they might work outside the home, which almost always means dropping out of school, which leads to the subsequent perpetuation of illiteracy and to the impossibility of breaking out of misery by way of education (see, for example, the interviews with Dona Luisa in Inhapí, in the sertão of Alagoas and Dona Palmira in Araçuaí, in the Jequitinhonha Valley). For this reason, it is important that a program like the BF should make demands on the families of grantees, such as the obligation to have children in school and to take care of their health. It must be remembered that these demands are common in European countries, where parents who do not send their children to school can even lose custody of them.

   However, it is no use offering schools of terrible quality which contribute to the reproduction of inequality in its broadest terms: social, cultural, economic and most of all political inequality. This calls into question the role of the local authorities (municipal and state)[21] who are those mainly responsible for primary education.[22] The role of education as a fundamental component in the development of people's autonomy and as an instrument for citizenship is universally recognized and we will not dwell on this point. We would like to emphasize the importance of education as a source of capabilities, not only in regard to professional training (excessively dominant in the pedagogical view of many professional educators, from the MEC to the city level secretaries) but mostly in regard to enabling people to broaden their vital and cognitive horizons. The lack of contact with ways of life other than those of their nuclear family and immediate social context, which are almost always marked by destitution and need, prevents the children of poor families from imagining any other life for themselves, from imagining that 1 day they might leave that environment or change it profoundly. The culture of resignation that we have already spoken of and to which we will return in point ten has some of its roots in the lack of knowledge and contact with other ways of life different from the atavistic family poverty.

4. *High birth rates*. Linked to the issue of child labor is the question of the high birth rate among poor families. According to a certain traditional view, a high number of children would represent more potential sources of income for the family and the promise of support for the parents in their old age. However, a large number of children augments the family's economic problems, particularly when they are young, or when the job market does not provide enough jobs for the adults. This leads to a vicious circle, according to Dieterlen (2005, 26 f.). Our research showed that high birth rates persist in the regions studied, due much more to disinformation about its control than to the instrumental view just described. Pregnancy still occurs frequently and without planning, due to the already mentioned disinformation, to family situations and, sometimes, to religious beliefs. The domination of women in a highly patriarchal society deprives them of almost any self-determination regarding their bodies. This proves that the lack of basic civil rights such as the right to the integrity of their very bodies may be rooted within a sexist and violent culture (we will return to this point below). Moreover, some Christian denominations (such as the Pentecostals and even Roman Catholics) generally condemn birth control. Some of the women we spoke with, especially in the rural regions like the *sertão* of Alagoas and the Jequitinhonha Valley, refer to their frequent pregnancies and the large number of children with expressions such as "Here's another gift from God" (that is what a resident of the rural part of Inhapi, in the Alagoas sertão, Dona Luisa, told us when she, a mother of eight, showed off her latest baby when we returned to her house 1 year after the first interview). On the other hand, we also encountered

[21] Translator's note: In Brazil municipal governments are responsible for primary education, state governments for secondary education, and the federal government for universities.

[22] The mechanisms for reproducing inequality in the cultural and educational contexts have been analyzed, among others, by Pierre Bourdieu and, in the Brazilian case, by Luiz Pereira and more recently by Jessé Souza (Bourdieu 2010, Pereira 1967 and 1969, Souza 2009).

women who had had their tubes tied and others who said that this was one of their dreams. This shows that birth control is ambiguous and complex, although what prevails is disinformation and strict religious sexual morals. We often are not dealing with the free choice on the part of these women, who are, in fact, subject to the imposition of maternity on the part of their husbands, their families, the priests or the pastors of their churches. This lack of freedom also leads to a dearth of basic functionings like the ability to plan their lives or even to have control of their very bodies.

5. *Accidents.* The poor are more subject to accidents, due to the precariousness of their homes and installations (precarious electrical connections), the poor quality of construction materials and the dangerous location of their property (e.g. beside rivers and along roadsides and even on the shoulders). Moreover, the roads in this part of the country are not maintained appropriately. This leaves these spots and the houses of many people inaccessible. It also increases the risk of transporting people, livestock and etc. Just like the major thoroughfares, the very means of transport are equally precarious. One example is that of the father of Dona Luana, from Peroba, on the Alagoas coast, who was the victim of an accident when he was working as a sugar cane cutter. "He was in a truck of sugar cane cutters and the truck turned over and he was up there on top and he was injured. Nobody died, you know? But he was injured." He suffered a broken hand and arm and so he was no longer able to work. It can be argued that this greater likelihood of suffering accidents results in a loss of freedom and autonomy since it hinders the exercise of many relevant functionings.
6. *Lack of access to credit.* The poor cannot get credit because they have nothing to offer as collateral, and they cannot find guarantors. The number of Brazilians without access to banking services is still quite large. This constitutes another form of exclusion to which the poor are subjected. For these reasons, an effective public program easing access to credit should be included on the public democratic agenda (e.g. with low or no interest rates, subsidies, etc.) together with other related services aimed at including this vast contingent of people into the dynamics of society and solidifying their ties of belonging to the national community, with all of its contradictions and deep conflicts (see Sect. 5.4 for more about this issue).
7. *Invisibility and muteness.* In the cities, the phenomenon of the hidden poor is well-known and has been analyzed. They are generally segregated into separate and far away neighborhoods (e.g. the favelas which are often built on incredibly steep hills so that the neighborhoods themselves have come to be called *morros,* or hilltops). They get by with precarious public infrastructure (such as pavement, leisure space, lighting and terrible sanitation facilities, namely a lack of sewage and treated water). Their jobs are the least skilled, and they do not use public transport either because it does not exist or because they cannot afford it.

   For these reasons, in some cases, their presence goes almost unnoticed in the everyday's life of the upper class (except in cities such as Rio de Janeiro). However, they can be noticeable in several situations, mainly when they break certain social conventions or even the law. Then, their invisibility turns into a dangerous visibility. Hegel had already stated in his work *Realphilosophie* that the act of breaking the law represents the response of those who feel excluded from society and who seek to achieve the recognition that had been denied to them, declaring themselves to be endowed with subjectivity (Hegel 1983; see Honneth 1996).[23]

In the countryside, the poor either live in isolated houses or in hamlets that are normally located far from the main or even secondary roads (e.g. many of the residents of the Jequitinhonha Valley and the Alagoas sertão). The distance from the town or the municipal center always makes it hard to get access to essential services (medical assistance, notaries, banks, schools, etc.). Oftentimes, we are speaking of communities without electricity, a fact which increases their isolation even more and weighs heavily on their quality of health and of life as well as on the training of their subjectivity. After all, isolation hinders bringing people together where they might exchange information. Dona Bernardete, who lived in Sítio Novo (RN), told us that during her childhood she had not had electric energy. When two street lamps were installed in the small square in front of the church of the next village she went out every night in her yard in order to watch those distant, feeble lights. She found it "the most beautiful thing I had ever seen".

This set of characteristics of the life of the poor mutes them, which is to say, their voices and their suffering are not felt, nor even listened to. Therefore, their right to voice is totally inexistent. Throughout our research, we often heard their complaints about being heard even by the local officials responsible for the BF: the "muteness" of the poor is aggravated by the "deafness" of the public officials. In most cases, they would tell us that they never got together nor did they talk among themselves, except when waiting in line, either at the bank when they went to withdraw their money, or when they went to renew their BF registration. Most of the city halls lack the ability to create a space for meetings and debates about the grantees' difficulties in understanding the procedures required by the program. So, the problem of their muteness persists. The mismatch between their cultural and material reality and that of the officials is, after all, abysmal. This became obvious when grantees showed us letters they had received from the city hall which were written in a highly bureaucratic style. Their illiteracy led them to miss the deadlines for the BF renewal or hindered them in their attempts to resolve any problems that arose with their BF cards. Just one example like this effectively demonstrates the loss of human functioning as well as communication. The damage caused by such an attitude on the part of public authorities transcends the material loss of the grant and evidently constitutes disrespect from the institution and the resulting humiliation. Once again, the situation described evokes the notion of the decent society of Avishai Margalit (Margalit 1996) and the causal link established by Martha Nussbaum between institutional

[23] During the Middle Ages and the first part of modernity, the poor were excluded from the political community, because they literally had nothing to lose. A classic republican argument of the sixteenth and seventeenth centuries (and revisited by Kant) justifies the exclusion of people without regular income and without economic independence for this reason.

lack of interest and the corresponding lack of capabilities that lead exactly to the creation of an indecent society (see Nussbaum 2004 and 2011).

The lack of communication between the women on the one hand and the institutions and public officials on the other, as sometimes happens with the local program managers, calls into question the representativeness of the elected public officials who should support their constituents' right to a voice. In the town of Itinga, in the Jequitinhonha Valley, as described above, we attended a meeting of BF grantees. Between 40 and 50 women talked to us about their problems. The most common ones were those related to the actions of the local BF manager and the contact with local elected officials, beginning with the mayor. As far as we were able to tell from our interviews over the years, this problem was common to many locations. It could easily have been corrected if the mayor, as the highest ranking representative of the locale and therefore the senior person responsible for the BF, had gone to the trouble to build spaces dedicated to discussions and debates among the grantees. These officials could, furthermore, have met periodically with grantees, encouraging them to organize themselves into representative counsels, after first explaining the meaning of representatives. Such initiatives did, in fact, take place in the city of Guarulhos, in the state of São Paulo.

8. *Inequality within families.* In very poor families, inequality usually ends up accentuated, whether it is that between men and women, adults and children, or youth and the elderly.[24] We would like to point out that the potential for freeing oneself from spousal oppression is very limited in the poor and backward regions of Brazil, due to the strict family control over the women. This control comes from several masculine figures and is amplified upon marriage. As the family expands, so does the reach of domination. This is to say that many of these women are subject to domination by the father-in-law and mother-in-law as well as by their husbands and fathers (for more about this issue, see Sect. 5.2).
9. *Shame.* Poverty itself generates feelings of shame and low self-esteem for the reasons discussed above (see Sect. 2.2). Once again, it is worth calling attention to the fact that poor and needy people end up being blamed, directly or indirectly, for their situation, although they can, in fact, do nothing to combat the lack of education, lack of jobs that arise from factual circumstances which they have no control over. The poverty in the regions we visited, for example, is not cyclical but structural. It is not caused by temporary economic crises but by structural factors – a fact that showcases the need to complement emergency social assistance programs (like the BF) with other programs and policies designed to alter the structure, such as programs dealing with culture and education, housing and electrification, etc. Even still, we witnessed that the subjectivity of these people was strongly marked by shame. Several times and in several different fashions, we witnessed its expression, e.g., we have already mentioned how they were often greatly embarrassed to invite us into their simple homes, which were gen-

[24] "A serious study of poverty ought to measure the inequality existing within households, which is frequently to the detriment of women and old people" (Dieterlen, 2005, 24).

erally lacking furniture, such as chairs for us to sit on or tables where we could make notes. Immediately, the owner of the house would apologize repeatedly for the lack of these things. Other times, we could tell the humiliation and shame stamped across the faces of the husbands, usually unemployed, who kept their heads down with sad and melancholy looks on their faces while their wives were interviewed. Sometimes, they would leave the house so as not to have to listen to their wives speak of their poverty.

After 5 years of interviews we could tell that the program had reached one of its main objectives, since the BF had guaranteed the right to life for millions of Brazilians. It had not, however, resolved the problem of poverty. This is particularly obvious when we look at the situation of the poor men in regard to regular income and the increase in self-esteem. In fact, the husbands normally had few hopes of working and improving their lives. They had no future in the part of the country where the research took place. The dominant pattern saw them traveling across the country in search of work which was seasonal and uncertain. These people lived a precarious life in all senses of the word: precarious ties, precarious emotions, precarious social relations because their underemployment was also precarious. In large part, they were illiterate, as were their wives, or they had had 2 or 3 years of schooling at most. Generally, they lacked the skills for any productive activity. At best, they might get a bricklayer's assistant job in the cities. In the countryside, they could work in seasonal harvests and earn R$15 or 20 per shift for work that was unpredictable and short-lived. On the other hand, there was the relentless alcoholism. It was a highly demoralizing condition that could make people turn violent. They were systematically rejected and, therefore, subject to many types of humiliation, by their families, by the local police officers who arrested them, beat them up and then released them even more humiliated than ever. This, of course, reinforced any violent tendencies and their eternal recidivism in relation to drink. There was no support program or assistance for them. Alcoholism was seen by everyone as a moral failure, so the path was already laid out leading to humiliation. The drunk, the irresponsible one, became their stigma that sometimes accompanied them throughout their lives. Faced with this situation, what did it mean for them to separate from their wives and lose their families? A separation made them even more destitute, even more vulnerable to society's humiliations. Having a wife and children ensured something at least: a home, food, a bed to sleep in, in short, a human sort of existence. Without this, they wandered through this world brutalized, little more than animals. They wandered around as "refugees from the earth". They were rejected by everyone, often appearing to have been kicked out of humanity itself.

The women, when they could, tried to free themselves from a family life with these men. Their reasons were obvious: they tried to live and to raise their children with some dignity, protect them from the violence of the drunk – impossible things that they are obliged to share with their children, the tragedy of having an alcoholic in the family. Unfortunately, this was a common and persistent problem, almost endemic to the situation of poverty.

10. *Culture of resignation.* The best Brazilian literature has always portrayed the poor, giving them a voice with which to express the emotions and sentiments that had been silenced by a culture of deep resignation. This culture came to the surface many times in our interviews, not only by way of words (at times an adverb, an interjection, an adjective, were enough to reveal it) but also in the gestures, an expression on the face, the tired bodies, the clouded look in the eyes, the fallen shoulders. They accepted their situation as a natural or inevitable fate. Their only hope was that their children might escape this from it, as they had no more hopes for themselves. In addition, there was a tendency to significantly reduce the scope of their desires and preferences. This phenomenon reflected a common experience: we tend to hope for things that are within our reach, foregoing in advance those that are unachievable. This tendency is especially evident among the poor, who are aware of the limitations of their situation. Sen says,

> Desires reflect compromises with reality, and reality is harsher to some than to others. The hopeless destitute desiring merely to survive, the landless laborer concentrating his efforts on securing the next meal, the round-the-clock domestic servant seeking a few hours of respite, the subjugated housewife struggling for a little individuality, may all have learned to keep their desires in line with their respective predicaments. Their deprivation are gagged and muffled in the interpersonal metric of desire fulfillment. (Sen 1985, 191)

People who can barely meet their most miserable needs are highly unlikely to develop desires that transcend those needs. Material deprivation corresponds to a subtraction of hope, to the impossibility to dream and to desire something different than a life limited to meeting their most basic needs. Once again, material misery leads to spiritual poverty. Little is hoped for, so that the suffering will be lessened if this little is not achieved. Any dream of substantial improvements in their way of life is renounced so that the inevitable failure of this dream might not destroy the naïve mind of those who dare to imagine the impossible.[25]

However, the same literature describing the spirit of resignation of the Brazilian poor has never failed to recount that, like all cultures, this socially produced set of mental habits, sentiments and emotions is susceptible to change. Historically, great social revolutions, as well as systematic and persistent democratic policies put into practice with the primary purpose to put an end to exclusion and poverty, have managed to alter significantly, and sometimes even profoundly, this traditional resignation.[26]

---

[25] For more on this topic, see Burstin et al. 2010.

[26] The mechanisms that lead to the fall of this culture of resignation may be the most varied. Examples can be found, even if in contexts very distinct from those under study, in the anti-colonial struggle as described by Frantz Fanon and Jawaharlal Nehru among others (Fanon 2004 and Nehru 2004). In Brazil, it is worth mentioning the popular revolutions that started during the Empire, the Peasant Leagues of the 1950s, and continuing on until the struggles of the Landless Workers' Movement.

11. *Exclusion from citizenship*. The poor remain excluded from citizenship in two senses, the formal and the material. In a material sense, they have neither work nor regular income, and therefore they have no permanent collective ties other than those of the family or neighborhood. Formally speaking, many of them lack updated documents. In some cases, they do not even have an identity card, which prevents them even from registering for the program. The civil existence of a person relative to the state is an important element in their constitution as a citizen. Without it, they cannot request services, because without that document they do not exist in the eyes of the state. The efforts of central and local officials to improve this situation (as witnessed in Piauí by the presence of mobile notaries that go out into the most remote regions to update people's documents) is an important step towards this formal inclusion. The latter, in turn, represents an indispensable step towards civic inclusion, as it allows people to participate in elections and political activity.

Chapter 5
Money and Autonomy

> [W]ages provide an altogether new freedom within the framework of his dependency. […] Since freedom means independence from the will of others, it commences with independence from the will of specific individuals.
>
> Georg Simmel[1]

> • Because we've got more freedom with money.
> • Why have you got more freedom?
> • Because we can buy more of what we want, you know?
>
> Interview with Dona Amélia,
> Pasmadinho (Jequitinhonha Valley), July 2008

After 5 years of interviews and traveling through the poorest regions of Brazil, which lack mostly in state services, we can attest to the fact that the BF program produced significant change in the lives of its grantees. One such change constitutes the first steps towards overcoming the culture of resignation, in other words, the resigned wait to starve to death or to die from diseases of poverty. This was a drama that was commonplace in this world: its lament was the subject of most of the songs and popular poetry of the region. The greatest Brazilian writers have written their masterpieces against the backdrop of the hunger and misery of our fellow citizens.

In the following section, we will take up once more and then develop more deeply a common thread that has run through our entire project: the relationship between money and personal autonomy. In doing so, we will present what we see to be the most important impact that receiving a regular monthly income has had on the people whom we studied.

[1] Simmel 2011, 324.

A. Pinzani, W. L. Rego, *Money, Autonomy and Citizenship*,
https://doi.org/10.1007/978-3-030-01361-5_5

5.1 Money and Individual Autonomy

In a large majority of families studied, the BF represented the only money these people received. In several cases, it was the first time these people had ever received a regular income. Beforehand, life had been limited to a daily struggle to find food, whether that might have come from hunting, or from the help of family members. At times, it seemed like one of the contemplations of Fabiano, a character in the Brazilian masterpiece *Barren Lives* by Graciliano Ramos, "That was what we hunted. It was miserly, but it put off the death of the group." (Ramos 1986, 14, our translation from the Portuguese). This is sufficient justification for saying that income in the form of money has historically been the very condition for beginning the process of freeing people up from the urgent drive to stay alive and, equally, the process of changing people's mentality. As Simmel says, the fact that people turn into "determined" people due to monetary income brings up paradoxical issues. For example, income allows for the depersonalization of subjects while simultaneously leading to their individualization. The person becomes a mere performer of a certain function (a consumer, for example). To this extent, the individual is as indifferent as "a guest in a hotel room" (Simmel 2011, 320). Contradictorily, this indifference frees the person from traditional ties that restrict their freedom of movement and freedom of profession. Thus, it permits something akin to the enjoyment of some civil rights. A relationship of personal domination almost inevitably entails the control of people's intimate desires and personal emotions. It limits the scope of the subject's activities to the point of depriving them of functional abilities and, moreover, of individuality, when this latter is taken to indicate an individual endowed with a certain level of autonomy. Thus, this terminology has many facets, including that which Marx called "extra-economic coercion." (see Marx 1964) In this sense, income frees people from relationships of private oppression and personal control over one's intimacy, while it also confers a socially determined function and enables greater movement and, thereby, novel experiences. In the case of the extremely poor, it may happen that such experiences end up incurring other types of social suffering that are experienced, in conjunction with greater personal freedom, which may be the freedom to "sell one's own skin". It could even be the tragic end of Macabéa, a character of the novel *The Hour of the Star* by Clarice Lispector (1992). She is one of so many poor, northeastern women who carry with them the *sertanejo* legacy of repression, hunger and abuse when they migrate to a big city like Rio de Janeiro in search of a better life. In her case, among her dreams, she cherishes that of becoming a movie star and, encouraged by a fortuneteller's prophecy, she hopes to marry a blond man with blue eyes. She had, as Clarice herself would have said, nostalgia for the future: she searches for her dream but finds it, allegorically, when she is run over by a car and goes on to vomit stars, those stars on the vehicle, which is a Mercedes Benz, made in a land of blond men with blue eyes.

In any event, all experience outside the domain of personal relationships and dependence confirms the role of money in dissolving the inside of this world. Money and its function as a method of payment dissolves the customary obligations linked to the private nature of personal relationships: obligations and the provision of services that constitute personal dependence between people who interact but who are endowed with unequal levels of power. It is not hard to imagine the magnitude of these forms of appropriating the other and their desires, such as in the case of poor women. These women are deprived of any training in self-expression and are taught just those functions linked to tradition and habit, as if these had been determined by nature. Mill reminds us that habit and tradition can be forms of despotism, as hard to destroy as any other. These habits exert a symbolic effect on people's subjectivity, which for its part legitimizes them and makes them even seem 'necessary', particularly when their content and their modes of implementation are naturalized.

5.2 Family and Domination

It bears repeating that it is rare for women to manage to free themselves from marital oppression in the poor and backward parts of Brazil, due to the tight control exerted upon these women by their families. The interviews revealed that it is possible to glimpse a few potential acts of liberation in this regard.

The fact that the BF card comes in these women's names was seen positively by almost all of them. The classic answer to this question was that they were better managers of the household economy and that their husbands either were incapable of making the adequate purchases to meet the family's needs, or they would spend the money on drink. According to Dona Graciele from Inhapi, if the money went to the husband, "well, he'd take it and would go drink *cachaça*." Dona Neusa from Maragogi reacted to the question, saying, "It's deadly. Men are sneaky.[…] We become more independent when you put the card in the name of the person herself..."

The grantees, in general, approved of the program. However, they did not fail to emphasize the insufficiency of the grant to achieve greater improvements in life and to gain greater freedom of choice regarding consumer goods. They called for more income, due to the almost total lack of potential regular jobs. It is worth pointing out that their expectations were limited, and that they only hoped to achieve a more dignified life including housing slightly better than their miserable huts which are typically poorly lit, poorly ventilated and much too small to house an entire family.

It is worth taking note of the small beginnings of autonomy in these women. We can say that these first steps represented new personal and collective achievements. However, we cannot say that the construction of a social identity based on their autonomy was a quick process. On the contrary, the deeply rooted nature of submission in these people's identities means that it will take a long, and arduous process before these shackles are broken. Another issue relates to gender difference. Seyla Benhabib reminds us, rightly, that the difference between the masculine and the feminine as a product of culture and civilization cannot be explained merely in terms of social roles:

> Liberal feminism takes a very superficial view of people and a very limited understanding of the relationships between gender and identity. Let us take one simple example: a woman may become a neurosurgeon but may suffer abuse in her private life. In that domain, she may be subjected to situations of inequality, be an abused woman and feel terrible insecurity and feelings of inadequacy regarding being a woman. In this sense, the theory of gender does not explain how gender is part of women's identities, their fantasies, their subconscious. In other words, what they are and how they perceive themselves to be in the world. It seems to me that the theory of roles is superficial in political and legal institutions. Their goal is the public person and for that reason, they do not inquire about the deeply individual identity that is behind the public persona. (Benhabib 1992)

In order to minimally delineate the domination women are subject to, we must turn once again to John Stuart Mill's *The Subjection of Women*. In this insightful work, Mill unravels a puzzle about the nature of women's domination and deciphers some of its main mechanisms. The most powerful relates to the lack of women's sovereignty over their own lives, their own bodies, as well as over the decisions made about them. These are prickly issues in and of themselves and they are, in fact, some of the most difficult studied by sociology. This is especially true when, as is the case in Brazil and particularly in the regions in question, you are dealing with women who are very poor and subject to many types of domination. Mill helps us to understand that women's subjugation is different from than that of other individuals and social classes. These observations lead us to perceive that personal freedom can be thought of as individual, subjective autonomy and, moreover, as having the ability to become an autonomous agent so that, for example, as an effective consumer, one might go into the market and decide on at least some of the purchases to make. The despotism of custom, as Mill called it, destroys all freedom, including the basic freedom linked to a minimum of financial independence, which is the first step towards realizing the goal of personal self-governance. The lack of this minimum acts at the deepest level of subjectivity and prevents people from acquiring the conditions to turn themselves into subjects of right who might demand social justice. This, once again, represents a deficit of capabilities.

We witnessed cases in which getting a regular monetary income permitted some women to leave difficult marriages, thus gaining greater personal liberty. That was the case, for example, of Dona Madalena, resident in the countryside outside of Inhapi, in the *sertão* of Alagoas (see Sect. 3.1.3). But the very story of Madalena, who got back together with her husband and then had to face the same old problems, demonstrates how difficult it is for these women to leave their marriages – whether due to social pressure or their incapacity to take control of their lives. This is one more example of the lack of capabilities and, therefore, a lack of freedom.[2]

---

[2] "The human faculties of perception, judgment, discriminative feeling, mental activity, and even moral preference, are exercised only in making choices. He who does anything because it is the custom, makes no choice. He gains no practice either in discerning or in desiring what is best. The mental and moral, like the muscular powers, are improved only by being used" (Mill 1991, 65). There is an artistic memory that relates here as well. Just think about the lines of Cesare Sterbini in *Barber of Seville*, the famous opera by Gioachino Rossini, when Fígaro says: "at the idea of this metal [money]…a volcano within me commences to erupt." The Italian philosopher Vittorio Mathieu says, "pay attention to the concept: that metal acts on his mind like an idea that gives him other ideas" (Mathieu 1991).

Freedom from the "dictatorship of misery"[3]and from the extensive control of their fates exerted by male family members affords these women a minimal ability to plan their own lives. To this extent, the BF enabled them to begin to gain autonomy regarding their moral lives. The latter element is the foundation of citizenship, if it is understood as an indispensable condition for the achievement of political autonomy by these subjects.

As was seen in the interview, a hint of choices, including moral ones, has just begun to be felt. The right to choose is exercised from the broadest aspect of planning one's own life, down to the ability to decide between more of one kind of food or another, or a piece of clothing, or a hair crème, and so on. This may set up an avenue to greater personal liberty – a totally different situation than that of a woman who was previously excluded objectively and subjectively from this sphere. Their fate, from birth to death, was recorded deeply within their subjectivities. They would be poor. At a young age, they would marry equally young men who were also poor. They would live in shacks, and they would not even be able to choose the number of children they wanted to have. As the Argentine philosopher Alejandra Ciriza said, we are faced with a "destiny anchored in our bodies". In other words, women are destined to live a certain type of life due to their biological and corporeal specifications (Ciriza 2002, 223). Body and destiny blend into an oppressive and fatal combination for these women. Wanting or even achieving an operation in order to have their tubes tied represents a first step towards controlling their own bodies and, therefore, controlling part of their destiny.

The women, from the moment they begin to receive monetary income, take command of some sort of human capacity, such as choosing between options, including, as mentioned above, making moral choices. Our humanity rests fundamentally on the permanent exercise of choice.[4] However, in situations of misery and deprivation of the most elementary resources in life, one does not choose. One lives in perpetual motion, the "vicious circle of poverty," which is characterized by the near impossibility of personally choosing the kind of life one wants to live. To paraphrase Graciliano Ramos, the deprived person lives always hearing the horn of death pushing him along all the time! Making him "dance on the asphalt like a crazy cockroach" (Ramos 1986a, 143 our translation from the Portuguese). This circle will only be broken in the future, specifically in the future of the children of these women. Several times we asked some of them if they could imagine a world that was fairer. They almost always answered in this way: if it exists, they arrived late to it. Now, their hopes lay in ensuring such a world for their children. Who knows? Maybe their children would become less destitute than they were. (See, e.g. the interviews with Dona Cássia and Dona Marinilda in Piri-Piri, PI in Sect. 3.3.4). As Fabiano, the character from *Barren Lives* observed,

> Could he change his luck? If they told him that it was possible to improve his situation, he would be surprised. He had come into the world to break horses, cure wounds by praying, fix fences from winter to summer. It was his fate. His father had lived like this, his grandfather as well. He had been born with this destiny, no one could blame him for having been born with a bad fate. What could he do? (Ramos 1986, 96, our translation).

[3] Hannah Arendt discusses this issue in several works.

[4] This idea is central to the thinking of Amartya Sen, as was discussed in Chap. 2.

5.3 Money and the Morality of Spending

Money frees people from the land they were born on, and it enables them to move. It permits them to migrate to other places, to leave a harmful family situation or a situation of personal dependency tied to a specific location. That is why Simmel reminds us that "money, as the most mobile of all goods, [...] is really that form of property that most effectively liberates the individual from the unifying bonds that extend from other objects of possession" (Simmel 2011, 383). Let us not forget as well the differentiation of social functions conferred upon people by the use of money as a method of payment. These functions constitute processes of differentiation and are, therefore, a strong factor in individualization. We should also recall that without people endowed with mobility, we cannot even think of citizenship and rights, especially regarding civil rights, since the ability to move and to circulate is part of the essence of the concept. Market capitalism would be unimaginable without this prerogative: the free movement of people from one place to another, whereby their very perceptions of time and place are altered. The world becomes wider, space spreads out and time expands, creating possibilities of greater command of the world on the part of free people. As the words of the song by Gilberto Gil says: "Time and space navigate all the senses". And who knows, the world will turn and again in the words of the singer "time, the king, transforms the old ways of living" (Gilberto Gil, *Tempo Rei,* our translation).

Let us remember that the fact that these women receive monetary income does not change their condition as poor people. Having greater assurance of being able to feed your own family, however, has an impact that surpasses the merely material. It is psychological as well. This effect is felt on at least two levels. Firstly, people no longer need to pass all their time thinking exclusively about how to find enough food, and they can pursue a wide range of activities (including economic ones). This is a way to gain autonomy, to free oneself from the most basic and immediate need, that of feeding oneself. At a second level, they gain autonomy, as they become responsible for the way they use the money in their pockets. In this sense, it is necessary to study closely the way that structuring factors such as culture, religion, social context and their condition as women constitute important influences on the way they use this money, how they allocate it to the economy of the home, thereby conferring significant meanings upon this act. This leads us to consider the symbolic dimension of money. We see an example of this in the story of Dona Carmen and her nephew the painter that we told in Sect. 3.4.1.

Viviana Zelizer (Zelizer 1989, 353) recalling other studies on this topic, mentions the existence of a type of morality of household spending, according to which, certain uses of money would be considered more legitimate than others for families, especially regarding its use by women. In the case of the BF, we perceived this, even if not immediately. Only after long conversations did we hear, in a confessional tone, stories about purchases not directly related to food for the family or school material for the children. The women were even more reticent when we asked if they used the money to buy anything for themselves. Some of the women 'confessed' with a visible, if unjustified, feeling of guilt that they occasionally used the BF grant to buy lipstick or hair crème. These attitudes constitute a sort of morality of spending that weighs heavily on their subjectivities.

Therefore, it should be stressed that the phenomenon of monetization of people's lives is very complex and multifaceted. As Simmel warned, the effect of money on people is not homogeneous, exactly because its multiple functions act in many ways on a multitude of subjectivities. There is a great temptation to react with express contempt in an ideological operation of imputing negative attributes to those whom you consider unequal. Frequently there is the danger of making aspersions against all of a group of people when faced with certain facts. This is especially so when dealing with poor people and how they deal with money, even more so when it comes from a state cash transfer programs. Ideological mental mechanisms are immediately triggered that disqualify the poor. "They" are freely given negative identities, as though they were preordained by nature: the poor are like this; they do this or that; they feel things like this. The differences in social conditions are sufficient justification for a prejudiced mind to speak judgmentally of others. On the contrary, there is the insightful intuition of Riobaldo, the philosophical bandit from *The Devil to Pay in the Backlands* by Guimarães Rosa. Based on a wealth of experience gathered throughout a tired life that had been full of torment and suffering and yet was luminous in its lucidity and finesse, he said "You, sir, look see: the most important and the most beautiful in the world is this: that people aren't always alike, they haven't been finished yet – but they are always changing. Coming into tune, going out of tune. Greatest truth. That is what life has taught me."

Therefore, supposing that anything that impacts people in their tremendous diversity, particularly the poor, and especially poor women, may have a homogeneous effect is nothing more than prejudice and elitist stereotyping. Understanding the differences among the epochs, the time of each person, demands another way of understanding a set of social relationships that surrounds the individuality of people, marking them as at once distinct and similar, a phenomenon, once more, well understood by Riobaldo who comments that:

> Are we all crazy in this world? Because people all got the same head. And the things that there are and those that will come to be are too many, too muchly greatly different, and we got to need to grow our heads to fit it all. All of the things happening, the strong feelings we have – that's what makes the wind blow. We can only live together with a body, know somebody, without hating them, if we got love. Any love is already a tad bit of health, a rest from the crazies (Our translation.)

5.4 Credit as Autonomy and Dignity

Many of the women told us that, from the moment they started getting a BF grant, they were able to get credit at the markets and the stores where they usually shopped. As Dona Inês, from Demerval Lobão in the state of Piauí, said, "the BF card is the only thing that's brought me credit in life, before I didn't have anything." Here we come across a meaning for the term "credit" that surpasses the merely economic and refers to a dimension of trust and reliability that are important steps towards the dignification of a person. A common saying in certain parts of the Brazilian countryside says, "If you can't run a tab, you don't exist."

The need is highlighted, therefore, for policies aimed at creating instruments of credit for the poorest segment of the population. In this context, it is worth mentioning the question of micro-credit that has gained much awareness and that we will discuss below.

Receiving monetary incomes brought to many of these women a decisive element, the dignification of their person and the personal emotions that experience provoked. We return, once again, to the interview with Dona Inês. This young woman told us that the BF card conferred upon her, in addition to reliability, more dignity in the eyes of the community. Let us refer back to the debate carried out in the monetary theory of economics about this issue. It points out that money serves as a guarantee of trustworthiness and that this aspect becomes an extremely strong psycho-sociological factor of an almost religious nature, particularly for the poor and the disinherited and especially for women (see Laidler and Rowe 1980, 99).

Generally speaking, the BF grantees were not familiar with the experience of having regular monetary income and the reliability that they then came to enjoy among local business people, in addition to so many other social demands that contribute to a dignified life. Achieving reliability was seen by almost all of them as one more positive benefit to the grant, since being a trustworthy person is an important value in these parts: it represent the acquisition of more respectability and is experienced as an increase in self-respect. Being the object of distrust bring them very negative emotions, as well as great personal suffering, because it imposes shame and humiliation, which are central elements in the processes of destroying their dignity as people. So, it is worth taking another look at the astute observations of Avishai Margalit about the effects of shame and humiliation (Margalit 1996). He points out that these feelings might incapacitate people to act and, therefore, to fight for their rights, thereby hindering even more the establishment of active citizenship.

The words of Dona Ines once again elucidate us. When asked about how she felt when she got her BF card, she emphasized, first of all, the value of money for anything that you might need or want to do: "Everything that you want to do in life is with money, it's paying." Ines's words reinforce our intent to emphasize as strongly as possible the importance of the BF coming in the form of money. This money serves as an enhancer of greater personal and inner freedom on the part of those who have gained a monetary income.

5.4.1 An Aside: Microcredit and its Limits

Microcredit has become the model of empowerment of the poor, and women in particular, in both academic and public discourse. India is the textbook example. However, our research there[5] showed us grave problems in its implementation. In

[5]This refers to a 2009 Ford Foundation research project comparing Indian microcredit with the Brazilian BF.

the first place, most of the Indian banks that carry out microcredit policies are private and not public. It is important to clarify that the loans are small, but the same thing is not true of the interest rates that users pay. NGOs serve as intermediaries between the women borrowers and banks. According to information we obtained from the NGO Ujjivan in New Delhi, the annual interest rate on a microcredit loans at that institution was 24% in 2009.[6] Banks practice interest rates between 10% and 20%, depending on the amount of the loan.[7] Default by the client can represent demoralization and, consequently, shame or even suicide.[8] According to Sudhirendar Sharma, a former World Bank analyst and now director of the Ecological Foundation in New Delhi, microcredit is part of the problem of suicide in the countryside, and it is affecting women who cannot repay their loans. Sharma complains about interest rates as high as 40% per year, which are tantamount to usury. Moreover, there are aggressive collection techniques such as social and moral pressure caused by the obligatory participation in self-help groups organized by the NGOs that are intimidating these poor women instead of empowering them.

For many critics of microcredit, the concept of empowerment becomes void of meaning, if it is limited mostly to the capacity to take responsibility for taking out and repaying loans. Although there were great expectations created around the promise of microcredit, many analysts have argued that the high expectations of improvements in the lives of these women are not something that depends only on the right to credit, as many enthusiasts appear to believe.

Other empirical analysts have shown that access to credit is not sufficient for these women to become empowered. According to Thelma Kay (Kay 2002, 71), responsible institutions often fail to pay attention to how the credit is conferred upon the client and how it is used by families. Many male businessmen continue having a prominent role in using the loans to women in their families. They become hidden participants, with enough power to maintain the distinction between typically male and female activities. This reaffirms the traditional roles of gender and the exclusion of women from family income. In our visit to Ujjivan, the person responsible for presenting the institution's work expressly stated that it is much more common for the husbands to administer the loans that the wives take out. This complacency with the unequal hierarchical division between male and female roles is a strong argument against the expectations by the proponents of microcredit that the initiative would contribute to female emancipation. David Hulme and Paul Mosley (1998) also showcased the perverse effects of the program also in cases where the clients met with success in setting up their microbusinesses. Research in the state of Gujarat showed that many women pulled their daughters out of school so that they could work to help support the family. The choice of the daughters is deliberate since the school-aged boys are not given such responsibilities.

---

[6] Data available at: http://www.ujjivan.com/monthly_newsletter_july_2009.htm.

[7] Data available at: http://www.gdrc.org/icm/icm-peoplebanks.html.

[8] It must be understood that suicide by Indian farmers is a problem. It is estimated that 87,000 farmers committed suicide in 2006. Default on debt is one of the reasons listed for such a desperate act. Information available at: http://knowledge.allianz.com/en/globalissues/microfinance/microcredit/microfinance_debt_trap.html. Accessed on 12/03/2008.

Obtaining access to credit does not necessarily lead to gaining a feeling of personal value or a belief in their potential to become entrepreneurs. In order to explain this lack of success, it was pointed out that there were problems in the relationships between the clients and staff at this NGO. Moreover, there was an almost complete focus on the economic well-being of these women. Ensuring their empowerment entailed much more than merely guaranteeing access to credit. From the point of view of the women, other factors that might contribute to their feeling greater dignity and quality of life seem equally important. This fiction about the right to credit seems to have been the weak spot in the Indian microcredit experiment. It must be understood that the rhetoric of growth and/or the rise of the idea of empowering women through microcredit has become the new orthodoxy in the discussion of Asian economic development. However, the actual interests of the women themselves seem to be often subordinated to the priorities of economic development and institutional profit and this is not always compatible with the expectations regarding women's rights. To conclude, these findings about the limitations of Indian policies of microcredit reveal that the demands of moral autonomy far surpass that which the narrative of access to credit seems to provide.[9]

5.5 The Multiple Functions of Money

The sociology of money has shown time and again that the many functions of money far transcend its practical roles such as those of measuring and saving, of serving as a method of payment, and as a universal instrument of exchange. Money has two faces, just like Janus: it frees people and it oppresses them. At the same time that is an instrument of freedom, it also produces interpersonal relationships that ensnare people more and more. With each increase in freedom, there is a subsequent rise in responsibility and a paradoxical loss of liberty. Georg Simmel described this contradictory process:

> The development of each human fate can be represented as an uninterrupted alternation between bondage and release, obligation and freedom. This initial appraisal, however, presents us with a distinction whose abruptness is tempered by closer investigation. For what we regard as freedom is often in fact only a change of obligations; as a new obligation replaces one that we have borne hitherto, we sense above all that the old burden has been removed. Because we are free from it, we seem at first to be completely free – until the new duty, which initially we bear, as it were, with hitherto untaxed and therefore particularly strong sets of muscles, makes its weight felt as these muscles, too, gradually, tire. The process of liberation now starts again with this new duty, just as it had ended as this very point (Simmel 2011, 305)

In our case, this means that there is a perception of monetary income that simultaneously brings more freedom to the BF grantees while it also weighs them down with

[9] We owe a debt to Márcia Baratto, a doctoral candidate from Unicamp, Brazil for the collection and organization of this data about the moral and political effects of microcredit among poor Indian women. She joined us during our research in that country.

the need to deal with the new situation. Whichever function of money we are dealing with requires human actors behind it in order to manipulate it. Furthermore, it allows them to develop the capacity to minimally plan their lives with complex strategies and calculations. The BF grantees are learning to deal with it, i.e. to overcome the lack of such strategies and calculation. As they recounted how hard it was to stretch their limited funds to the end of the month, they sometimes gave a nervous laugh as if to highlight the fact that they were used to a shortage of cash. Even more often, their faces clouded over and took on an expression of distress.

The monetization of life, which is marked by the wide spectrum of possible uses of money, points primarily to learning its symbolic function. This is particularly true in the case of the BF and the experience of women getting regular income for the first time. Along these lines, Enrico Donaggio and Peter Kammerer wrote about Marx's theory of money,

> "the magic of money is the most real thing that can be. Its power arises in the nocturnal sacrificial rites in the temples. From there it moves into the mundane worship of the circulation of goods and takes on more strength, capable of turning all flaws and vices into virtue. In this manner, the possession of money supplants the strategies of happiness prescribed by the great religions, who then defame it as being the devil's dung" (Donaggio & Kammerer, in Marx 2007, 98, our translation from the Portuguese).

Money is an empty form, so it can be coated with numerous capacities and functions as we have already said. One of these roles is precisely that of symbolizing the relationship between objects, or between objects and the world. In this role, money orients and measures people, because social needs are not fixed. They change, and they do so constantly due to the general development of society. As part of this process, the monetary patterns of acquiring life's basic essentials transform, as do the relationships between people and these basic goods, due to the new cultural and symbolic changes within society (see Pollock 1973, 69 and ff., especially 76). Adam Smith had already perceived that the relationship between culture and the possibility of acquiring goods was constantly being redefined by new habits and he also realized how this redefinition acted upon people's subjectivities, "Custom… has rendered leather shoes a necessary of life in England. The poorest creditable person of either sex would be ashamed to appear in public without them" (Smith 1976, 870).

Money as a mere method of payment puts objects and their owners on the same level, as Marx reminds us about people who purchase things, "[...] a worker who buys a loaf of bread and a millionaire who does the same appear in this act as simple buyers, just as, in respect to them, the grocer appears only as seller. All other aspects are here extinguished. The *content* of these purchases, like their extent, here appears as completely irrelevant compared to the formal aspect" contained in the money (Marx 1993, 251; see also Smelt 1980, Zelizer 1989 and Deutschmann 1996). In this case, Marx argues that money is once again fulfilling its role as a radical leveler.

In short, money showcases its broad social nature. It is full of nuances and paradoxes and even contradictions. It can bring people together while also fulfilling other social functions. One of these, and one of the most important, is that which both Marx and Simmel called the power of dissolution. If, on the one hand, money dissolves traditional ties of time and space, on the other hand, it can bring people together in new social configurations, e.g. as subjects of their own volition who can come together to overcome certain historical situations. About this Simmel said, "In that the purely monetary relationship ties the individual very closely to the group as an abstract whole and in that this is because money [...] is the representative of abstract group forces, the relationship of individual persons to others simply duplicate the relationship that they have to objects as a result of money" (Simmel 2011, 324).

Thus, money contributes to the process of individuation by imposing more mobility on subjects but also by introducing more emotional instability into their lives. A similar process is enough to effect important changes of their subjectivities. It is worth remembering that money is neither culturally nor morally neutral. Its symbolic influence is allocated in unexpected ways on the emotions and sentiments of people (in our case the BF grantees). Something along these lines can be seen in the words of several of them, i.e. in the words of poor women who traditionally have faced many obstacles to the liberation of their personality and the expression of their most intimate feelings. Let us hear once again the words of Dona Fátima and Dona Rosangela, from the neighborhood of Anjo da Guarda, in the outskirts of São Luís do Maranhão (see Sect. 3.4.1). The former emphatically exclaimed "Look! This money is mine. Lula gave it to me to take care of my children and grandchildren. So, am I going to give it to my husband? I am not!" The second woman told us, "The grant has really changed my life. Look! It's been great!" Regarding the fact that she was now receiving regular money, she stated, "Ah! It was the first time that's happened to me! And that's how it should be because women are more careful with money than men."

The BF is not governmental charity (see our remarks above about Simmel). Instead, it ends up creating the conditions for a profound change in the emotional structure of the grantees. In their way, the women told us that in the interviews, as we saw above in the words of Dona Amélia, a resident of Pasmadinho, in the Jequitinhonha Valley. We asked her if she felt that this income had changed her hard life. She answered yes and added, "We've got more freedom now with the money."

Moreover, in this inventory of the multiple functions of money, we should remember that there are communicative functions as well, a long-debated issue. Why does it play a communicative role? It demands both the actual and potential circulation of people. In other words, it inevitably requires greater contact with the world, especially in the case of the women we are looking at. They felt that, and they told us so clearly. In many places, in fact, their isolation was to a certain extent broken. We cannot neglect the cultural factors that weigh on these women and that impede their free circulation. Martha Nussbaum, recounting her experience of researching women in India, talks about how tradition and culture can serve as factors of oppression and injustice, thereby, restricting women's movements (Nussbaum 2000, 15 ff.). However, having a certain sum of money helps people to circulate more widely and more freely.

> "Ah! Money in my pocket brought me out of the house!" said Dona Maria Joaquina, a 24 year-old mother of five children. "Now I have to leave my lair more often. I go shopping, and experiment with things I wasn't familiar with."

"Such as?"
"The other day I bought my kids yogurt and pasta."
"So, you like the program?"
"I think it's really good."

5.6 Money and Political Autonomy

Many of the women, when asked, did not know what 'citizen' meant. They did not, therefore, see themselves as citizens, as members of a broader community than that of their city, which continued to be their political point of reference. From this perspective, the BF created a tie of belonging to a political community, at least a potential one. Nevertheless, it becomes essential to implement a policy of civic education aimed at better integrating these people. Their feelings of belonging need to be nurtured, as does their sense of belonging to a greater community, that of the nation.

The question about whether the BF is a favor or a duty of the state is one of the most difficult for them to understand. Some of them just looked at us in surprise and said, "Ah! It's a favor because nobody's done this for us before." The past without any assistance at all from the state appears to support the idea of a favor, of the BF constituting a gift. This notion will only change when there are citizenship policies instituted similar to those described throughout this manuscript, i.e. integrative policies intended to create public spaces for people to come together, debate and deliberate, in short, all of that which Tocqueville called the "school of freedom".

Public policies, even those that are compensatory, are to some extent able to better prepare citizens in the substantive sense, due to the moral and ethical dimensions inherent to governmental cash transfers. This fact, in and of itself, is key to redefining the patterns of democratic life in society. According to testimony gathered from some people in the region that have been active in social movements, the re-election of President Lula da Silva in 2006, after an intense media campaign attacking his government and his party, highlighted the beginning of a change in the traditional electoral maps in Brazil. Several patronage-based politicians and political parties whose strongest base was in this region began to suffer important losses in the subsequent local, regional and national elections. At differing rates, the references and the political patterns deeply rooted in the structures of many people's sentiments and mental habits have begun to change.

The French political scientist Bernard Manin has called our attention to this process of people's growing political autonomy as they break out of isolation:

> The less isolated people feel, the more they realize their potential strength, and the more capable they are to organize themselves and exercise pressure on the government. Awareness of a similarity of views may not always result in organization and action, but it is usually a necessary condition. Moreover, public expression of an opinion generates momentum. People who silently harbor an opinion that is voiced aloud by others become more self-confident when they discover that they are not alone in thinking that way, and thus they become more inclined to express that opinion. (Manin 1997, 171)

The complex configuration that results from these processes is what imposes difficulties on those people because their precarious human development has not enabled them to respect the collective agreements of civic conduct, which is one of the prerequisites of democratic life. This prevents them from developing what John Stuart Mill called the "capacity to cooperate" and that, according to Sen, could be called political capabilities. In this way, it becomes difficult to commit an entire collective to certain civilized patterns of social relations. This, in and of itself, puts at risk whatever economic development a country may hope for.

These observations are intended to show that, throughout this research, we took note of the fact that, despite its small scale, the federal BF program can be seen as a policy of "moral urgency" to use the words of Fraser (1997, 22 ff.). Nevertheless, its first results allowed us to discern the rudimentary conditions for turning it into a public policy of citizenship, thereby bringing about in Brazil a development that is not only economic but also political, and that is distinct from that which took place between 1930 and 1970. Now, it is possible to see this political development as part of a substantive enhancing of our democracy.

To varying extents, and still at an incipient level, it can be said that Brazil has taken the first steps towards building a democratic citizenship. This would be a decisive factor in the democratization of our society. This will certainly be a long and painful journey since we still lack specific cultural policies intended to free poor women and men, as well as blacks, nor have we erased century-old stereotypes and prejudices that weigh on their lives. In the case of the women, their freedom from the dictatorship of misery and from male family control of their fate might permit them a modicum of control over their moral lives. We do not intend, however, to state that this outline of autonomy is anywhere near the normative demands inherent to the Kantian concept of moral autonomy, which is a fundamental element of the so-called project of modernity and its promises of individual liberty. Nevertheless, it is commonly accepted that, without any level of moral and political autonomy, we cannot speak of citizenship. Active and autonomous citizens result from a long and determined democratic policy aimed at their construction.[10] Freedom, rather, the real possibility of experiencing it (according to the Senian idea of capability as freedom), is closely tied to the broadest social, economic and cultural conditions of society. In large part, they determine people's very ability to express themselves. As the historical leader of the Italian labor movement, Bruno Trentin states in a speech,

> At the origin of the most terrible inequalities there has always lain the denial of the freedom of those people who have been excluded from the distribution of resources, many times with the same force with which they have been denied the right to speak, to organize; in other words, they have been denied the very ability to even assert their very arguments (Trentin 1998, our translation from the Portuguese).

In a Brazilian democracy that is still immature and highly deficient regarding questions of citizenship, we briefly reaffirm the urgent need for further initiatives of this type, especially those consistent with what is currently called "cultural citizenship"

[10] For more on this long story, see, among others, Zincone 1992, Bendix 1964, Tilly 1990 and Costa 1999–2001.

because it depends on cultural policies which are intended to free from shame and humiliation that vast majority of people who are poor and deprived of their rights in innumerable ways. It is obvious that this set of policies refers to education understood in its broadest sense rather than that of mere literacy or professional training. It means adopting a policy that takes the quality of education into account and that targets the content transmitted by the media (especially by television). We are talking about a policy that provokes public debate, and that creates spaces for people to come together for discussion.

5.7 Basic Universal Income: Brief Reflections

For all the reasons discussed above, we would like to repeat our call for the institution of a conditional basic universal income (see Sect. 2.5) as an ongoing, fundamental right. This would contribute to realizing the potential on the part of all Brazilians, but particularly, the poorest ones and to ensure that they might live a dignified life. The guarantee of such an income would be the first step in a broad social process of moral and political change for those involved. To build a true democracy and to bolster it as a way of life, universal democratic citizenship must constantly be nurtured, and one of the mainstays of this process is generalized monetary income. This would increase the level of freedom and autonomy of all, especially those of the poor. This would bring into the realm of rights the husbands of the women BF grantees, the vast majority of whom are either unemployed or work only sporadically.

The guarantee of a universal basic income would be a decisive step towards recognizing the status as citizens of those large majorities of Brazilians who until today have been excluded from enjoying their basic civil, social and political rights, rights that give shape to human dignity and democratic citizenship. The right to monetary resources coming from state programs such as the BF and basic universal income could be incorporated into the notion of basic fundamental rights (cf. Ferrajoli 2002).[11] These would be similar to the citizenship rights defined by Bertram Pickard, who considers them to be equal to the right to land and the right to life (apud Pateman 2004).

It must always be emphasized, however, that within the set of rights, the right to life is the most basic, as it substantiates the right of a person to have rights (Arendt 1968, 296 f.). This must be the framework in which to place the current BF. Without the state allocation of resources that might ensure the minimal material conditions, a large number of poor Brazilians are in effect expelled from humanity, as Hannah Arendt so dramatically put it (Ibid.; see also Gourevitch 1986).

[11] The debate regarding the theoretical legal merit of the contemporary constitutional debate is beyond the scope of this work. As is well known, there is great controversy in this respect among the various schools of constitutionalists, especially regarding the type of basic and secondary rights that require basic and secondary guarantees by the state.

Thus, the state program of cash transfer in Brazil is not just a morally urgent policy that guarantees the right to life, but it represents the first step towards giving substance to our democracy. Throughout history, and in different national situations, it has been moral imperatives that, when recognized as such by the state, have led to the deepest democratic transformations. The experience of seeing one's life improve, as little as it may have, engraves itself deeply into people's souls. It opens their world up so that greater demands for freedom might arise. This is how what Marshall has called the "virtuous circle of rights" takes off (Marshall 1950): one right expands and triggers new demands for others and so on, indefinitely. This can be seen in the fact that the women interviewed never quit complaining about the insufficiency of the grant. They wanted more income. Perhaps the Gordian knot of the culture of resignation has begun to loosen. As Gramsci would say about what can be known a priori about the history of humans: the only certainty is the endless, arduous struggle. It is on the political plane, in the broadest sense, that the common destiny of the human race will be decided. (see Gramsci 1999 121ff.)

However, we must highlight an important issue. We have already seen that these women's range of choices expanded. As is known in democratic theory, exercising the right of choice and, thereby, having the ability to plan one's own life, may lead these women into the sphere of greater personal choice.

For all of these reasons, the anti-hunger policy and the BF can be seen as recognition on the part of the state of the moral and political calamity these women and their families live in. We cannot even speak seriously about democracy without resolving these predicaments. The resources dedicated to date have been limited, but this represents a new social process for Brazilians whose end and magnitude are still hard to evaluate.

It is good to remember that it is essential that democracy take root in the soil of society's institutions. However, this is not enough. The realization of the constitutional principles, i.e., putting into practice the rights established by said principles, demands struggle at various levels of social life. What is more, it demands that this struggle take place daily. We are dealing with a complex process of political and social construction that is long and difficult. Not only does it take a long time for rights to become demanded as such, but, as one of the founders of the Italian nation-state, Giuseppe Mazzini, has already warned us, said rights are born amid uproar (Mazzini 2002). So, it is a long road leading to their transformation into effective legal norms. This huge political, legal and social construction that brings together innumerable political subjects will be most profound if it can alter the mental and emotional structures of a given nation.

Closing Remarks

> The ugly hell of this world is that you will never see strength carrying justice on its back, nor the highest powers embracing only the greatest good.
>
> Guimarães Rosa
>
> *Grande Sertão: Veredas* [*Devil to Pay in the Backlands,* our translation from the Portuguese]

In previous chapters, we showed how our research verified that, despite its limited scope, the BF could be seen as a policy of moral urgency capable of setting up the minimal conditions for the development of political and ethical autonomy (this represents an important development of the concept of autonomy presented in Sect. 2.4). Notwithstanding, it contains the germ needed to transform itself into a public policy for citizenship, which might result in an economic development committed to the substantive enhancing of our democracy. As the democratic process gains strength, the chance of developing citizens who are more civically and politically autonomous grows. We are speaking of citizens who demand their rights and who are aware of their duties to the body politic.

Monetary Income and Civic and Political Autonomy

The distance between the spheres of ethical-moral autonomy and the civic-political one emerged from the interviews when the women spoke about their commitments to their families, on the one hand, and to the government on the other. The latter naturally included not only the conditions that had to be met for them to receive the grant but also the duty to vote. All of the women said they participated in elections, but some said that they did so just to avoid paying fines, while others told us they enjoyed voting. Not all of them, however, demonstrated enough awareness of the importance of their vote to their lives, although they did recognize the central role of Lula's government in setting up the BF and other social programs. Such contradictions can be explained by the tendency to identify the government with the figure

A. Pinzani, W. L. Rego, *Money, Autonomy and Citizenship*,
https://doi.org/10.1007/978-3-030-01361-5

of the president and to think that the assistance afforded by the BF had been given to them by Lula himself. Only a few of the women (the more literate and more articulate ones) expressed the idea that they had a right to the BF and that, as citizens, they had the right to receive help from the government so that they might escape hunger and misery. One of them even pointed out the fact that she was a citizen since she paid taxes (which is, in fact, true, if we consider indirect taxes on consumer goods) and that the government, therefore, had an obligation to her. Others said that their duty to vote corresponded to the right to receive assistance from the state, such as the BF. They did not say this because they considered it a form of vote exchange, as claimed by some critics of the program who have called it "the new patronage." In most cases, they understood that the state was requiring something of them, i.e., that they vote in every election, without, however, seeing them as citizens in the periods between elections. From their point of view, the state only saw them as voters, not as the subjects of rights and needs requiring responses from public policies.

The possible ramifications of the broadening and deepening of citizenship will be much more effective if the local authorities are committed to the issue, if the grantees are also the subject of local policies designed to encourage political participation. Local governments might, for example, set up various types of councils with different purposes, such as the social monitoring of the program, monitoring its implementation and registration and, most of all, listening to grantees' demands and denunciations of potential irregularities (such as enrollment fraud) and other problems that arise in everyday life. It is worth remembering the meeting we had with the women of Itinga, in the Jequitinhonha Valley. It came out that the management of the program lacked a democratic approach which might lead them to greater political autonomy. The local authorities, generally, limit themselves to managing the program; in other words, they merely register the users. There were innumerable complaints about the lack of preparation on the part of local managers. The fact that these positions were political appointments shielded them from any accountability. The majority of mayors did not see themselves as politicians concerned with creating stimulating environments for the development of their citizens. They had no interest in encouraging their citizens to participate more actively in the political life of the city or, in the case of the grantees, in the management of the program itself. This lack of local political authority (occasionally an actual physical absence, such as in the case described in Inhapi) and the fact that mayors rarely acted as civic politicians, explains, in part, the strong identification that these people felt with the figure of President Lula. It is our opinion that there is great room for local authorities to contribute to broadening the program to strengthen democracy and citizenship. There is truly the potential to make it a policy for citizenship. When this takes place, as we witnessed in a few places, the BF gains a new democratic nature, a new civic one.

It is important to look here at the various notions of the state that emerged in our interviews. The women saw the grant as a favor and as a gift. They had a clientelistic view of power, which they probably are familiar with and had experienced in their local context. According to such a view, power is an asset in the hands of one person or a group (*coronéis*, mayors, large landowners, local power bosses, etc.) who, arbitrarily and at whim, distribute favors among family members, friends, colluders, bosom buddies, etc. In exchange, the leaders demand loyalty, even political loyalty, from those favored (see Franco 1969). In this case, it is the culture of the client and not that of the citizens that takes precedence.

On the other hand, the women who thought of the grant as a right saw the state as an abstract entity but which gave and guaranteed rights and, theoretically, legal equality, "If I pay taxes then I'm a citizen like all the other taxpayers," one of the women said. These women demonstrated the likelihood (but not necessarily the truth) of the hypothesis just stated that economic independence was experienced as a condition for becoming a political citizen. Public social programs did not represent just assistance measures, as they aimed to include their grantees within the body politic. For this reason, they were programs of citizenship in the broadest sense of the word.

Citizenship, when seen as a process of people acquiring rights and the capacity to enjoy them, thereby, as the right and capacity to participate in the material and cultural legacy of civilization, sets up the possibility of implementing democratic political processes that are in constant expansion as more rights are written into legislation. This leads citizens to experience more fully their status as participants in an integrated and cohesive human community which might be a nation, but that is measured by universal patterns of values and material well-being.

Monetary Income and Ethical-Moral Autonomy

Regarding their commitments to their families, all of the women interviewed declared having obligations that resulted from being mothers. Furthermore, the vast majority of their expenditures other than for family food were destined for the children (clothes, school material, medications, sometimes toys, cookies, candies, etc.). The fact that the women had a positive reaction to the BF card coming in their name shows, in addition to the problems linked to the role of the men, that they considered themselves to be responsible for the management of the household economy. When the husband cooperated in this management (e.g., going shopping), the women still saw themselves and the true "head" of the household. This view of their position in the family did not appear to us to be a mere expression of the social roles resulting from a certain social and educational context (e.g., from that of their role as women and as mothers in the social environment specific to the Alagoas or Jequitinhonha society). Instead, it appeared to be a genuine commitment of responsibility to the children. This view is an expression of moral autonomy, if this is defined in the terms mentioned above.

This brings us to another issue: the relationship between the subjects' economic and moral autonomies. It appears that the former is understood by these women as a condition for the latter. Indigence and the lack of economic independence translate into the sensation that one's personality remains incomplete, unfinished. In our opinion, this far surpasses a simple feeling of frustration and achieves a much deeper level: How can I see myself as an active subject if I am unable to autonomously ensure my very existence (not to mention that of my family)? Political subjects themselves are normally seen (by normative theories and in the daily debate in the media) as economically autonomous players, or at least, they must be above the poverty line. It is important to bring up once more the thoughts of Amartya Sen and Martha Nussbaum about this topic. They believe there exists an unconditioned duty of public institutions to guarantee the capabilities needed to achieve the minimum levels of a dignified life. Nussbaum emphasizes that the fact that some people fail to achieve this level results not only in their loss of autonomy and freedom (in the Senian sense) but also in a lack of dignity and even humanity. We have already spoken of how the experience of hunting food equates humans with animals. It is only by achieving some degree of economic independence that people become dignified human beings rather than simply a member of the species *Homo sapiens* engaged in a ceaseless search for nutrition and shelter. By ensuring their survival, the BF humanizes its grantees, a fact which represents the first and decisive step toward achieving autonomy.

Another consideration relates to the incipient liberation from shame as a step toward achieving citizenship. Shame, arising from the awareness of being in an impoverished state, led many of these women to not want to speak, at first, or at least not speak freely. This emotion demonstrated their low self-esteem and, consequently, the fact that they did not see themselves as citizens. Otherwise, they would not have had a reason to feel shame when speaking about a state program designed for them and, in some cases, that they still thought of as being a gift from the president.

Public Policy and the Nation-State

We know that we are dealing with a Brazilian national experiment that illustrates the importance of the nation-state, at a moment in history when misconceptions of globalism have created the impression that such states have not only lost their regulatory functions but also those of promoting development (this restriction of the role of the state has worked to the advantage of powerful economic and financial interests). According to this view, it would seem as if the state had lost any regulative or functional meaning.

For decades, we had heard a well-tuned chorus singing a dirge. Voices in the media and those of opinion makers preached in unison the obsolescence of the institutions that had founded modernity, such as the nation-state and citizenship. This funeral buried, as well, the idea that democratic policy might serve as a common language with which to deal with the universal right to citizenship, for recognition of differences, and the demand for the civilized resolution of conflict. These egalitarian impulses had given rise to the most universal and most democratic nations. But recently, there has been the attempt to bury this impulse and substitute it with civic apathy by erasing one of its most important dimensions: that of providing measures and meaning to power and to the struggle for power within national communities.

As the civilizing achievements of modernity were being silenced, an ancient moral and political grammar reemerged together with its ally, market deregulation and the resulting end of the public functions of the state. This "new" lexicon valued individuals seeking to achieve the greatest self-interest. It mandated the disassembly of any pact of solidarity between generations for the enjoyment of rights. Between the lines of this process, democracy was emptied of its meaning and of its means to resolve disputes between different social groups. Following this naturalization of social life, distributive inequalities increasingly took on the aura of being inevitable and necessary for the country to launch itself into modernity.

A uniform political and economic recipe book that ignored any differences between the varied political and cultural traditions of each people spread across the world like wildfire and led to the privatization of public assets. The selling off of public patrimony was proclaimed to be the proper reform. It imposed its own rules and values, which, although originating from very particular interests, proclaimed themselves to be universally valid because they were supposedly in sync with the "natural" order of the world. A crudely ideological and political operation took us back to a medieval essentialism, in which nature replaced history. Naked individuals, deprived of their rights and humanity, a subject of Marx's critique of capitalism, were reinstated as the moral assumption behind the public justification for dismantling any idea of the common good and collective ethics. A well-known Brazilian economist even wrote, "Enough of compassion!" This was said to defend the dismantling of public pensions for poor retirees who had not made contributions to their pensions. Since they had almost always lived outside of labor regulations, they had not saved toward that pension. Therefore, they should not have welfare rights! He wanted, in addition to canceling a constitutional prerogative, to expel them from humanity.

The idea of a nation as a political force and that of a country as a political arena for debating plans for civic coexistence, including the embedding of democratic citizenship, was abolished as a historical abnormality. After all, why invoke this anachronism if its structures of sentiment had disappeared, been swept away, and been destroyed by the uncontrollable whirlwind of globalism? In this rhetorical ruse, the gravediggers of the national community kept even quieter about the duties of the state relative to the community itself, and, in the same ideological operation, they concealed the true *modus operandi* of social domination.

National and international hegemonic powers (fundamentally, central banks and financial institutions in general, economic groups, rating agencies, etc.) and their ideological staff prescribed absolute freedom of movement. Their "rationality" admitted no limits and no social control. On the contrary, they openly demanded the despotic exercise of their power.

The most visible and dramatic of these ideological constructions and of this political action was the weakening of citizens, figures who had already arrived late in Brazil. They were replaced by mere consumers of private services. Their prerogatives represented an attack on freedom, which was mandated to be associated with the absolute commodification of life. However, the force of things brought to the surface, with empirical evidence, the urgent need to resuscitate the unburied dead. Today one studies and debates across the world the need to recuperate the state as an analytic category, as an indispensable protagonist of distribution, and as an agent contributing to the recognition of social, cultural, and civil rights. This rescue is seen as the only way to prevent the majority from sinking, broken up by the destructive forces of globalization. The nation is being restored, and it is once more bringing people together and training citizens who are dedicated to democratic methods for resolving their conflicts of interests. The nation is restoring itself, at least as a transversal community in the words of Partha Chatterjee (1993, 2004). Such a community is morally and politically equipped to implement egalitarian patterns of social integration, based on the deepening of the republican public sphere. This is a decisive factor in our fragile democracy.

The denial of the role of the nation-state resulted in the denial of politics itself, in the sense of Arendt, seen as the action of a free community that organizes its coexistence not based on naturalized economic rules but by continually reinventing itself. Political autonomy is the fruit of uninterrupted production over time, a construction that takes place over a long period as the old learn to cope with the new. It is a process in which social subjects confront each other so that they might say *who they are and what they want out of life.* This, in and of itself, presupposes a tridimensional form of time: the time of memory, the time of the project, and the time of desire and of the future. Only politics, as a collective endeavor with a common language, can bring these three dimensions of time together. It is only by way of politics that differences can be recognized and conflicts resolved with a minimum of civility. As we said above, it is the civil and symbolic aspect of politics that establishes the measure and the meaning of power and the struggle for it.

This process of the continual reinvention of the community itself is marked by the struggle of citizens dedicated to improving their lives, not only in the material but also the immaterial sense. This relates to their hopes for the future, to the recognition of their dignity, to their specific cultural and expressive dimension, and to their sense of justice and decency. Political action is essentially linked to a decent society (in the sense of Margalit). A state that excludes and humiliates its citizens is dismantling politics as a sphere of understanding and misunderstanding among them. It denies a fundamental aspect of the lives of its citizens: their civic and political autonomy.

At the same time, we cannot imagine political action without the life of the state. The state is still the principal institution for satisfying conflicting interests and for formulating and achieving different views of community, such as those identified in the preamble and the articles of the Constitution of 1988 mentioned earlier. Forgetting this is to bury the long and hard fight of Brazilians for democracy – a struggle that did cost many people their lives.

To the contrary of what is preached by neoliberal dogma, the state is still the primary instrument for organizing and managing life in society – including that of the market which never has been and never will be self-regulating. As we have commented in another occasion,

> [t]he state is the public agency that confers, recognizes and guarantees rights. It has played and continues to play a central role in training and maintaining contemporary citizenship. Its acting through its institutions in their normative role is indispensable for ensuring full citizenship. (Leão Rego 2008, 156)

After all, the history of the twentieth century showed us that it is only the state that is capable of carrying out those processes of distribution that are needed so that a fairer community of citizens can be built.

Shifting Paradigms

In many societies, it is thought that poverty is the result of individual moral failure or that the poor themselves are to blame, due to their laziness, incompetence, indolence, etc. In short, the poor are defined as incompetent buyers and imprudent consumers. Consequently, they must either be kept as far away from money as possible, or there must be strict controls on how they should spend it. This is an old stereotype. Viviana Zelizer recalled that the 1893 amendment to the general statutes of 1878 in the American state of Minnesota stipulated that "in no such case should money be given to the poor." (Zelizer 2011, 162 f.). Zelizer discusses throughout her research the motives behind such a refusal to grant monetary aid to the poor. She analyzes the ideology of charity as being one of the strongest constructs opposing monetary aid to the poor. However, she tells us, "in the beginning of the 20th century [...] a paradoxical twist took place: the managers of charity foundations began to speak of the need to carry money to the homes of the poor, arguing that it was better than leaving them without a cent" (IBIDEM, 178). This turnaround is actually linked to concrete experiences, in certain circumstances and specific locations in which cash donations by social workers freed people up more. Nevertheless, the ideology of the control of expenditures continued almost as a social dogma.[1] Once again, as Zelizer warned, it was shown, as it continues to be shown, that the poor develop unpredictable and unexpected ways to manage their money. They come up with a wide variety of ways to account for their money, as they also choose specific purposes for the little money they have. For example, some families attribute different places for the money intended to meet their social and emotional obligations. They save it in different places within the home: money to be spent on the children, given to the church, or to certain saints, to be used for certain festivals, etc. The multiplicity of cultures and social experiences plays an important role in earmarking this money.

In the Brazilian case, the debate about the BF is a good example of the historical replay of prejudice and the force of stereotypes. In a wide range of settings, the poor are accused of preferring to live off the grants instead of working, of having children

[1] Regarding this, see, principally, Chaps. 1 and 4 of the book cited. As for the stigmatization of the poor as being responsible for their own destiny, due to their poor conduct and irresponsibility, see as well Rosanvallon (2011, 127 ss).

so they can get more state aid, of using the money to buy *cachaça*, etc. These accusations come, in most cases, from people who are not familiar with the program (about the amount of the grant, which will certainly not replace that of a regular salary, or about the fact that the families receive a maximum for three children, recently for two more school-aged children and one or two teenagers between 16 and 17 years of age, while the others are excluded; or the fact that the money is paid to the women and not the men, etc.). This type of argument is very common in the general public, who cannot accept that the poor are not to blame for their situation.[2] The stigma they are stuck with is based on the neoliberal premise that each one is responsible for their socioeconomic position as an adult. This premise, however, fails to take into account the fact that most of the people that belong to the elite or the upper classes were born in wealthy families and that they are therefore not responsible for their situation of well-being or of power. The few stories of *self-made men* who started with lowly positions and climbed until they owned huge companies are precisely the exceptions that confirm the rule that Gaetano Mosca set out at the beginning of the twentieth century: The elite tend to reproduce. They monopolize wealth and education, which they hand down to their descendants while excluding other society members as much as possible (Mosca 1896). The rule is the exclusivity of social and economic power, and the exception of the "self-made man" is a welcome one because it reinforces the dominant discourse that says that everyone gets what they deserve: wealth or poverty.

As we have already discussed, democracy is based on the idea of equal respect, and it therefore rejects the possibility of humiliation[3]. However, humiliation is precisely what takes place in many countries where poverty is a serious problem, such as in Brazil. The same situation is beginning to arise even in the so-called developed countries where poverty is no longer temporary and has ceased to be corrected by the market or without state intervention. However, a determined effort by the state is precisely what the dominant political discourse is vigorously condemning. Each public program designed to help the poor is labeled as paternalist, and, as we have seen above, it is common to lament the effect of such programs on the moral attitudes of the poor. There is an absolute lack of empathy and the capacity to see the world from the point of view of the other (What would I have done, if I had been born in a poor family? What kind of person would I have become?). This is a lacuna of the very faculty that is at the base of any true democracy as John Dewey and George Herbert Mead argued (Dewey 1966; Mead 1934). If the citizens are not able to see things from the point of view of their fellow citizens, and if they assert that a certain lifestyle and the related values are the only ones possible and that they

[2] An exception is usually made for children, who are seen as victims of circumstance. It is an interesting exception, as it reveals an implicit premise: if the children cannot be blamed, as they have had the bad luck to be born into poor families, the same cannot be true for the parents who, in the vast majority of cases, were also born poor. This means that according to this view, each person who was born in poverty has a chance to escape from it and, if this does not happen, she is the only one who should be blamed.

[3] Society can accept the idea of punishing acts that it considers illegal, but it cannot accept that citizens (including criminals) be humiliated by other citizens.

should be adopted by everyone, democracy will quickly degrade into an ethnic tyranny of certain groups where people who live differently from those of the model are disdained and disrespected.

One of the ways that this disdain is communicated is by the exclusion of the poor from the discussion about their very poverty. This disavowal of their voice is equal to the lack of recognition of individuals as subjects by those very people who have silenced them, or do not want to listen to or even see them. It is as if, in addition to silence, the poor have had invisibility imposed upon them as well. In public antipoverty programs, there must always be a place for a public education campaign targeted at other social classes about respecting the poor. Even in a social welfare state, society can fail to be civilized, if its members humiliate or disrespect each other. The struggle against material poverty by a part of the population should always be accompanied by the struggle against spiritual and moral poverty by the other parts.

As innumerable empirical studies (including ours) have shown, the poor frequently internalize the negative image constructed by the rest of society and blame themselves for their situation, becoming victims of the self-legitimizing discourse of the dominant groups. Sometimes they blame bad luck or certain individuals or even God, but they almost never blame society in general or its institutional organizations. It seems that they do not feel themselves to be victims of an unjust social organization or an unfair distribution of resources, rather of occasional injustice or a lack of luck. This may explain the extremely passive attitude that the poor have in many countries or the fact that, when they fight for their rights, they do so in connection with just one specific cause (e.g., against the privatization of water or common lands). They rarely aim to effect more generalized social or economic change.

The biggest obstacle to effective political participation on the part of the poor is due exactly to the lack of self-respect arising from the internalization of an image created by others. The lack of self-respect is a consequence of a form of humiliation that stigmatizes poverty and blames the poor for their situation. In other words, the exclusion of the poor produces feelings of self-exclusion. In the interviews, we commonly heard expressions like "This isn't for us" or "I know my place." These are traditional phrases the Brazilian poor use to express their resignation with their situation. Once again, we encountered the gap between the normative promise of modernity and its actual achievements. Technological, economic, and legal modernization does not correspond to true freedom for the people. Social mobility still encounters almost insurmountable goals within the structure of a society that – in many places and for many people – remains unchanged centuries later. There are a variety of obstacles, not only the economic or material ones (lack of regular income or education) but also of the immaterial and subjective type: The feeling of otherness vis-à-vis the rest of society means that in the colloquial language of the women interviewed we heard terms like "us" and "them" to refer to groups seen as immutable and in inevitable opposition. We could make out, however, clear signs of changes in this situation. The case of children of illiterate parents who were enrolled in universities may still seem exceptional, but most of the women interviewed were very hopeful about the future of their children. This means that the women excluded the children from their negative view of themselves and of life. In this sense, the BF has created positive expectations, and this has changed the age-old feeling of resignation. We also witnessed a profound change in the subjectivity of the women grantees. The future was no longer immutable and predetermined. The atavistic misery and suffering were no longer stuck in eternal repetition. Instead, as Celso Furtado (1962, 115) dreamed, the future can now be seen as an option and a challenge for our generation. This opening up of new possibilities for the future represents an increase in freedom, if we can identify it, as Amartya Sen taught us, as an incremental increase in the capacity of choice, i.e., the capacity to plan one's own life. It obliges us to look once more at the categories of time we discussed above: the time of memory, the time of the project, and the time of desire and future. The BF deals with all three and not merely the last two. By offering hope to the next generation, it means that their parents' generation, when looking back on their own suffering, can manage to see some meaning in it, according to the notion of Benjamin that the suffering of past generations only acquires meaning at the point in time at which its social transformation eliminates its causes (see On the Concept of History, Benjamin 2003). After all, "the future has an ancient heart" as Carlo Levi said (Levi 1956).

In conclusion, we must reaffirm that a nation composed of free and equal subjects (an ideal sought ever since the French Revolution) can only exist if there are bonds of belonging that link fellow countrymen, such as language, memory, and cultural traditions, but also bonds of solidarity between them. The latter is the result of political processes rather than a natural fact. Therefore, they depend on policies of citizenship implemented by the state that are intended to nurture bonds of social and cultural solidarity that are indispensable to building a just community, namely, policies of distributive justice and cash transfers to their members and components. It is only in this way that the society predicted in the preamble of our constitution will become a reality.

References

Ackerly, Brooke A. *Political Theory and Feminist Social Criticism*. Cambridge: Cambridge University Press, 2000.

Adelman, Irma; Taft Morris, Cynthia. *Economic Growth and Social Equity in Developing Countries*. Stanford: Stanford University Press, 1973.

Adorno, Theodor W. et al. *The Positivist Dispute in German Sociology*. Translated by G. Adey and D. Frisby. London: Heinemann, 1976.

———. *Negative Dialectics*. Translated by E. B. Ashton. London: Routledge, 2004.

———. *Philosophische Elemente einer Theorie der Gesellschaft*. Frankfurt a. M.: Suhrkamp, 2008.

Agamben, Giorgio. *Homo Sacer. Sovereign Power and Bare Life*. Stanford: Stanford University Press, 1998.

Anand, Paul; Santos, Cristina; Smith, Ron. "The Measurement of Capabilities". In: Basu, Kaushik; Kanbur, Ravi (eds.). *Arguments for a Better World. Essays in Honor of Amartya Sen. Vol. I: Ethics, Welfare, and Measurement*. Oxford: Oxford University Press, 2009, 283–310.

Anderson, Elizabeth. What is the Point of Equality?. *Ethics*, 109/2, 1999, 287–337.

Arendt, Hannah. *On Revolution*. New York: Viking Press, 1963.

———. *The Origins of Totalitarianism*. New Edition with Added Prefaces. New York: Harvest Books, 1968 [1st edition: 1951].

———. *The Human Condition*. Chicago: Chicago University Press, 1958.

Bendix, Reinhard. *Nation-Building and Citizenship. Studies of Our Changing. Social Order*. New York, London, and Sydney: John Wiley and Sons, 1964.

Benhabib, Seyla. *Intervista con Seyla Benhabib: La filosofia politica femminista (15/07/1992)*. Acessível em http://www.emsf.rai.it/interviste/interviste.asp?d=381 (acessado em 26/06/2011).

Benjamin, Walter. On the Concept of History. In: *Selected Writings. Vol. 4 (1938–1940)*. Cambridge (MA): Belknap, 2003, 389–400.

Bercovici, Gilberto. Os Princípios Estruturantes e o Papel do Estado. In: Cardoso Jr., José Celso (org.). A Constituição Brasileira de 1988 Revisitada: Recuperação Histórica e Desafios Atuais das Políticas Públicas nas Áreas Econômica e Social. Brasília: IPEA, 2009, vol. 1, 255–291.

Bichir, Renata Mirandola. O Bolsa Família na berlinda? Os desafios atuais dos programas de transferência de renda. In: *Novos Estudos Cebrap*. N° 87, Julho 2010, 115–129.

Boltanski, Luc; Honneth, Axel. *Soziologie der Kritik oder Kritische Theorie? Ein Gespräch mit Robin Celikates*. In: Jaeggi, Rahel; Wesche, Tilo (Hrsg.). *Was ist Kritik*? Frankfurt a. M.: Suhrkamp, 2009, 81–114.

Boltanski, Luc. *Soziologie und Sozialkritik. Frankfurter Adorno-Vorlesungen*. Berlin: Suhrkamp, 2010.

A. Pinzani, W. L. Rego, *Money, Autonomy and Citizenship*,
https://doi.org/10.1007/978-3-030-01361-5

Bourdieu, Pierre (ed.). *The Weight of the World*. Stanford: Stanford University Press, 1999.

———. *Distinction. A Social Critique of the Judgment of Taste*. London: Routledge, 2010.

Brown, Larry (ed.). *The Link Between Nutrition and Cognitive Development in Children*. Medford (MA): Center on Hunger, Poverty and Nutrition Policy, School of Nutrition, Tufts University, 1993.

Burstin, Verónica; Fascioli, Ana; Modzelewski, Helena; Pereira, Gustavo; Reyes, Augustin; Salas, Gonzalo; Vigorito, Andrea. *Preferencias adaptativas. Entre deseos, frustración y logros*. Montevideo: Fin de Siglo, 2010.

Calamandrei, Piero. *On the 1947 Constitution. Freedom regained and always to be regained, 2010*. At: http://explorehumanrights.coe.int/wp-content/uploads/2010/11/Italia_ehr.pdf

Calogero, Guido. Intorno al concetto di giustizia. In: ————. *Difesa del liberalsocialismo*. Roma: Atlantica, 1945.

Cardoso, Fernando Henrique *Capitalismo e escravidão no Brasil meridional: o negro na sociedade escravocrata do Rio Grande do Sul*. São Paulo: Difusão, 1977.

Castro, Josué de. *Geografia da Fome. O dilema brasileiro: pão ou aço*. 7ª edição atualizada. São Paulo: Brasiliense Editora, 1961.

Chang, Ha-Joon. *Kicking Away the Ladder. Development Strategy in Historical Perspective*. London & New York: Anthem, 2002.

———. *23 Things They Don't Tell You About Capitalism*. London: Penguin, 2010.

Chatterjee, Partha. *The Nation and Its Fragments*. Princeton: Princeton University Press, 1993.

———. *The Politics of the Governed. Popular Politics in Most of the World*. New York: Columbia University Press, 2004.

Ciriza, Alejandra. Pasado y presente. El dilema Wollstonecraft como herencia teórica y política. In: Boron, Atilio A,; Vita, Álvaro de (orgs.). *Teoría y filosofía política*. Buenos Aires: Clacso, 2002, 217–246.

Cohen, Gerald A. Incentives, Inequality, and Community. In: Darwall, Stephen (ed.). *Equal Freedom*. Ann Harbour: University of Michigan Press, 1995, 331–397.

Comim, Flavio; Qizibash, Mozzafar; Alkire, Sabina (eds.). *The Capability Approach. Concepts, Measures and Applications*. Cambridge: Cambridge University Press, 2008.

Costa, Pietro. *Civitas. Storia della cittadinanza in Europa*. Roma; Bari: Laterza, 1999–2001.

Deneulin, Séverine; Nebel, Mathias; Sagovsky, Nicholas (eds.). *Transforming Unjust Structures. The Capability Approach*. Dordrecht: Springer, 2006.

———; Shahani, Lila (eds.). *An Introduction to the Human Development and Capability Approach. Freedom and Agency*. London: Earthscan, 2009.

Deutschmann Christoph. Money as Social Construction. In: *Thesis Eleven*, Vol. 47, November.1996, 1–19.

Dewey, John. *Democracy and Education. An Introduction to the Philosophy of Education*. New York: Free Press, 1966.

Dieterlen, Paulette. *Poverty. A Philosophical Approach*. Amsterdam; New York: Rodopi, 2005.

Diniz, Eli (org.). *O Brasil no rastro da crise*. São Paulo: Hucitec, 1994.

Disraeli, Benjamin. Sybil: or Two Nations. London: Henry Colburn Publisher, 1845 (also available at: www.gutenberg.org/dirs/etext03/sybil10.txt, accessed on 1/5/2010)

Easterly, Williams. *The Elusive Quest for Growth*. Cambridge (MA): MIT Press, 2001.

Ellison, Ralph. *The Invisible Man*. New York: Random House, 1952.

Fanon, Frantz. *The Wretched of the Earth*. New York: Grove Press, 2004.

Fernandes, Florestan. *A integração do negro na sociedade de classes*. São Paulo: Dominus : Ed. Univ. S. Paulo, 1965.

Ferrajoli, Luigi. *Diritti Fondamentali*. Roma e Bari: Laterza, 2002.

Forst, Rainer. *The Right to Justification. Elements of a Constructivist Theory of Justice*. New York: Columbia University Press, 2011.

Franco, Maria Sylvia Carvalho. *Homens livres na ordem escravocrata*. São Paulo: Editora UNESP, 1969.

Fraser, Nancy. (1999). Social justice in the age of identity politics: redistribution, recognition, and participation. In: L. Ray & A. Sayer (Eds.), *Culture and economy after the cultural turn*. London: SAGE, 25–52.

———; Honneth, Axel. *Redistribution or Recognition? A Political-Philosophical Exchange*. London e New York: Verso, 2003.
Furtado, Celso. *Desenvolvimento e subdesenvolvimento*. RJ, Fundo de Cultura, 1961.
———. *A pré-revolução brasileira*. Rio de Janeiro: Fundo de Cultura, 1962.
———. *Subdesenvolvimento e Estado democrático*. Recife, Condepe, 1962 (1962a).
———. *Dialética do desenvolvimento*. RJ, Fundo de Cultura, 1964.
———. *Subdesenvolvimento e estagnação na América Latina*. RJ, Civilização Brasileira, 1966.
———. *Teoria e política do desenvolvimento econômico*. SP, Editora Nacional, 1967
———. *Brasil, a construção interrompida*. SP, Paz e Terra, 1992
Galeotti, Anna E. *La politica del rispetto*. I *fondamenti etici della democrazia*. Roma & Bari: Laterza, 2010.
Gerth, Hans; Mills, C. Wright. *Character and Social Structure. The Psychology of Social Institutions*. New York: Harcourt, Brace & World, 1964 [1953].
Goerne, Alexander. The Capability Approach in social policy analysis. Yet another concept? In: REC-WP 03/2010 (in: http://www.socialpolicy.ed.ac.uk/recwowepudiac/working_papers/rec-wp_ 03_10; acessado em 24/05/2012)
Goffman, Erwing. *The Presentation of Self in Everyday Life*. New York: Anchor Book, 1959 [1956]
Gourevitch, Peter. *Politics in Hard Times. Comparative Responses to International Economic Crises*. Ithaca: Cornell University Press, 1986.
Gramsci, Antonio. Caderno 11 (1932–1933): Introdução ao estudo da filosofia. In: ———. *Cadernos do cárcere. Volume I*. Edição de Carlos Nelson Coutinho. Rio de Janeiro: Civilização Brasileira, 1999.
Habermas, Jürgen. Modernity – An Unfinished Project. In: M. Passerin d'Entrèves and S. Benhabib (Eds.). Habermas and the Unfinished Project of Modernity. Oxford: Polity Press, 1996.
———. *The Inclusion of the Other. Studies in Political Theory*. Cambridge (MA): The MIT Press, 1996 (1996a)
Harris, David. *Justifying State Welfare*. Oxford: Blackwell, 1987.
Hayek, Friedrich A.: *Law, Legislation and Liberty. Volume 2: The Mirage of Social Justice*. Chicago: Chicago University Press, 1976.
Hegel, G. W. F. *Hegel and the Human Spirit. A Translation of the Jena Lectures on the Philosophy of Spirit (1805–6) with Commentary*. Ed. by L. Rauch. Detroit: Wayne State University Press, 1983.
Hofbauer, Andreas. *Uma história do branqueamento ou O negro em questão*. São Paulo: Editora da Unesp, 2006.
Holanda, Sérgio Buarque de. *Raízes do Brasil*. Rio de Janeiro: José Olympio, 1936.
Honneth, Axel. *Unsichtbarkeit. Stationen einer Theorie der Intersubjektivität*. Frankfurt a. M.: Suhrkamp, 2003.
———. *The Struggle for Recognition. The Moral Grammar of Social Conflicts*. Cambridge (MA): The MIT Press, 1996
Hulme, David; Mosley, Paul. Microenterprise Finance: Is There a Conflict Between Growth and Poverty Alleviation? In: *World Development* Vol. 26, No. 5, 1998, 783–790.
Ianni, Octavio. *As metamorfoses do escravo*. São Paulo: Difel, 1962.
Kant, Immanuel. *To Perpetual Peace*. Edited by T. Humhprey. Indianapolis: Hackett, 2003.
Kay, Thelma. Empowering women through self-help microcredit programmer. In: *Bulletin on Asia-Pacific Perspectives*, vol. 20, 2002, 69–78 (www.unescap.org/drpad/publication/bulletin%202002/ch6.pdf)
Kuznets, Simon. Economic Growth and Income Inequality. In: *American Economic Review*. Vol. 45, 1955, p. 1–28.
Laidler, David; Rowe, Nicholas. Georg Simmel's Philosophy of Money. A Review Article for Economists. In: *Journal of Economic Literature*. Vol XVII, March 1980, 97–105.
Lambert, Jacques. *Os dois Brasis* (Coleção Brasiliana). São Paulo: Companhia Editora Nacional, 1967.
Lassalle, Ferdinand. On the Essence of Constitutions (1862). *Fourth International*, 3/1,1942, 25–31.

Lavinas, Lena. A mulher pobre. In: *Estudos Feministas*, IV/2, 1996, 464–479.
———. Pobreza e exclusão: traduções regionais de duas categorias da prática. In: *Economica*, 4/1, 2002, 25–59.
———. Gasto Social no Brasil: programas de transferência de renda versus investimento social. In: *Ciência & Saúde Coletiva*, 12, 2007, 1463–1476.
———. Aspectos teóricos das políticas de cidadania: uma aproximação ao Bolsa Família. In: *Lua Nova*, n° 73, 2008, 147–185.
Levi, Carlo. *Il futuro ha un cuore antico*. Torino: Einaudi, 1956.
Lispector, Clarice. *The Hour of the Star*. New Directions, 1992.
Lousao, Antoine. Sobre a importância intrínseca das decisões democráticas para a realização da justiça – uma abordagem comparativa das teorias de Amartya Sen e Nancy Fraser. In: *Revista Redescrições – Revista on line do GT de Pragmatismo e Filosofia Norte-americana*. 2/2, 2010 http://www.gtpragmatismo.com.br/redescricoes/redescricoes/ano2_02/4_lousao.pdf (acesso em 26 de abril de 2012)
Manin, Bernard. *The Principles of Representative Government*. Cambridge: Cambridge University Press, 1997.
Margalit, Avishai. *The Decent Society*. Cambridge (MA): Harvard University Press, 1996.
Marshall, Thomas H. *Citizenship and Social Class and Other Essays*. Cambridge: Cambridge University Press, 1950.
Martuccelli, Danilo: Les trois voies de l'individu sociologique. In: *EspacesTemps.net*, 2005 (http://www.espacestemps.net/document1414.html – acessado em 11/24/09).
Marx, Karl. *Grundrisse. Foundations of the Critique of Political Economy*. London: Penguin, 1993.
———. *Pre-capitalist Economic Formations*. New York: International Publishers, 1964.
———. *Critique of the Gotha Program*. Rockwille (MD): Wildside. 2008
———. *Economic and Philosophical Manuscripts of 1844*. Amherst (NY): Prometheus Books, 1988.
———. *Antologia. Capitalismo, istruzioni per l'uso*. A cura di Enrico Donaggio e Peter Kammerer. Milano: Feltrinelli, 2007.
Mathieu, Vittorio. Filosofia del denaro. In: *Enciclopedia Multimediale delle Scienze Filosofiche*, 1991, http://www.emsf.rai.it/aforismi/aforismi.asp?d=118 (acesso em 26 de abril de 2012).
Max-Neef, Manfred et al. *Desarrollo a escala humana: Una opción para el futuro*. Uppsala: Dag Hammarskjöld Foundation, 1986.
Mazzini, Giuseppe. *Dei doveri dell'uomo*. Milano: Rizzoli, 2002.
Mead, George H. *Mind, Self and Society*. Chicago: Chicago University Press, 1934.
Mill, John Stuart. *Subjection of Women*. Oxford: Oxford University Press, 1911.
———. *On Liberty and Other Essays*. Oxford: Oxford University Press, 1991.
Mills, C. Wright. *The Power Elite*. New York: Oxford University Press, 1956.
Moore Jr., Barrington. *Reflections on the Causes of Human Misery*. London: Penguin, 1972 [1ª edição: London: Allen Lane, 1970]
———. *Injustice. The Social Bases of Obedience and Revolt*. London: MacMillan, 1978.
Mosca, Gaetano. *Elementi di scienza politica*. Torino: Bocca, 1896.
Mosca, Gaetano. *The Ruling Class*. London & New York: McGraw-Hill, 1939.
Narayan, Deepa et al. *Voices of the Poor. Can Anyone Hear Us?*. Oxford: Oxford University Press, 2000 (2000a).
———. *Voices of the Poor. Crying Out for Change*. Oxford: Oxford University Press, 2000 (2000b).
Nehru, Jawaharlal. *An Autobiography*. New Dehli: Penguin India, 2004.
Nussbaum, Martha. Aristotelian Social Democracy. In: Douglass, R. B.; Mara, G. R.; Richardson, H. S. (orgs.). *Liberalism and the Good*. New York e London: Routledge, 1990, 203–252.
———; Glover, Jonathan (orgs.). *Women, Culture, and Development. A Study on Human Capabilites*. Oxford: Clarendon Press, 1995
———. *Women and Human Development. The Capabilities Approach*. Cambridge: Cambridge University Press, 2000.

———. *Hiding from Humanity. Disgust, Shame, and the Law*. Princeton: Princeton University Press, 2004.
———. *Creating Capabilities. The Human Development Approach*. Cambridge (MA): Belknap, 2011.
Okin, Susan Moller. *Justice, gender and family*. Princeton: Princeton University Press, 1987.
———. Humanist Liberalism. In: Rosenblum, Nancy. *Liberalism and the Moral Life*. Cambridge (MA): Harvard University Press, 1989, 39–53.
Pareto, Vilfredo. *The Mind and Society*. New York: Harcourt, Brace & Co., 1935.
Pateman, Carole. Democratizing Citizenship. Some Advantages of a Basic Income. In: *Politics and Society*, 32/1, 2004, 89–105.
Paugam, Serge. *La diqualification sociale*. Paris: PUF, 1991.
Pereira, Luiz. *A escola numa área metropolitana*. São Paulo: Livraria Pioneira, 1967.
———. *O magistério primário numa sociedade de classes*. São Paulo: Livraria Pioneira, 1969.
Pogge, Thomas. *World Poverty and Human Rights*. Cambridge: Polity Press, 2002.
———. *Politics as Usual. What Lies Behind the Pro-Poor Rethoric*. Cambridge: Polity Press, 2010.
Polanyi, Karl. Wirtschaft und Demokratie, *Der Österreichische Volkswirt*, XXV/13–14, 1932, 301–303
———. *The Great Transformation*. New York: Farrar & Rinehart, 1944.
———. *La libertà in una società complessa*. Torino: Bollati Boringhieri, 1987.
Pollock, Friedrich. La teoria marxiana del denaro. In: ———. *Teoria e prassi dell'economia di piano. Antologia degli scritti 1928–1941*. Bari: Di Donato, 1973.
Prebisch, Raúl. *El desarrollo económico de la América Latina y algunos de sus principales problemas*. Santiago: CEPAL, 1949.
———. *Crecimiento, desequilibrio y disparidades: interpretación del proceso de desarrollo económico*. New York: United Nations,1950
Ramos, Graciliano. Barren Lives. Austin: University of Texas Press, 1965.
Ramos, Graciliano. *Vidas Secas*. 57ª edição. São Paulo: Record, 1986.
———. *Insônia*. São Paulo: Record, 1986 (1986a)
Rawls, John. *A Theory of Justice*. Cambridge (MA): Harvard University Press, 1971.
Renault, Emmanuel. *L'expérience de l'injustice. Reconnaissance et clinique de l'injustice*. Paris: La Découverte, 2004.
———. *Souffrances sociales. Philosophie, psychologie et politique*. Paris: La Découverte, 2008.
Rosa, Hartmut. Kritik der Zeitverhältnisse. Beschleunigung und Entfremdung als Schlüsselbegriffe der Sozialkritik. In: Jaeggi, Rahel; Wesche, Tilo (Hrsg.). *Was ist Kritik?*. Frankfurt a. M.: Suhrkamp, 2009, 23–54.
Rosanvallon, Pierre. *La societé des égaux*. Paris: Seuil, 2011.
Rowntree, Benjamin. Poverty. A Study of Town Life. London: Macmillan, 1901.
Sales, Teresa. *Trama das desigualdades, drama da pobreza no Brasil* (Tese de livre-docência, IFCH, UNICAMP). Campinas, 1992.
Sen, Amartya. Well-being, Agency, and Freedom. The Dewey Lectures 1984. *Journal of Philosophy*. 82, 1985, 169–221.
———. *The Standard of Living. The Tanner Lectures 1985*. With contributions by J. Muellbauer, R. Kanbur, K. Hart, B. Williams. Ed. by G. Hawthorn. Cambridge: Cambridge University Press, 1987.
———. *Inequality Reexamined*. Cambridge (MA): Harvard University Press, 1992.
———. *On Economic Inequality*. Expanded Edition with a substantial annex by James E. Foster and Amartya Sen. Oxford: Clarendon Press, 1997.
———. *Development as Freedom*. Oxford: Oxford University Press, 1999.
———. *The Idea of Justice*. London: Allen Lane, 2009.
Sennett, Richard. *Respect in a World of Inequality*. New York: Norton, 2003.
Shue, Henry. *Basic Rights. Subsistence, Affluence, and U.S. Foreign Policy*, 2nd ed. Princeton: Princeton University Press, 1996.

Sieyes, Emmanuel. *Political Writings*. Indianapolis: Hackett, 2003.
Silva, Maria Ozanira S.; Yazbek, Maria Carmelita; Di Giovanni, Geraldo. *A política social brasileira no século XXI. A prevalência dos programas de transferência de renda*. 4ª edição. São Paulo: Cortez, 2008.
Simmel, Georg. The Poor. *Social Problems*, 13/2, 1965, 118–140.
———. *The Philosophy of Money*. London: Routledge, 2011.
Smelt, Simon. Money's Place in Society; In: *British Journal of Sociology*, 31, 1980, 204–223.
Smith, Adam. *The Wealth of Nations*. Oxford: Oxford University Press, 1976.
Sonderegger, Ruth. Wie diszipliniert ist (Ideologie-)Kritik? Zwischen Philosophie, Soziologie und Kunst. In: Jaeggi, Rahel; Wesche, Tilo (Hrsg.). *Was ist Kritik?*. Frankfurt a. M. : Suhrkamp, 2009, 55–80.
Souza, Jessé. *A construção social da subcidadania. Para uma sociologia política da modernidade periférica*. Belo Horizonte: Editora da UFMG; Rio de Janeiro: Editora UPERJ, 2003.
———. (org.). *A invisibilidade da desigualdade brasileira*. Belo Horizonte: Editora da UFMG, 2006.
———. (org.). *A ralé brasileira. Quem é e como vive*. Belo Horizonte: Editora da UFMG, 2009.
Streeten, Paul P. *Thinking About Development*. Cambridge: Cambridge University Press, 1995.
Taylor, Charles. *Philosophical Arguments*. Cambridge (MA): Harvard University Press, 1995.
Tilly, Charles. *Coercion, Capital, and European States*. Oxford: Blackwell, 1990.
Tocqueville, Alexis de. *Recollections. The French Revolution of 1848*. Edited by J. P. Meyer and A. P. Kerr. New Brunswick (NJ): Transaction, 1987.
Todaro, Michael P. *Economic Development*. 5th edition. New York: Longman, 1994.
Trentin, Bruno. L'ingiustizia sociale. Entrevista para a revista *Il Grillo*, 10/12/1998.
Urbinati, Nadia. *Mill on Democracy- From the Athenian Polis to Representative Government*. Chicago: Chicago University Press, 2002.
Vanderborght, Yannick; Van Parijs, Philippe. *Renda básica de cidadania. Argumentos éticos e econômicos*. Rio de Janeiro: Civilização brasileira, 2006.
Van Parijs, Philippe. *Real Freedom for All. What (if Anything) Can Justify Capitalism?*. Oxford: Oxford University Press, 1995.
Veca, Salvatore. *Dell'incertezza. Tre meditazioni filosofiche*. Milano: Feltrinelli, 1997.
Walzer, Michael. Philosophy and Democracy. In: *Political Theory*, Vol. 9, 1981, 379–399.
———. *Intepretation and Social Criticism*. Cambridge (MA): Harvard University Press, 1987.
Wanderley, Luiz Eduardo W. Enigmas do social. In: Castel, Robert; Wanderley, Luiz Eduardo W.; Belfiore-Wanderley, Mariângela. *Desigualdade e a questão social*. São Paulo: Educ, 2007, 163–234.
Wolff, Jonathan; De-Shalit, Avner. *Disadvantage*. Oxford: Oxford University Press, 2007.
Zelizer, Viviana. The Social Meaning of Money: "Special Monies" In: *American Journal of Sociology*, 95/2, 1989, 342–377.
———. El Dinero de los Pobres. In: *El Significado Social del Dinero*. Mexico: Fondo de Cultura Economica, 2011.
———. *Da sudditi a cittadini*. Bologna: Il Mulino, 1992.

MIX
Papier aus verantwortungsvollen Quellen
Paper from responsible sources
FSC® C105338

If you have any concerns about our products,
you can contact us on
ProductSafety@springernature.com

In case Publisher is established outside the EU,
the EU authorized representative is:
Springer Nature Customer Service Center GmbH
Europaplatz 3, 69115 Heidelberg, Germany

Printed by Libri Plureos GmbH
in Hamburg, Germany